M000313369

LETTERS OF
ST. PAULINUS OF NOLA

Ancient Christian Writers

The Works of the Fathers in Translation

EDITED BY

JOHANNES QUASTEN   WALTER J. BURGHARDT

THOMAS COMERFORD LAWLER

No. 35

LETTERS OF
ST. PAULINUS OF NOLA

TRANSLATED AND ANNOTATED

BY

P. G. WALSH
Department of Humanity
University of Edinburgh

VOLUME I

Letters 1–22

NEWMAN PRESS

New York, N.Y./Ramsey, N.J.

De Licentia Superioris S.J.
 Nihil Obstat:
  J. Quasten
     Cens. Dep.
Imprimatur:
  Patricius A. O'Boyle, D.D.
     Archiep Washingtonen.
        die 19 Maii 1966

COPYRIGHT 1966
BY
REV. JOHANNES QUASTEN
AND
REV. WALTER J. BURGHARDT
AND
THOMAS COMERFORD LAWLER

Library of Congress
Catalog Card Number: 66-28933

ISBN: 0-8091-0088-6

PUBLISHED BY PAULIST PRESS
Editorial Office: 1865 Broadway, New York, N.Y. 10023
Business Office: 545 Island Road, Ramsey, N.J. 07446

PRINTED AND BOUND IN THE UNITED STATES OF AMERICA

CONTENTS

LETTERS OF
ST. PAULINUS OF NOLA

INTRODUCTION

The prose letters of Pontius Meropius Paulinus, whose birthplace and family estate were near Bordeaux but who established a monastic house at Nola near Naples and ultimately became bishop there, extend over approximately the second half of his life.[1] There are none dating from his early years in Aquitania, where he was born in or shortly before A.D. 355.[2] Nor have any survived to shed light on the course of his secular career, the high point of which was his appointment as governor of Campania in his early twenties.[3] The absence of such documentation makes it impossible to reconstruct the detail of his tenure of that important post, or of the circumstances under which he relinquished it to return to private life in Aquitania, probably late in 383. And no letters survive to explain the circumstances under which he shortly thereafter journeyed to Spain to marry Therasia, or to describe their comfortable life on his wealthy estates near Bordeaux.[4] The immediate reasons impelling him to seek baptism and to return to Spain in 389 are likewise obscure.[5]

The first of the extant prose letters of Paulinus were written during the ensuing five-year period in Spain, during which Therasia bore a son, Celsus, who died within a few days. These six letters from Spain, reinforced by the evidence of the poems,[6] allow some insight into the spiritual development of Paulinus during the years of his life near

Bordeaux. The picture emerges of a Christian formation firmly rooted in the Scriptures, an effective complement to his secular education in literature and rhetoric. When one notes in his later correspondence the impressive number of Paulinus' former circle who gave up careers and wealth for a rigorous Christian life, it becomes clear that Ausonius' "cold and conventional deference to the Christian faith,"[7] which has left the pervasive impression of a purely nominal Christianity in fourth-century Bordeaux, has overshadowed the vitalizing influence of such figures as Bishop Delphinus and Amandus, the confessor of Paulinus. Whatever may have been the immediate stimulus to Paulinus to sell his property and enter the monastic life, whether the sanctity of Therasia or the death of his son, the fundamental motivation was his understanding of what real Christianity entailed, and this he had learnt at Bordeaux.

In addition to the six letters written from Spain, there are forty-five[8] extant letters of Paulinus, all of which originated from his monastery at Nola during the thirty-six years between his arrival there in late 395 and his death in 431.[9] The writing of these letters he regarded as an indispensable part of his monastic life, for they represent a continual meditation on the relevance of scriptural exhortation and exemplars to his own life. His Roman literary education had trained him to focus and formalise his thoughts by expressing them in artistic prose and in verse. But whereas the great Roman poets had been his earlier models, after his conversion the Scriptures are largely his sole guide, moulding his patterns of thought and modes of expression.

The surviving letters represent a mere fraction of those Paulinus actually wrote. He did not keep copies, and in fact frankly states that he does not recognize his own letters when he sees them.[10] They survived only if received by persons who regarded them as of permanent value. It is no accident that most of those extant were sent to Gaul, where the name of Paulinus was specially celebrated. He frequently mentions letters of his which have not survived. The loss of those to Jerome,[11] Anastasius,[12] Ambrose,[13] Venerius,[14] and Aurelius of Carthage[15] is particularly unfortunate.

THE CORRESPONDENTS OF PAULINUS

Of the surviving letters, thirteen are addressed to Paulinus' most intimate friend, Sulpicius Severus.[16] Severus played a most influential part in the development of Gallic monasticism while Paulinus was in Italy. From Paulinus we learn how his friend, a noble Aquitanian a few years younger than himself, had won a great reputation as an advocate before deciding to sell his property and follow Paulinus into the monastic life. He attached himself as disciple to Martin, the founder of monasticism in Gaul, and made frequent visits to Tours for spiritual advice; later, in 397, he wrote his *Vita s. Martini*[17] which has immortalised the saint. With his mother-in-law Bassula he established a monastery at Primuliacum[18] where his community lived in accord with Martin's rule; a remark of Paulinus suggests that there was also a monastic school there.[19] Severus further stimulated interest in monasticism by his *Dialogues*,[20] in which a certain Posthumianus recounts his visit to witness eremitic life in Egypt. We do not know how early Severus' friendship with Paulinus began, but they were intimates by the time of Paulinus' retirement to Spain in 389. In his letters to Severus, all written in the decade following Severus' conversion to monasticism,[21] Paulinus repeatedly stresses the uniqueness of their relationship, a friendship founded in the secular world but crowned with the *caritas Christiana*.[22]

Of the remaining letters the most frequent addressees are Delphinus and Amandus. Though Paulinus always sends them separate letters, he invariably writes to both by the same courier, and reveals that the two were close associates. Six letters to Amandus and five to Delphinus have survived. The details of their activities and characters we owe entirely to Paulinus. Towards Delphinus, bishop of Bordeaux and a man considerably older than himself,[23] Paulinus adopts a tone of devoted deference appropriate for a spiritual father. Delphinus emerges from these pages as a man of saintly humility, immensely proud of the illustrious convert whom he had baptised; he is constantly asking Paulinus for news of his activities, or for the scriptural meditations which he so much admired.[24] And it is touching to observe how Paulinus attempts to introduce Delphinus to the great ecclesiastics of Italy, writing to the bishop of Milan to invite him to correspond with Bordeaux, and promising to elicit for Delphinus a letter from Pope Anastasius.[25]

Towards Amandus, the priest who had been his catechist at Bordeaux, Paulinus reveals himself as an intimate friend. His letters to Amandus are longer than those to Delphinus, and allow him to develop his speculations on the significance of various scriptural passages. We may assume that Paulinus is here resuming with the pen discussions which had engaged Amandus and himself in the period before his baptism.[26]

On arrival at Nola, Paulinus took the initiative in corresponding with the great Fathers of the West. Apart from the connexions with Ambrose and Jerome already mentioned, he corresponded regularly with Augustine. The four letters of Paulinus to Augustine which have survived (Nos. 4, 6, 45, 50) do not offer much new information about the bishop of Hippo,[27] but they do provide interesting insights into the cordial relations between the two men, and especially show the respect Augustine accorded Paulinus not only as a distinguished ex-senator but also as a Christian thinker. Augustine consults Paulinus, for example, on what he thinks life in heaven will be like[28]—the right kind of question for Paulinus, requiring poetic speculation more than theological learning.[29]

A single letter, No. 3, survives of Paulinus' correspondence initiated with another African bishop, Alypius of Tagaste, and in it Paulinus acknowledges a gift of books written by Augustine. This Alypius was the friend of Augustine immortalised by the Saint of Hippo in his letters and in the Confessions. Augustine and Alypius wrote at least two joint letters[30] to Paulinus, the first about 398 asking for a treatise of Paulinus, the second some twenty years later warning him of the dangers of the Pelagian heresy.

Of less importance is another African correspondent, to whom Paulinus may have sent only the single letter, No. 7, in which he informs him of Augustine's elevation to the episcopate. The addressee here is Romanianus, the wealthy patron of Augustine, and the main reason for the letter may have been to enclose a communication (Letter 8) to Romanianus' son Licentius. This young man had been with Augustine at Cassiciacum during the famous discussions there, but had begun to lose interest in the Christian life. Paulinus wrote to Licentius because Augustine had expressed disquiet about Licentius' worldly tendencies.[31]

Pammachius, to whom Paulinus addresses a *consolatio* (Letter 13) on the death of his wife Paulina, is a much more interesting and important figure. A member of the Patrician house of the Furii, Pammachius amongst Christian leaders "stands almost alone in having stayed at Rome and dedicated himself to the normal religious life of the city."[32] The Roman Senate of the late fourth century, of which he was a member, had been dominated by the non-Christian element headed by Symmachus; Paulinus' eulogy shows that Pammachius during his secular career was isolated in his full commitment to a Christian life.[33] This commitment, deepened by the sanctity of his wife, led him after her death to take the monastic habit and to devote his considerable wealth to works of charity, amongst them a *xenodochium* or pilgrims' rest house at Portus near Ostia.[34]

Rufinus of Aquileia is another regular correspondent whom Paulinus mentions in tones of affection and respect.[35] Only two letters to this important figure have survived, Nos. 46 and 47, both of them written about 406/8, shortly before Rufinus' death. The replies of Rufinus to Paulinus are also extant.

The addressee of Letter 49, ostensibly one Macarius, who is asked to intercede with appropriate officials in having the cargo of a shipwreck returned to its owner, was clearly a high imperial official. It is worth noting that there was a Macarius with the status of deputy prefect amongst the friends of Pinian, husband of the younger Melania, and that he was keenly interested in Christian theology.[36] Moreover, it is known that Paulinus wrote a *consolatio* to a certain Macarius on the death of his wife.[37] It would seem reasonable to assume that this is the same Macarius; the only doubt is whether Letter 49 was sent to Macarius at all.[38]

Most of the other letters were sent to friends in Gaul. Of these the most noteworthy is Victricius, bishop of Rouen, one of the most influential missionary figures of his age,[39] to whom Letters 18 and 37 are addressed. These two letters are of considerable importance, the first providing the sole documentation of Victricius' conversion and evidence of his missionary activity in northern Gaul, the second offering details of the charges of Apollinarianism laid against his orthodoxy, which was vindicated in a special decree of Innocent I.

Other Gallic clerics in correspondence with Paulinus include the brothers Florentius and Alethius. Florentius, bishop of Cahors,[40] had taken the initiative in writing to Paulinus, whose Letter 42 is addressed to him. The one surviving letter to Alethius, No. 33, was sent before Alethius succeeded Florentius in the see of Cahors.[41] This latter letter has been partly lost, but it is clear that Alethius had requested an exemplar of sacred eloquence; so when a superscription on two manuscripts intimates that Letter 34, which is actually a sermon, was sent to Alethius, we may assume that it was enclosed with Letter 33.

Letter 26 is addressed to one Sebastianus, about whom nothing further is known. He represents perhaps the earliest evidence of eremitic life in Gaul as distinct from the coenobitic monasticism practised at Marmoutier, Primuliacum, and elsewhere. Sebastianus was not strictly a recluse, because he was attended by a deacon who made provision for his food. The notable feature of this letter is Paulinus' uncritical enthusiasm; his initiative in writing shows that he had given little thought to the relative merits of the two kinds of monasticism.[42]

In contrast to these ecclesiastics is Jovius, the sole correspondent of Paulinus who, it would seem, was not a Christian. Letter 16 is our sole evidence of his character and interests. From it there emerges a sympathetic portrait of a man who had thought deeply about man's relationship with God but could not accept the Christian claim about the universal activity of Providence. This letter, as we shall see below, has in its content a general significance for the cultural history of the age; but we may also note here the phenomenon of Jovius himself, representing the more courteous and constructive Gallic pagan, who unlike many nominal Christians could see the point of Paulinus' retirement from the world.[43]

The two letters to Crispinianus, Nos. 25 and 25*, also are of interest more for the general significance of Paulinus' advice therein than for the person addressed. Crispinianus was a young and unimportant soldier in the imperial army in Gaul. When Paulinus heard that Crispinianus believed he might have a monastic vocation, he took the trouble to write on two different occasions to stress the incompatibility of serving Christ and Caesar, and to urge on Crispinianus the importance of a prompt and incisive decision.[44]

Other letters are sent to Paulinus' friends in Gaul, a group which provides impressive testimony to the spiritual awakening in Aquitania, for they have all renounced promising careers for religious poverty. One of these is Aper, to whom Letters 38, 39, and 44 are addressed. Paulinus lays emphasis on the wealth and fame which Aper had enjoyed as lawyer and provincial governor;[45] and he praises the wife of Aper, Amanda, who took on her husband's secular responsibilities when he withdrew from the world. The most interesting feature of this correspondence is perhaps the attitude it reveals to a woman who encouraged her husband to enter monastic life—a situation which soon became common enough to demand canonical regulations.[46]

Another such example is provided by Eucher and Galla, to whom Letter 51 is addressed. Though these two were not former intimates of Paulinus, they followed the example of Paulinus and Therasia in together entering monastic life. They retired to the island of Sainte Marguérite, close to the monastery founded by Honoratus, future bishop of Arles and yet another correspondent of Paulinus.[47] From there they exchanged letters with Paulinus. Eucher later became bishop of Lyon.[48]

Letters 40 and 41 were sent to a former intimate of Paulinus named Sanctus. We can presume that Sanctus also had entered religious life, for these letters are wholly devoted to scriptural meditation on points raised by Sanctus and his friend Amandus (not the catechist of Paulinus). The same presumption can be made about the "holy Desiderius" to whom Letter 43 is sent. The addressee here may well be the Desiderius to whom Severus dedicated his *Vita s. Martini*, and the priest who urged Jerome to write his polemic against Vigilantius.[49]

Finally, there is a fragment of another letter, No. 48.

Presumably this letter also was sent to a friend in Gaul, for it praises the spiritual depth of the great Gallic bishops of the early fifth century.

IMPORTANCE OF THE LETTERS

What is the chief importance and interest of these letters? It may seem audacious, in view of the pervading emphasis on spiritual and devotional topics, to claim any historical value for them. In consulting them, the secular historian feels that he has been diverted "from the unambiguous 'realities' of imperial legislation and senatorial politics into a hot-house world of piety."[50] This is certainly the opinion of the most recent English authority on the period.[51] Though Paulinus lived at Nola during the critical years of the fifth century when Rome collapsed before the barbarians, no hint of the political and military crisis emerges from these letters.[52] Again, there is an infuriating indifference to the ideological struggle which was being waged in the Senate between the Christian and the pagan elements. Paulinus had deliberately turned his back on this world.[53] Even when writing of political figures like Pammachius and the senator Publicola, son of the elder Melania, his words are directed to their souls and not to their activities at Rome.[54]

There are, of course, certain ecclesiastical topics treated by Paulinus in which the secular historian is keenly interested. But here, too, lies much frustration. Paulinus has little interest in the rigorous vocation of the historian. "My studies," he writes, "were never directed towards the investigation and collation of historical facts. Even in my early days, when doubtless I read more widely than I needed to, I always steered clear of historians."[55] Everything that he writes is glossy with the rhetorician's polish, *ornate compositum*.[56] In describing an escape from shipwreck, he inserts details derived from the account of Paul's deliverance in the Acts of the Apostles.[57] He presents the history of how Helena found the Holy Cross in a wholly emotive and uncritical manner, with a wealth of edifying but incredible detail.[58] The account of Victricius' conversion to Christianity is unfolded with the dramatic touches so beloved in rhetorical historiography; the picturesque description of the scene on the parade ground as Victricius renounced Caesar for Christ is marred by the absence of names, dates, and chronology which would allow the historian to set the event in a precise historical context.[59]

Yet these letters contain a massive amount of incidental information of importance to the ecclesiastical historian. They assist in the compilation of lists of occupants of episcopal sees, especially in Gaul,[60] with greater detail of the diocese of Bordeaux.[61] Some information can be gleaned as well on leading Italian ecclesiastics, such as, for example, Pope Siricius and his successor Anastasius.[62] The student of fourth-century liturgy will find an interesting description of an alms-feast held at Saint Peter's Basilica in Rome.[63]

The main weight of such detailed information, however, naturally centres on monastic life, especially at Nola but also in Gaul. We are afforded glimpses both of eremitic practice in Gaul and at the coenobitic monastery at Primuliacum, the two basilicas at which are mentioned, with some detail on the more recent one.[64] The information about the buildings at Nola is much more comprehensive. Paulinus mentions five basilicas and a guest house. There is a detailed description of the newest buildings which has allowed modern scholars, assisted by the impressive archaeological remains at Cimitile, to attempt a detailed reconstruction of the whole complex of buildings.[65]

Considerable information on the monastic routine can also be assembled. So far as worship is concerned, there is mention of assembly in church in the late afternoon for hymn-singing, and also of the practice of night vigils, of which something is known also from Milan.[66] It is interesting to find Paulinus acknowledging the gift of a Gallic hymnary;[67] it will be remembered that Hilary of Poitiers had been the pioneer in this composition in the West.

Clothes are described in some detail, since Paulinus has a characteristic interest in their symbolic importance and in scriptural warrant for the monastic habit. The approved garment of goat hair or camel's hair is contrasted with the more flamboyant uniform of soldiers, and a similar contrast is drawn between secular hair styles and the close-cropped head of the monk.[68]

There is also detail of meals. In accordance with general fourth-century practice in monasteries in both the East and West, only one daily meal was taken at Nola, even outside Lent. The community assembled for this evening meal, at which only vegetarian food was served. It seems that with this simple meal Paulinus permitted the company to drink a little wine.[69]

Unfortunately we get no clear picture of the size of the community at Nola or of its activity outside the life of prayer. From Paulinus' letters it appears that scriptural study must have had a central place. Paulinus himself spent some time in translation and in working up his Greek. There is also a possible allusion to the copying of texts.[70] The less literate members of the community were doubtless occupied with the church-building, the scale of which suggests that it provided regular tasks during Paulinus' lifetime. Paulinus shows that his passion for the welfare of the poor extends beyond his sermons to practical help for local indigents, and his community may have devoted time to such charitable works.[71] Some monks and brothers acted as couriers, taking letters and gifts (especially of blessed Campanian bread)[72] to his correspondents in Italy, Gaul, Africa, and Palestine.

Besides this abundance of information on monastic life, Paulinus provides evidence of some of the great spiritual leaders of his time. Many have already been mentioned amongst his correspondents, notably Sulpicius Severus, Augustine, Victricius, Rufinus. Amongst others there is an especially valuable portrait of Melania the Elder. Paulinus tells of her early years and conversion, her departure to Jerusalem and defiance of the Arian persecution in the East, and her return many years later. Paulinus' descriptive powers find a worthy subject in her triumphal visit to Nola; the extraordinary procession is memorably described, with a telling contrast between the empress of monasticism in her garb of poverty and her aristocratic relatives in their ostentatious finery.[73] Another great figure of the age to receive mention is the Dacian bishop Nicetas, probable author of the *Te Deum*.[74] There are also allusions to the great Gallic figures of monasticism, Martin and his successor Clarus.[75]

Above all, there is the portrait of Paulinus himself as it emerges from these pages. His feelings are recorded both at dramatic moments and during periods of uneventful solitude. We read of his distress at his brother's death because the brother had died indifferent to his spiritual welfare,[76] his forcible ordination at Barcelona when he was still reluctant to be ordained priest,[77] his rebuff by Pope Siricius at Rome when en route to Nola,[78] his yearly visits to the shrines of the martyrs at Rome, his illnesses and anxieties, and his joys at receiving messages from friends. But much more than surface details of the daily round is revealed in these letters. From them we also gain insight into Paulinus' spiritual development in the heroic life of poverty, chastity, and charity enjoined by the Scriptures. In this sense the true value of these letters is as spiritual autobiography.

PAULINUS AND THE SECULAR WORLD

To say, therefore, that the letters of Paulinus have no historical value is to set far too strict a limit on the word "historical." Aside from the points already made, these letters help to document fundamental fourth-century attitudes, a grasp of which is vital for an understanding of the nature of the conflict between the humanism shaped by centuries of Roman tradition and the Christian humanism represented by such figures as Augustine and Jerome, Ambrose and Paulinus. In short, these letters have importance in the history of ideas at one of the critical junctures in the intellectual history of Europe. Paulinus is readily aware that he is fighting a protracted engagement in company with Augustine, Ambrose, and Jerome against the intellectual forces of the pagan world.[79]

For Paulinus true Christianity resides in the utter renunciation of all the aspects of the secular world. He sees no merit in involvement in that world. When he writes to the soldier Crispinianus urging him to abandon his military career and follow Christ, he is well aware that Crispinianus is serving a Christian emperor, Honorius. This makes not the slightest difference. "You cannot serve two masters," he writes, "the one God and Mammon, Christ and Caesar, even though Caesar himself is now keen to be Christ's servant. . . . For it is not an earthly king who reigns over the whole world, but Christ and God."[80]

This rejection of the contemporary world entails not only contempt for its wealth and arms and political power, but also for its culture. In a significant passage to his friend Aper, Paulinus writes: "Let the rhetoricians keep their literature, the philosophers their philosophy, the rich their wealth, the princes their kingdoms. Our glory, property, and kingdom is Christ."[81] The literature and philosophy are closely associated with the wealth and power. But like Jerome, Paulinus could not shake off the formative influences of his education. Repeatedly he apologises to his friends when he finds himself quoting Virgil or Terence. "Please do not blame me for quoting a poet whom I do not now read, and for appearing to break my resolution in this respect."[82] And again: "Why do I use the language of foreigners, when our own tongue is sufficient for everything?"[83]

Just as the Christian tongue rejects the literature, so Christian "foolishness"—as in St. Paul's I Cor. 1.18—abandons the philosophy of the world. Much of this worldly philosophy Paulinus regards in any case as casuistry and linguistic trickery.[84] But his Letter 16 to Jovius is a central document for the Christian attitude towards pagan philosophy. Here Paulinus mounts attacks on the prevalent views which would reject the Christian claim of an all-knowing, all-merciful God. After a scathing attack on Platonic necessity, Stoic fate, Epicurean chance, and that deification of abstractions to which the Romans were traditionally addicted, he sets against them the reasonableness (*ratio*) of Christian truth, especially the Pauline teaching that adversity and danger are a merciful dispensation of divine Providence to combat human indifference.[85] It is interesting to note that in this instance Paulinus suspends his determination to avoid the language of the pagans, and readily uses arguments from secular philosophy which Jovius would best appreciate. And the style in which this letter is written is more consciously classical, with reminiscences of Homer and Virgil but virtually no scriptural quotation; we are reminded of the contrast between the Latin of Augustine's sermons and that of the *City of God*.[86]

STYLISTIC PRESENTATION

When Paulinus writes to Christian friends on his staple scriptural topics, his stylistic presentation is dominated by constant quotation from the Old and New Testaments, especially from the Psalms and Saint Paul, so that frequently his paragraphs take on the appearance of a verbal mosaic, with sentences and phrases gathered from various books of Scripture and linked ingeniously together. The firm impression of easy familiarity with the Bible should not mislead us into the notion that the introduction of such texts was rapid and mechanical. The technique of building up a narrative in this way was the fruit of his literary training at Bordeaux. Inherent in this training, after the selection of a topic, is the collection of passages from earlier authors where a similar subject is treated.[87] The characteristic approach of Paulinus is not to attempt systematic exegesis of a Psalm or a chapter of the Epistle to the Romans, or a personal exposition of a theological subject like the Redemption. More normally, he takes his correspondent's or his own existential situation, selects a broad scriptural image with which to depict it, and then gathers together and links the scriptural passages which enable him to develop the implications of the image. In a sense his talent here lies more in the literary than in the theological treatment.

The reader will note how often Paulinus derives his imagery from the scenes of his early life in Aquitania. Repeatedly he draws together scriptural passages where the symbolism is agricultural. Letter 10 sustains the farming image throughout. Writing to Delphinus, he reminds the bishop that at baptism he had implanted the seed of truth in Paulinus, and now confidently awaits the harvest. But Paulinus in his own eyes is barren soil, or the blighted crop produced in such soil. He is grateful for the enclosing wall built by Delphinus, and begs him to pray to the Lord of the vineyard that He may grant respite to the barren fig tree. Delphinus' prayers will act as fertilising dung, so that Paulinus may not be burnt as so much dead wood, but become wheat for the Lord's barn. This agricultural imagery he frequently employs.[88] Other striking images include those of the athlete and the swimmer, lightening themselves of their encumbering garments before running or before swimming through the troubled waters of the world, and that of building to describe spiritual progress.[89]

Unfortunately Paulinus does not always discipline his literary talent, and at times what starts as a fruitful biblical meditation degenerates into a riot of dissonant metaphors and extravagant conceits. "Ce fut toujours le défaut du bon Paulin, dans sa prose et ses vers, d'être interminable."[90] The dangers of such prolixity are apparent in the agricultural symbolism just quoted, where he calls himself successively barren soil, blighted crop, stunted fig tree, and wheat of the harvest. But there is at any rate a coherence there which is fatally absent elsewhere. Letter 40, for example, discusses the theme of the repentant sinner with a striking series of images from scriptural bird-life. Paulinus likens the sinner in his repentant retirement to the pelican in the desert and to the night raven. The pelican, we are reminded, is the foe of snakes, and the night raven's keen vision can pierce the darkness engulfing it; so we as sinners are to overcome our desires, and find light in the darkness of this world. This original parallel is then vitiated by further elaboration. He tells us that by acting like the pelican and the night raven, we shall become as the sparrow on the housetop, that is, attain the heights of perfect virtue. Christ is such a sparrow (for the sparrows fall by God's will, and Christ died saying: *Thy will be done*), and we are to emulate this Sparrow by walking in the footsteps of the evangelists till we attain the housetop! It is a ludicrous image with which we are finally left, though the message is sufficiently clear. Even more devious is his treatment of Samson and the dead lion, and his discussion of the meaning of Samson's hair,[91] in Letter 23, where again he is too prolix and too ingenious in the interconnexion of scriptural ideas. When Paulinus writes in this letter: "It is pleasant to give free rein to words,"[92] we are reminded of Macaulay's judgment on an earlier author: "Ovid has two insupportable faults: the one that he will be clever, the other that he never knows when to have done."

In his comments on Scripture, Paulinus constantly emphasises the typological significance of biblical figures. We recall that it was a Gaul, Hilary of Poitiers, who half a century earlier had inaugurated such exegesis in Latin with his *Commentary on Matthew*.[93] Paulinus depicts the Queen of Saba, or again Mary Magdalen, as a type of the Church; the death of Rachel at Bethlehem symbolises for him the death of the synagogue; the five wise and foolish virgins are seen as presenting the purity and the corruption of the five senses; Christ is depicted in Samson, or in the lion, or in the lion's whelp.[94]

Paulinus also compares his own or his addressee's situation with apposite scriptural contexts. When he writes his letter of consolation to Pammachius, it forms a most impressive scriptural meditation on the Christian attitude towards death. He exhorts Pammachius to ponder on the reaction of the patriarchs to the death of loved ones, and he successively examines Abraham, Jacob, Tobias, Joseph, and David, and even Christ Himself. And he concludes that the grief of love must be tempered by faith; like David, we should lay aside our grief and live in Christian hope.[95]

AUTHORITIES

These brief illustrations of Paulinus' characteristic presentation of the lessons of Scripture suggest that we need not concern ourselves with searching out authorities to whom to ascribe a close and continuous debt. Though some exceptions may be noted, the contents of these letters would seem for the most part to be his original thoughts on and compilations from the Scriptures. Yet the general question remains of who or what inspired his interest in the symbolic and typological facets of scriptural interpretation.

An important consideration here is the extent of Paulinus' knowledge of Greek.[96] Ausonius' list of great teachers in Aquitania suggests that Greek was a regular feature of the curriculum in the fourth century.[97] That Paulinus had been taught Greek is indicated by his translation of individual words and his citing of material from such works as Plato's *Republic*.[98] But he had little inclination to develop his knowledge of the language in mature life. A comment in a letter to Rufinus is especially revealing. In reply to a suggestion from Rufinus that he should tackle an early patristic text,[99] Paulinus pleads general inadequacy and ignorance, and adds: "I have rendered certain passages, where I could not understand or translate the words, by taking or (to be more truthful) hazarding the general sense."[100] The letter then notes that Rufinus has been assisting him in the difficulties of translation.

We are, therefore, probably justified in assuming that Paulinus did not draw his inspiration directly from Origen or from the great fourth-century Greek exegetes. The similarities with their approach which these letters evince were most likely achieved through study of the work of intermediaries. We may hazard that these were Hilary, Rufinus, and above all Ambrose. It can in fact be demonstrated that Paulinus did on occasion follow Ambrose closely. In Letter 23, for example, there is a long discussion of how Mary Magdalen, in her role as repentant sinner winning pardon and justification, is a type of the Church. Throughout this section there are verbal echoes of Ambrose's *Expositio in Lucam*. The dependence is especially noticeable in the discussion of Judas' objection that expenditure on costly ointments was money wasted, and again in the exposition of the symbolic meaning of Magdalen's use of her hair as a towel. There is no doubt that Paulinus has had the treatise of Ambrose at his elbow throughout.[101] Elsewhere, in describing how we must strip ourselves of worldly goods before we run the race, there are echoes of a passage in Ambrose's *De officiis ministrorum;* and a comment on the opening of the Gospel of Saint John suggests the influence of Ambrose's *De incarnatione.*[102]

More surprising is the borrowing from a passage in a letter of Augustine when Paulinus writes to Aper and Amanda. In a letter written to Paulinus in 396, Augustine lauded in a series of highly rhetorical exclamations an epistle sent to him by Paulinus, and he continued with praise for the sanctity of Paulinus and for the invaluable moral support of Therasia. Much of this is incorporated verbatim into Paulinus' letter to Aper and Amanda. For those who read Paulinus' letter with awareness of this plagiarism, there is splendid irony in the opening words: "O, that someone would give me literary powers like yours, so that I could reply adequately to your letter!"[103]

Such borrowings as these by Paulinus have been noted to suggest that where Paulinus presents extended commentary on Scripture or a narrative of historical events, he may well be drawing upon the work of others. But the fact remains that his more usual method of presenting his meditations on Scripture suggests an original approach.

The Framework of Christian Thought

What is the general framework of Christian thought which underpins these meditations?[104] Two main points must be made here. When Paulinus presents Christian dogma, he is thoroughly orthodox, carefully avoiding the heretical doctrines current in his day;[105] secondly, dogmatic exposition as such is not his major concern.[106] Though in both letters and poems he gives a sound outline of the doctrine of the Trinity, for example, and indicates the orthodox teaching on Christ's dual nature,[107] his is not the academic approach. Like his spiritual mentor Saint Paul, he is fiercely devoted to the person of Christ. For him the prime fact of life in this world is that Christ saved mankind by His death on the cross, and that He continues to dwell and perform His saving work in us.[108] With a wide range of scriptural images he constantly depicts Christ as the sole necessity of our lives. Christ is the living Bread we must eat, the good Samaritan who heals our wounds, the Light dispelling the darkness of the world, the sacrificial Lamb who died for us, the Gate and the Way by which we attain eternal life, the Cornerstone of our building, the Vine of which we are the branches, and the Bridegroom of the Church.

The world is a battlefield between the forces of God and the legions of Satan. Paulinus sometimes envisages this world as a sort of Roman empire over which God presides as eternal emperor and in which the saints are allotted their special provinces. But it is interesting to observe that he gives much more prominence to this role of the saints and to their relics in his poems than in these prose letters.[109] Even his patron Saint Felix, who is never far from his thoughts when he composes his poetry, is mentioned in barely half a dozen letters and hardly ever in his role as miracle-worker.[110] It is almost possible to speak of two different religious attitudes, one in the letters and another in some of the poems. In the letters he continually concentrates on the truths of Scripture as they impinge on sinning mankind; many poems, on the other hand, hymn the sanctity of saints like Felix and see them as beneficent patrons over their flocks. The letters show Paulinus in his daily contemplation, a disciple of Paul confronting the central Christian mysteries; the *Natalicia* show him on holiday, as it were, the ward of Felix singing the praises and kindnesses of his patron on the anniversaries of his completion of the race.

In these letters, then, there is little emphasis on the miraculous mediation of angels and saints in the warfare with Satan. Here the saints are more regularly depicted as the "mountains of God" or the "beautiful black firs" which serve as exemplars directing us towards heaven.[111] The struggle against the wiles of the devil is conducted solely with the resource of divine grace.[112] God refuses this grace to none, and He wills that all men be saved.[113] If men do not attain salvation, it is because with their God-given freedom they have refused the gift of that grace.[114] Prayer is the means of conscious assent to salvation. Almost every letter of Paulinus is an exhortation to his friends to pray to God in praise or supplication, and above all to intercede for himself, that he may win pardon for his sins and growth in perfection.

Such intercession for fellow Christians has been made possible by baptism, by which God's love, descending through His Son, creates in us a kinship stronger than that of blood.[115] This love of Christ is as strong as death and cannot be loosed.[116] On this base Paulinus propounds the doctrine of Christ's mystical body, his grasp of which is impressive in its completeness. Repeatedly he emphasizes that we are the limbs of the one body, and that Christ is our head.[117] Repeatedly he explores the implication of this —that as members of the same body we must all be of one mind, and must all feel the same joys and the same pains as each other.[118] Such unity of heart and of mind has no need of physical confrontation.[119] Here is one of the four pivotal notions of Paulinus' thought, developed as so often from his meditations on the Pauline epistles.[120]

The other dominant notions revealed in his letters are likewise centred on the *ratio bene vivendi*, the Roman pre-occupation with the good life now translated into terms of Christian duty. The first of these is the need for Christian asceticism in all its forms, with the renunciation of wealth, luxurious living, marriage, and secular literature. But Paulinus has more to say about the disposal of riches than about the rest, because he has developed a theory about the divine economy of riches in this world. This theory he characteristically presents enshrined in a group of scriptural texts. He is concerned not only with the perfection of the individual as shown by compassion to his neighbour, but also with the *justice* thereby achieved in the community. Especially emphasised is the notion that the rich are stewards of their wealth, being lent it by Christ;[121] they are to lend support to the poor in this life, *that there may be an equality*,[122] and by donating their possessions to the poor they loan Christ His own gifts.[123] Even when Paulinus has begun on other topics, he often returns to this theme; thus in Letter 16 to Jovius, he begins with an exposé of the falsities of pagan philosophies, but ends by stressing the need to share our wealth.

Yet in this as in the other facets of his doctrine of asceticism, Paulinus is remarkably balanced in an age when extreme attitudes were by no means uncommon. He condemns not wealth itself, but the wrong and selfish use of it.[124] And in a most perceptive passage he stresses that the relinquishing of riches does not itself imply perfection, but only the beginning of the ascent towards surrender of self.[125] Likewise witness his views on marriage. He devotes a poem[126] to proclamation of its blessings, yet at the same time he stresses that the chosen life of virginity and the renunciation of marital relations are sacrifices more pleasing to God.[127]

Humility is the third keynote of Paulinus' thought, and in a striking meditation on its nature he is concerned to bring out its quality as a positive and magnanimous virtue. We are to humble ourselves before God alone. "There are such things as saintly pride and wicked humility. . . . That humility is condemned which is complaisant to men not from faith but from mental cowardice, which cares more for popularity with men than for salvation."[128] Humility of heart is in fact allied to that exaltation of spirit which rises above earthly thoughts and seeks the glorious realm of God.[129] This is the humility which Paulinus praises in his patron Felix and in his noble friend Melania; this is the humility to which he constantly aspires himself.[130]

The final dominating notion pervading these letters, which is in a sense the culmination of all that goes before, is that of the *caritas Christi*, the *agape* which is to govern all our relations with each other. Visualised at the lower and material level it is the charity which the rich owe to the poor. But in his analysis of such passages of Scripture as the parable of Dives and Lazarus,[131] Paulinus shows himself well aware that the giving must be invested with compassion and concern. He suggests that Dives' tongue suffered more than his other members because his words of scorn for the poor were the most terrible feature of his indifference towards his neighbour. Only the *caritas* which is both charity and love can open the gates of heaven.[132] Again it is the Pauline text which is the basis of his teaching and which he repeatedly invokes: *The love of our neighbour worketh no evil. Love therefore is the fulfilling of the law.*[133]

*   *   *

The text followed in the translation of these letters is that established by Hartel in *Corpus scriptorum ecclesiasticorum latinorum* 29 (Vienna 1894). The Hartel text represents a substantial advance on earlier editions, but much work still remains to be done.[134] I have indicated in the notes certain passages where Hartel's reading seems indefensible.

These letters have never previously been translated into English. The only complete translation of which I am aware is the eighteenth-century version in French of C. de Santeul,[135] and this has not been accessible to me. The letters of Paulinus to St. Augustine have been translated

into Dutch by A. P. Muys, and Letter 32 has been translated into English by R. C. Goldschmidt.[136]

In rendering the passages of Scripture quoted by
Paulinus, I have as far as possible used the Challoner revision of the Douay-Rheims version, with changes as
necessary to accord with the Latin of Paulinus. Since
Paulinus quoted Scripture frequently from memory, and
moreover was a contemporary of St. Jerome, it is hardly
surprising that in his scriptural quotations there are
numerous divergences from the Vulgate. I have not considered it necessary to cite all the textual variations in the
notes.

*   *   *

It remains for me to acknowledge with thanks the help
of my brother, the Rev. James Walsh, S.J., in the interpretation of certain passages and in the identification of scriptural allusions. He has not, however, read the work as a
whole, and, of course, is not responsible for the imperfec-
tions which remain.

LETTER 1

To Severus[1]

Paulinus, the servant of Christ Jesus, sends greetings to his dearest brother Severus,[2] in accord with their common faith in God the Father and in Christ Jesus our salvation.

1. *How sweet are thy words to my palate, sweeter than honey and the honeycomb to my mouth!*[3] In my heart, which was smeared as it were with the honey of your words, I distinctly felt the truth of that saying of Holy Scripture: *Let goodly words make thy bones fat.*[4] Not, of course, the bones whose structure provides the framework for the movement of the body, but the bones by which the strength of the inner man is maintained—hope, faith, and charity. These are the entrails of mercy, the bones of patience, the limbs which carry all our strength. These are the bones, limbs, and entrails which you have enriched with your holy messages of hope, faith, and charity. By these you have taught me that the hope of your faith trained upon the Lord, the unwavering faith of your hope in the Lord, and the fullness of your charity in Christ abide even as God's love for us.

For in answer to my prayer (I was troubled, yet my faith remained constant in you, or rather in God who wields and brings to perfection His power even amongst the weak) you revealed the increase of your inheritance amongst the saints.[5] This you did by your wholesome disposal of the burdens of this world, for you have purchased

heaven and Christ at the price of brittle worldly goods.[6]
You have true understanding *concerning the needy and the
poor,*[7] for you came to believe that they reside in Christ,
and that Christ, as He Himself taught us, is clothed and
fed and lent money when they are.[8]

2. *Let them that perish* regard this as an *odour of death
unto death.*[9] For them the flesh and the cross of the living
God are foolishness, or a stumbling block;[10] for flesh and
blood, to which they are slaves, do not reveal to them[11] that
Christ Jesus is the Son of God. But may our belief in the
flesh and death of God *become the odour of life unto life.*[12]
Dearest brother, let not our feet be diverted from the ways
of the Lord or from treading the narrow path, should the
wicked or foolish voices of worldly men from time to time
bark around us.[13] For the Sacred Scriptures have given us
sufficient teaching about them and about ourselves. In
speaking of worldly men the blessed Apostle tells us that
*we therefore labour and are reviled, because we hope in
the living God, who is the salvation of all men, especially
of the faithful.*[14] In His very own words in the Gospels,
God has foretold both the venomous conversation and the
deserved punishment of these men, to whom you wish to
render an account of your actions: *Woe to them that shall
scandalise one of these little ones that believe in Me; it
were better for him that a millstone should be hanged
about his neck, and that he should be drowned in the depth
of the sea.*[15] But to us He says: *Blessed are ye when men
shall revile you and speak all that is evil against you,
and shall cast My name as an evil thing in your faces; be
glad and rejoice, for your reward is very great in heaven.*[16]

My brother, let us remember these words of the Lord
and be strengthened in our faith, and let us ignore the

taunts or hatred of the pagans. For *they walk on in darkness*,[17] because *the sun of justice has not risen unto them*.[18] *The venom of asps is under their lips*,[19] it infects the mind and kills the soul, once the ears give assent to it and it penetrates the heart. *Their heart is vain*, says Divine Scripture, *and their throne is an open sepulchre*.[20] Let us be careful that their leaven does not affect the whole mass. For it is written: *Neither shall the wicked dwell near thee*.[21] And again: *With the holy thou wilt be holy, and with the perverse thou wilt be perverted*.[22] Further: *Let him depart from iniquity who nameth the name of the Lord*.[23] My brother, block and *hedge in thy ears with thorns*[24] at their words, which are the thorns and arrows of the devil. He lurks in their hearts, *he lieth in ambush that he may catch the poor man*[25] of Christ and hunt the soul of the Christian. But, in the words of Scripture, *their iniquity shall be turned on their own heads, and they shall fall into the hole which they are making*.[26]

3. *But thou, O man of God, fly from these men*,[27] and do not strive to render an account to them as if they were wiser. For you know that the beginning of wisdom lies in your fear of the Lord.[28] If they think our course is foolish, be thankful in your awareness that you perform the work of God and the command of Christ. Remember that *the foolish things of the world hath God chosen that He may confound the things that are wise*, and that *the foolishness of God is wiser than men*.[29] The desire to be rid of this foolishness is presuming to deny Christ Himself. If any are ashamed to confess His name before the world, He in turn will be ashamed to confess them as His before the Father.[30]

4. You write that you are taking pains to explain my course and your own. But what will you do if you fail to

persuade the men who argue with you about God's work, not for their instruction but for your destruction? First you will blush, and then you will grow pale, as though you are defending the worst cause. Dislodged from your position, you will stumble on the way of the Lord, and slip back from heaven to earth, once you destroy what you have built.

The identity of the inquirers to whom you must render an account greatly affects the issue. If a man comes in eagerness to learn and admits his ignorance, sprinkle upon him the seed of the faith, reveal God's commandment. If he embraces the word, *thou hast gained a brother*[31] for the Church and a sheep for Christ. But the bud which sprouts from the good seed may be imperfect. If the enemy of our heavenly Master has oversown cockle by night amongst the wheat, the pernicious blade and the barren crop will have to be separated from the good produce at the time of the harvest. Consigned not to the barns but to the furnace, the crop will burn as fuel feeding the eternal fire, whilst now it thrives with the flames which lie within it.[32] If your inquirer is such, avoid him and keep him away from your conversation and your sight, so that if he cannot be healed by your faith, he may not wound you by his lack of it.

5. Even though he be a brother and friend and closer to you than your right hand and dearer than life itself, if he is a stranger and an enemy in Christ *let him be to thee as the heathen and the publican.*[33] Let him be severed from your body as a useless right arm if he is not united to you in the body of Christ. Let him be plucked out like a harmful eye[34] if he overshadows your whole body with his

blemish or blindness. For it is better *that one member should perish* for the safety of the whole body *rather than that the whole body pass into hell,* as the Lord says,[35] because of the love of one diseased limb. We must not fear the displeasure of such men; indeed we should desire it, for from their taunts and curses is born the abundant reward which God has promised in heaven. Christ says: *The disciple is not above the master nor the servant above his lord. And if they have called the master of the house Beelzebub, how much more them of his household?*[36] If they have come to love the Lord and God whom we follow, they will love us also. *If they have persecuted Him, as they will also persecute us,*[37] what is there for us in the favour of the world, which is the same as hatred for Christ? *If you had been of the world,* says Christ, *the world would love its own.*[38]

6. So realise what you are longing for when you seek to render an account to men such as these unbelievers. It is unquestionably the favour of men that you seek, that is, the favour of the world. But you cannot please the world unless you prefer to displease Christ. For *if I pleased men,* says Paul, *I should not be the servant of Christ.*[39] So let us displease these men, and be thankful that we displease those who find God displeasing. For, as you know, it is not our work that they assail in us, but that of our Lord Jesus Christ, who is almighty God. It is He they reject in their actions and in our deeds. Too late will they say: *Lord, when did we see Thee naked and did not cover Thee? Hungry, and did not give Thee to eat? Sick, and did not visit Thee?*[40] Then they will hear these words: *Depart into everlasting fire, which God has prepared for your father*

and his angels.[41] For what they deny to the needy, they deny to Christ, *who being rich became poor, that through His poverty we might be rich.*[42]

7. Meanwhile let them enjoy their pleasures, high offices, and wealth, if indeed these are theirs. For they prefer to have these on earth, where our life ends, than in heaven, where it abides. Let them keep their wisdom and happiness, and leave us what they think is our poverty and stupidity. Let them claim wisdom if they wish and condemn our stupidity in regard to the words of our God Himself, whom *they profess to know in name, but in their works deny Him, having an appearance of godliness but denying the power thereof.*[43] For the Lord says: *The children of this world are wiser than the children of light;* but He added: *in this generation.*[44] Let them be wiser, provided they are not children of light. Let them be wise in this one generation, provided they are seen to be witless in the regeneration which we enjoy. Let them be blessed, or rather fortunate, now, borne along through unlimited prosperity in a complaisant world, clad in soft garments, dwelling in the houses of kings,[45] provided *they are not in the labour of men nor scourged like other men.*[46] Let them abound in the world's riches because they are paupers in God's. Of them it is written: *The rich have wanted and have suffered hunger,* just as the same passage adds about us: *But they that seek the Lord shall not be deprived of any good.*[47]

8. I pray, my brother, that we may be found worthy to be cursed, censured, and ground down, and even to be executed in the name of Jesus Christ, as long as Christ Himself is not killed in us.[48] Then at last *we would walk on the asp and the basilisk, and trample underfoot the head*

of the dragon[49] of old. But we dissociate ourselves from a world which still shows friendship to us and is therefore worse, and we find delight in Christ. We love to obtain praise only in His name, and we refuse to be dejected and oppressed, which is the more useful course. Remember that if the grain of mustard seed, from which we are sprung, is trodden underfoot, its creative heat increases and it is at last roused to exploit its power. So in this we ought to do justice to our nature. When we are trodden down by hostile talk, we ought to issue forth in flaming faith and burn the men who seek to break us because they regard us as the least of men, *the grain of mustard which is the least of all seeds.*[50] If indeed these outsiders demand from you a reason for your holy work, and from vipers' hearts wave venomous tongues at your heart, *give not that which is holy to dogs, and do not cast your pearls before swine. For what part hath the faithful with the unbeliever? Or what fellowship hath light with darkness? What concord hath Christ with Belial?*[51]

9. You are a soldier of Christ. Paul has armed you with *the helmet of salvation, the breastplate of justice, the shield of faith, the sword of truth, and the power of the Holy Ghost.*[52] Stand unflinching in your heavenly arms, and quench the glowing weapons of the enemy with the waters of wisdom and the stream of living water within you. *Keep that which is committed to thy trust, preserve the faith, pursue justice, keep the charity of Christ, strive after patience, practise yourself in the godliness which is profitable to all things, be sober, labour in all things, fight the good fight, finish the course, so that you may lay hold of that for which you have been chosen. As to the rest, there shall be laid up for you a crown of justice, which the Lord,*

the just judge, will render on that day to them that love His coming.[53] But avoid those who *consent not to sound teaching,* and *love pleasures rather than God.*[54] They advance always towards the worse course, leading others astray and being themselves misled. They are depraved in mind, strangers to the truth, and therefore slaves to the evil longings of their hearts, to the snare, to the many desires which cause men to be wrecked from the barque of faith and drowned in death and destruction.[55] This is because they have preferred the creation to the Creator. In other words, they hold *gold and silver, the idols of the Gentiles,*[56] dearer than God; they preserve their souls in this world, but lose them in Christ. Depart from such men, avoid their irreligious and fashionable arguments, so that you may not begin to grow sick whilst considering vapid problems and empty or impious disputes.[57] Avoid them, so that you may not be in danger from false brothers and wicked, depraved philosophers, so that the devil may not jump for joy as all who look on you say: *This man began to build and was not able to finish.*[58] May we avoid this fate, for we have dared to attempt our work of perfection relying not on our own deeds and strength but on the power and mercy of God. Since He is almighty, He can complete in us the work of His perfection. Now that He has deigned to lay the foundation and to begin building with the first scaffolding, He can construct it according to His measurements and complete it by roofing it. For when even His apostles were confounded at the enormity of such a task, He deigned to say that it was impossible in men's eyes, but not in God's.[59] For those who believe in Him, nothing is impossible.

10. But in order that we may console each other with

the words of the Lord and progress in our works, *go forth out of thy country and from thy kindred,*[60] so that imitating Abraham by the faith of your departure, you may be worthy of his blessed bosom. Hasten to come to me, so that you may both receive and impart reinforcements of faith for our common profit. For this is acceptable in God's sight, that a brother who helps a brother shall also be exalted.[61]

As I wrote previously, I am now staying in the city of Barcelona.[62] After my letter which you answered, on the day on which the Lord deigned to be born as man,[63] I was ordained into the priesthood. The Lord witnesses that it happened through the sudden compulsion of the crowd,[64] but I believe that I was forced into it at His command. I confess that I was unwilling. Not that I despised the rank (for I call the Lord to witness that I longed to begin my holy slavery with the name and office of sacristan),[65] but since I was bound elsewhere and had my mind, as you know, firmly intent on another place,[66] I trembled at this strange and unexpected decree of the divine will. I offered my neck, then, to the yoke of Christ, and now I see myself engaged on tasks which are too great for my deserts and for my understanding. I know that I have now been admitted and accepted into the secret shrines of the highest God, that I partake of heavenly life, that brought nearer to God I dwell in the very spirit, body, and illumination of Christ. With my puny mind I can as yet scarcely understand the sacred burden I bear, and aware of my weakness I tremble at the weight of my task. But He *who has given wisdom to little ones, and out of the mouth of infants and sucklings has perfected his praise,*[67] is capable of achieving His work and adorning His gift even in me, so that having summoned me from unworthiness, He may make me worthy of Himself. But you are to know that the plan on which we were both[68] set is unaffected, since the Lord has also granted us this. For I was prevailed upon to be ordained in the church at Barcelona only on condition that I was not attached to that church. I was dedicated to the priesthood of the Lord only, not to a particular place in the Church.[69]

11. So please come here preferably before Easter, so that now I am a priest you may join me in celebrating the sacred festival.[70] But if you wish to meet us, God willing, at the start of our journey, set out in Christ's name after Easter. But I have faith in the Lord that He will fire you with a greater longing for me, so that you do not contemplate postponing until after Easter the time you plan to spend with me. Your loving servant, who told me that he took only eight days to get here from Eluso,[71] will tell you the length of the journey. The journey is so short and easy that it provides no difficulty even in the Pyrenees, the bulwark between Southern France and Spain which inspires awe more in name than as a mountain range.

But why should I mention the distance? If you long for me, the journey is short; but if you are indifferent, it is long.

LETTER 2

To Amandus[1]

Paulinus greets his lord and most beloved brother Amandus.[2]

1. I have finally received the letter which you affectionately sent me. The longer it had been desired, the more eagerly did I take hold of it. For *as cold water is sweeter to a thirsty soul and good tidings from a far country are more pleasant,*[3] so your sweet words lent richness to my bones and *filled my hungry soul with good things.*[4]

How can I make a reply worthy of such words? For my eloquence and intellect are slight, my mind is dull, my lips lack fluency, and in the words of Scripture *my belly is slothful.*[5] But though I am inferior in every way, charity alone gives me equality with you. The affection which you show to me I strive to match with like mind, and indeed it is implanted in my heart, fixed in my breast, and mingled with my very soul through the spirit of the Lord, *who maketh men of one manner to dwell in a house,*[6] who joins countless thousand of believers in a single heart, for He alone is *filled all in all.*[7]

2. Now it has pleased the Lord to place His treasure in an earthenware vessel.[8] *He has called me by His grace, raising up the needy from the earth and lifting up the poor out of the dunghill that He might place me with the princes of His people,*[9] and clothe me with salvation[10] amongst His priests. So *in hastening to the odour of His ointments*[11] I

may become a drop of that ointment which *ran down upon the beard of Aaron.*[12] Out of awareness of my deserts, I tried to refuse (or rather, I did not dare to consent) to become a servant in the Lord's house and *to bless the Lord from the fountains of Israel.*[13] I admit that I, *a worm and no man,*[14] was unwillingly forced by sudden coercion, compelled by the crowd with their fingers at my throat. Though I desired my chalice to pass from me, still I was compelled to say to the Lord: *Yet not my will but Thine be done,*[15] especially when I read that the Lord Himself had said of His own person: *The Son of man is not come to be ministered unto, but to minister.*[16] Therefore, restrained by the Lord and *apprehended by Him whom I do not yet apprehend,*[17] I attend God's altar. I serve at the table of salvation as one now senior[18] in title and office, but as still a child in sense and a suckling in speech.

3. Reverend lord, brother and lord in Christ, pray to the Lord, who is rich in every blessing, that I may discharge my ministry well and attain a station that is good for me, that I may know how to deport myself in God's house and conduct the sacrament of fatherly love. Pray that *I may abound in faith and word and knowledge and all carefulness,* and also *in your charity towards us, so in this grace also you may abound.*[19] Moreover, with your letters give me frequently the fresh resources that I need. For *nourished up in the words of faith and of the good doctrine*[20] which you have attained in Sacred Scripture from boyhood, fashion me in accordance with your rule of direction, feed me with the spiritual food which is the word of God. He is the true and living Bread; we live more on Him than on bread, for He is the food of the just who

live on faith.²¹ Do not because of my ordination be less careful in your care for my formation. For we are separated by our place in the Church, but not in its body. For *there is one God and one mediator of God and men*²² who is the head of the Church. Since we are all one, we live in this Church as in one house. I cannot say that I am deprived of you, since we belong to the one Spirit, and dwell in the One who is one. So *keeping the unity of the spirit in the bond of peace as one body and one spirit,*²³ let us toil together as with limbs allied with each other, that we may grow *unto the edifying of that body*²⁴ whose head is Christ.

4. Since, then, I am no longer an enemy but a citizen, no longer afar but close at hand, no longer sheep but shepherd, and since I have been set on the foundation of apostles and prophets,²⁵ school and strengthen my hands in the knowledge of building. So I may learn to join both walls to *the stone which is become the head of the corner,*²⁶ and to build up body and heart cleansed with faith into the holy temple and dwelling of God; to lead captive, by the armour of Paul and the power of God, all pride which exalts itself against the knowledge of God, and all understanding towards obedience to Christ; to apply the axe of the Gospel to the roots of the trees; to kill earthly sinners with the sword of the spirit, which is the word of God; to quench all the glowing darts of the most wicked one with the shield of the Catholic faith; and when the contest is fought out and the course run, when the faith has been kept and the ministry fulfilled, *to await what the Lord, the just judge, will render on that day to all that love His coming.*²⁷ So look upon me in spirit and hold fast to me as yours, as one who abides with you.

Instruct, help, encourage, and strengthen me. As one born of you, and through you of God, I should be your especial care in Christ. For if I am unworthy, I shall be a reproach to you; but I shall be your joy if I am recognised by my good fruit as a branch of your tree.[28]

LETTER 3

To Alypius[1]

The sinners Paulinus and Therasia send greetings to their most blessed father and rightly esteemed lord Alypius.[2]

1. You have shown, my lord, that you bear within you true charity and perfect love towards my lowly person. You are truly holy, deservedly blessed, the object of true affection. For my courier Julianus on his return from Carthage brought me the letter which conveyed to me your shining sanctity; it was such that I seemed to hear of your love for me not for the first time but as something already experienced.

Undoubtedly this love of yours has welled forth from Him who *has chosen us in Him from the foundation of the world*,[3] and in whom we were made before we were born. For *not we ourselves but He made us*,[4] for He made all that is to be. So fashioned by His foreknowledge and His creation, we have been joined together by the love that anticipates acquaintance, in identity of desires and in unity of faith, or the faith of unity. Thus we know each other through the revelation of the Spirit before meeting in person. So I give thanks and I glory in the Lord, who is one and the same throughout the world, encompassing His love in His people through the Holy Spirit, which *He has poured out upon all flesh.*[5] *With the stream of the river He maketh His city joyful*,[6] among the citizens of which He has placed you deservedly in your apostolic see *as a*

43

prince with the princes of His people.[7] And He has wished
me, whom He raised when I was cast down, and lifted
from the earth when I was destitute,[8] to be numbered
amongst your associates. But I am more thankful for that
gift of the Lord by which He has placed me to dwell in
your heart and allowed me so to steal into your affections
that I claim for myself a personal trust in your love. I have
been so impressed by your kindnesses and your gifts that I
cannot have any doubtful or slight regard for you.

2. For I have received as an outstanding token of your
love and regard the work, written in five books,[9] of our
holy brother Augustine, who has attained perfection in
Christ the Lord. I admire and revere it so much that I
believe the words have been dictated by divine inspiration.
So reassured by your friendliness, so worthy of my esteem,
I have presumed to write to him as well.[10] I take it for
granted that you will make excuse to him for my inexperi-
ence and commend me to his affection as to that of all
holy men. For it is by their services, far away though they
are, that you have deigned to secure my salvation; and I
am certain that with like affection you will ensure that they
are greeted in turn with my humble salutations through
your holy lips. I include both the clergy who accompany
your holy person and those in the monasteries who imitate
your faith and virtue. For though you work amongst
peoples and over your people, an unsleeping shepherd
guiding with anxious watchfulness the sheep of the Lord's
pasture, yet you have made for yourself a desert by re-
signing from the world and rejecting flesh and blood. You
are set apart from the many, and are called amongst the
few.

3. Though I cannot match you in anything, on your

instructions I have made arrangements for the great universal history of Eusebius, the venerable bishop of Constantinople.[11] It is in fact a gift to some extent provided by another. The delay in meeting your request was attributable to the fact that, not possessing the book, I found it on your instruction at Rome, in the possession of our most holy father Domnio.[12] Doubtless he obliged me all the more readily with this kindness because I told him it was to be conferred on you. Since you have kindly informed me of your whereabouts, I have followed your instructions and written to our father Aurelius,[13] your revered associate in the rank of bishop,[14] with the request that if you are now staying at Hippo Regius, he should have the parchment transcribed at Carthage, and kindly send it with my letter to you at Hippo. I have also asked the holy men Comes and Evodius, whom I know because your words reveal their charity, to be sure to write to the same effect, so that father Domnio may not be too long without his book, and so that once your copy has been sent to you, you may keep it and not have to return it.

4. Now I make a particular request, since you have filled me with great love for you though I did not deserve or expect it, that in return for this history of the world you send me the whole account of your holy person, "from what race and house"[15] you were summoned by so great a Lord. Tell me of your beginnings, when you were first sundered from your mother's womb, how you renounced the ties of flesh and blood, how you passed to the mother of God's sons who rejoices in her children, and how you were translated to *the race of kings and priests.*[16]

As for your information that you had already heard my insignificant name at Milan when you were baptised there,

I confess, in my eagerness to know everything about you
so that I may add to my felicitations, that I am rather
curious to learn whether you were either received into the
faith or ordained priest by our father Ambrose, who is so
worthy of my esteem. If so, it appears that we have the
same adviser. For though I was baptised at Bordeaux by
Delphinus, and ordained at Barcelona in Spain by
Lampius,[17] when the people there were suddenly fired to
put compulsion on me, yet I have always been nurtured
in the faith by Ambrose's affection, and now that I am
ordained priest he cherishes me.[18] In fact, he wanted to
claim me as one of his clergy, so that even if I live away
from Milan I may be regarded as a priest of his.

5. You must, however, know everything about me and
realise that I am a sinner of long standing. It is not so
long since *I was brought out of the darkness and the
shadow of death*[19] and drank in the breath of the air of
life, nor so long since I put my hand to the plough and took
up the cross of the Lord that I cannot be helped by your
prayers to endure to the end. If by your intercession you
lighten my burden, this will be added to your merits as
reward. For the holy man who helps the toiler (I do not
presume to call myself brother) *will be exalted as a great
city*.[20] You indeed are a city built on a mountain, a lamp
burning on a candlestick and shining with seven-branched
brightness,[21] whilst I lurk beneath the bushel of my sins.
Seek me out with your letters, bring me into the light
where you yourself shine on golden candlesticks. *Your
words will be a light to my path*,[22] and my head will be
anointed with the oil of your lamp; and my faith will be
fired when I take from the breath of your mouth food
for my mind and light for my soul.

6. The peace and grace of God be with you. May the crown of justice await you on the day of judgment, my venerable lord and father who are so rightly loved and longed for. I ask you to greet with great affection and allegiance the blessed companions and imitators of your holiness (perhaps they will allow me to call them brothers in the Lord) who serve the Lord in the faith in churches and monasteries in Carthage, Tagaste, Hippo Regius, and in all your parishes and places in Africa known to you.

If you have received the parchment of holy Domnio, please have it transcribed and return it to me. I ask you also to tell me by letter which hymn of mine you know. I have sent a loaf to your holy person to symbolise our unity; it also embraces the substance of the Trinity.[23] By deigning to accept it you will make it a blessing.

LETTER 4

To Augustine[1]

The sinners Paulinus and Therasia[2] send greetings to their loving lord and brother the venerable Augustine.

1. *The charity of Christ, which presseth us*[3] and binds us together, separated as we are, in the unity of faith, has itself lent me the confidence to banish my shyness and to write to you, and through your writings to take you to my heart. Meanwhile I cling to those writings to heal and sustain my soul, for they draw richness from your practised fluency and sweetness from heavenly honeycombs. I have obtained five books of them through the gift of my friend, the blessed and venerable bishop Alypius, not merely for my instruction but also to be of service to the church in many cities.[4] So now I have these books to read. I delight in them, and from them take sustenance—not the food that perishes, but that which achieves the essence of eternal life[5] by our faith through which we have become one in body with our Lord Jesus Christ. For our faith, which disregards the world before our eyes and looks with longing at the world unseen[6] through the love which believes all things according to the truth of almighty God, is strengthened by the writings and example of the faithful. You are truly the salt of the earth[7] by which our hearts are seasoned, so that they cannot grow empty through the delusions of the world. You are a candle worthily set on the candlestick[8] of the Church; from your seven-branched lamp[9] you

pour out light, nourished by the oil of joy, far and wide over Catholic cities. You dispel the mist of heretics however thick it lies, and with the brilliance of your brightening words uncover the light of truth from the disorder of darkness.

2. My loving brother, so admirable and venerable in Christ the Lord, you see with what friendship I acknowledge you, with what great wonder I marvel at you, with what great love I embrace you. Every day I enjoy a dialogue with your writings and take nourishment from the breath of your lips. For I could rightly call your mouth the pipe of living water and the course of the eternal spring, since Christ has become in you *a fountain of water, springing up into life everlasting.*[10] Out of longing for this water, my soul has thirsted for you, my soul has desired to be drunk with the richness of your stream.[11] So, since you have provided me with sufficient armour against the Manicheans with this Pentateuch, if you have written any defences of the Catholic faith against other enemies as well (for our foe, "who has a thousand means of working harm,"[12] must be encompassed by weapons as varied as the ambushes from which he attacks), I beg you to provide me with the arms of justice from your armoury, and do not refuse to bestow them upon me. For I am a sinner toiling even yet under a great burden, a veteran in the ranks of sinners but a new recruit for the eternal King in spiritual warfare. Up to now I have admired in my wretchedness the world's wisdom, and in God's eyes, through my useless writing and depraved sagacity, I have been foolish[13] and dumb. Now that *I have grown old amongst my enemies* and been *vain in my thoughts, I have lifted up my eyes to the mountains,* looking up to the commands of the law

and the gifts of grace, *from whence help has come to me*[14] from the Lord. Without punishing wickedness He has enlightened the blind, released the fettered,[15] and humbled one who was perversely haughty, so that being made humble and dutiful I might be raised by Him.

3. Accordingly, with steps yet unsteady I follow the glorious traces of the just, in the hope that through your prayers *I can apprehend wherein* by God's pity *I have been apprehended.*[16] So guide this puny creature as he creeps uncertainly along, teach him to advance by your steps. For I would have you compute my age not by bodily development but by my spiritual growth. In the flesh I have reached the age at which the lame man was healed by the apostles, at the gate called Beautiful, through the power of the Word.[17] But if I measure my soul's birthdays I am still at the age of the infants who were slain by wounds intended for Christ, and who by their worthy blood anticipated the sacrifice of the Lamb and foretold the passion of the Lord.[18] So nurture me as one still a child in the word of God and a suckling in spiritual life; I look with admiration to your words which abound in faith, wisdom, and love.

If one thinks of the office we share, you are my brother.[19] But if one considers your maturity of mind and thought, you are my father though you may be younger in years.[20] For your venerable wisdom has advanced you while still young to maturity of worth and the acclamation of your elders. So cherish and strengthen me, for I am a novice in the sacred writings and in spiritual studies, and therefore after my protracted perils and many shipwrecks I am not adept at handling them, since I am barely emerging from the breakers of the world. Since you now stand on firm ground, take me safe into your care, so that if you think it meet we may sail together in the harbour of salvation. Meanwhile, as I strive to escape from the hazards of this life and from the depths of sin, support me with the plank of your prayers so that I may emerge naked from this world as from a shipwreck.

4. For I have deliberately lightened myself of baggage and of oppressive clothing that I may swim unencumbered through this rough sea of the present life which bars our way to God with baying sins like hounds between. At Christ's command and with His help I have cast off all garments of the flesh and anxiety of the morrow. I do not boast of having done this. If I could boast, I would boast in the Lord, *who has the power to accomplish what we can merely will.*[21] But as yet my heart longs only to desire the Lord's judgments; you will realise how late the attainment of God's wishes must come for one who as yet can only long for the longing. Yet I have loved to my utmost the beauty of His holy house, and I chose so far as I could to be an outcast in the house of the Lord.[22] But as *it pleased Him to separate me from my mother's womb* and from the friendship of flesh and blood, *and to draw me to His grace,*[23] so also it has pleased Him to lift me, devoid of all merit, from the earth, and to raise me from the lake of wretchedness and the muddy scum *that He may place me with the princes of His people,*[24] and connect my portion with your lot. In this way, though you excel me in merit, He made me to share with and be equal to you in the task we perform.

5. So it is not through my own presumption, but at the decree and command of the Lord that I have claimed this compact of brotherhood with you. Though unworthy of

this great honour, I count myself worthy because I am sure that in your holiness you *do not mind high things but consent to the humble*,[25] for you are wise in truth. So I hope you will with ready friendship accept my humble love; indeed I trust you have already accepted it through the most blessed bishop[26] Alypius, who does not disdain to be my father. He himself has surely been a living example to you of how to love me, without knowing me, more than I deserve. For I was unacquainted with him, and separated from him by huge distances of land and sea; but through the spirit of true love, which penetrates and pours into all places, he found it possible both to look upon me by love and to reach me by words of greeting. By the gift of books which I have mentioned he has bestowed on me the first proofs of his regard and the pledges of your affection. He has made a great effort to ensure that my love for your holy person, which I have come to know not only through his words but more fully through your own eloquence and faith, goes beyond moderate bounds; and I believe he has striven equally that you should imitate him and love me greatly in return.

I pray that the grace of God remain with you, as now, forever. I hail you as my loving and venerable brother in Christ the Lord, and I greatly long to see you. I greet your whole household, and all who accompany you and imitate your holiness in the Lord, with the greatest regard of loving brotherhood. I ask you to take this single loaf[27] and so to bless it; I send it to your dear person as evidence of my brotherly love.

LETTER 5

To Severus[1]

Paulinus greets his brother Severus.

1. Did you think, my dearest brother, that because you did not come as promised and as we expected you need to be excused? In fact the part of you which arrived here was preferable to the part which stayed; for only your body remained at home, whereas your will, spirit, and conversation came here. And you were not even wholly absent physically, for limbs of your body came to us in the persons of your servants, who are joined to you by holy service in the Lord. Therefore, my truly holy and deservedly loved brother so devoted to me in Christ, there is already *laid up for you in heaven a crown of piety which the just judge will render on that day to you,*[2] and to all like you that with perfect charity love their neighbour in Christ, or Christ in their neighbour. For your personal qualities give me insight into those of your spirit; from that open affection which you show to your visible brother, I can easily infer the faithful, perfect, heavenly love you have for the invisible God.[3] This love we prove by the obedience of our faith; that is, we must prove by loving each other (as you indeed do) that we are disciples of the Master who *loved His own unto the end, and laid down His life for His friends*[4] with the same power by which He assumed it.

2. Therefore, my truly holy and deservedly blessed

53

brother, your place and your reward will be in the land of the living, above the southern queen.[5] For she was a sinner, since she lived in companionship with races then unvisited, yet she was the predecessor of those who were soon to be visited. She did not possess the law in writing, but she had faith in the law, a faith incised by the spirit of wisdom and piety in *the fleshly tablets of her heart*.[6] So in her own interest, and in her desire for the great gain which would bring salvation, she was roused to leave her remote country at the edge of the world. She desired to hear God's wisdom that she might obtain what she did not possess, and imbibe the light of knowledge which she lacked. Even as early as this a queen, *surrounded with variety, in gilded clothing*,[7] was to come from the Gentiles in longing for her bridegroom, to attain the odour of Christ whose breath was widely diffused by the prophet. Forgetful of her people and her ancestral home, she hastened forth. Her nation was barbarous, but not her spirit; on the surface she was a foreigner, but secretly at heart a Jew she desired to become a citizen amongst the saints. So she was accounted worthy not only of the reward of blessed resurrection in heaven, but also of the apostles' power to pass judgment on Jewish adulterers by the words of the Judge Himself. For she admired Christ in the person of Solomon, and so she fulfilled the true love of the heavenly queen, as a mystical representation of the wise Church.[8]

So if a divine reward awaits her in the future, though here on earth she then obtained her reward in large measure by hearing the divine wisdom which she greatly desired, what rewards, I ask, will be repaid to you? For you have longed for me with equal kindness and with greater pains, since your aspiration had less expectation of immediate profit. For what did you see in me worth longing for? What did you hope to obtain from me which you did not already possess? What good can you get from conversation with a novice? What help from looking on a sinner? What could you obtain from me, a wise man from a fool, an upright man from a wicked one, a blessed man from a wretch, a brave man from a weak, a man rich in the Lord from a beggar?

3. Truly you do not seek your own advantage, but Christ's, for you have taken thought not for what you deserve or may gain from me, but only for the charity which is the fulfillment of the Gospel,[9] whether in the project of your journey or in the trouble caused to your servants. *Thou art blessed because I have not wherewith to make thee recompense; but recompense shall be made thee at the resurrection of the just* by Him who bears witness that He is loved and welcomed in the persons of the least of His brethren.[10] By His own words He makes Himself a debtor on behalf of even a false or useless servant who belongs to His name, saying: *He that receiveth a prophet in the name of a prophet shall receive the reward of a prophet.*[11] Not that my burden will be removed on this account, though I, a sinner, receive a just man's honour from a just man. But as reward for your goodness you must be credited with the justice of your belief, for by what was a pious error but a genuine feeling of devotion you honoured the good Lord even in the person of His wicked servant.

4. What, then, shall I do in my wretchedness, since I shall owe an account and a penalty for receiving honours undeserved and for being praised by those who fulfill the law while I passively listen to it?[12] This is doubtless so that

my sluggish and blameworthy sloth, the poverty of my
barren soul, my hands unproductive of good works, may
be rebuked the more strongly when I hear from your lips
the praise which holds good for worthy servants of Christ
like yourself, and is therefore untrue of me. I recognize
the extent of the debt which binds me, for when I compare
your assessment of me with my own actions I do not find
in myself the qualities you ascribe to me.

What can I boast of resembling your sacrifice? Though
I must boast in the Lord, since all that I have received is
His gift, yet I was older than you, and the distinctions
accorded my person from my earliest years could have
made me more serious and more mature than you.[13]
Further, my physical frailty was greater, and my flesh
more wasted, and this destroyed my appetite for pleasures;
besides, my life in this world, often tried by toils and
labours, learned to hate what perturbed me, and increased
my practice of religion through my need for hope and my
fear of doubt. Finally, when I seemed to obtain rest from
lying scandal[14] and from wanderings, unbusied by public
affairs and far from the din of the marketplace, I enjoyed
the leisure of country life and my religious duties, surrounded by pleasant peace in my withdrawn household.
So gradually my mind became disengaged from worldly
troubles, adapting itself to the divine commands, so that I
strove more easily towards contempt for the world and
comradeship with Christ, since my way of life already
bordered on this intention.

5. But you, my most beloved brother, were converted
to the Lord by a greater miracle. For you were closer to
your prime, you were winning greater eulogies, the burden
of your inheritance was lighter, yet you were no poorer

in store of wealth; you were still prominent in the fame of the forum which is the theatre of the world, and you held the palm for glory of eloquence. Yet with a sudden urge you shook off the slavish yoke of sin, and broke the deadly bonds of flesh and blood. Neither the additional riches brought by your marriage into a consular household nor the easy tendency to sin after your marriage which followed your celibate youth could draw you back from the narrow entrance to salvation, from the steep path of virtue to the soft, broad road trodden by many. *Blessed are you who have shunned the counsel of the ungodly, who refused to stand in the way of sinners, and who disdained to sit in the chair of pestilence,*[15] so that with lofty humility you lay at the feet of the crucified Christ.

6. You are indeed a doer of the law, and not a deaf hearer of the Gospel.[16] For you nailed your body and the world to the cross,[17] and you avoided the pleasures of youth and evil joys of the present life as poisonous and grievous. You refused the burdens of your inheritance as though it were excrement. You deservedly won as your mother forever the holy mother-in-law[18] who is more noble than any parent; for you put your heavenly Father before your earthly one, and following the example of the apostles, you left your father on the tossing and uncertain ship of this life. Leaving him with the nets of his possessions,[19] enmeshed in his ancestral inheritance, you followed Christ. You rejected men's praise of your talent, which was no smaller than your family wealth, and, sublimely indifferent to empty glory, you preferred the preaching of fishermen to all the fine writings of Cicero and yourself. You took refuge in the silence of worship to escape the din of wickedness. You wished to be dumb before men

so that you could speak the words of God with pure lips, and, by the praises of Christ and the very mention of His name, atone for polluting your tongue with abusive eloquence.

7. You are truly an Israelite,[20] for with such faithful mind you looked on the God of Jacob,[21] and strengthened by what one might call your struggle with the Lord Himself,[22] you prevailed *against the princes of this world and you warred on the spirits of wickedness in the high places, with the shield of faith and the armour of justice.*[23] Preferring to please Christ rather than men, and to be foolish before men rather than before God,[24] you put the stumbling block of the cross before all the eloquence and the wisdom of this world;[25] so that when you were adopted amongst them that are saved, you realised that *what is foolishness to them that perish is the power and wisdom of God.*[26] This is clear to all that are to be saved. *Blessed art thou*, brother, *for flesh and blood hath not revealed this to thee, but our Father who is in heaven*[27] through our Lord Jesus Christ, who has made foolish the wisdom of the wise, and *has chosen the weak and foolish things of the world, so that He may confound the world,*[28] by means of the very elements which lead the world to disdain God. Therefore, since you are straining with your richer merits to make your prayers efficacious, be more mindful of me. For I am still hidden under a bushel of sins; but the lamp has been lit by the light of Christ,[29] and I long to be led forth by your hand. You are bright with the light not only of good works but equally of faith and grace; you gleam on the seven-branched candlestick of the Lord.[30] I desire my head to be anointed with your oil, so that I may no longer smoulder with smoking wick (though the Lord

in His mercy does not snuff it out), but shine forth with a light pure and fit even to be manifest before the rest, providing an example of faith for them. Yet the grace of God which shines in the darkness, and the brightness of His name, prevents me from being hidden in the shade, though as you have heard I live a sequestered life. For, as the prophet says, *it is good for a man to sit solitary and hold his peace.*[31] So the Lord Himself has taught us to be silent even in pleading our case, for *He did not open His mouth before His shearer*, but said: *I have kept silence, but I will not be silent for ever.*[32] So I dumbly endure His will and His judgment, for He is able even now to maintain His silence in my person, and to make intercession for me when He wills.[33]

8. Meanwhile, however, I have realised that my sins have so harmed me that I have not deserved to see you; moreover, I believe I have added to my store of evils by being a source of temptations to you. For, as you mentioned, you have twice suffered a double illness, and have been afflicted whenever you tried to come to me.

But I take hope from your faith rather than mine, because often, as Scripture says, *the Lord Himself our God trieth us to prove our love*[34] which we feel for each other in the peace of Christ; so that if the temptation which was set before you put you successfully to the proof, it cannot further make vain the prayers of love which were so tested. I know that the spirit in you is so willing I need not fear that the flesh, which is always weak,[35] will succeed in hindering our longing for each other. You will strengthen your flesh by faith and make it subservient to your mind, so that it cannot but have the power to do in Christ what it cannot do of its own accord, if only you say to it: Do not war on the spirit, *be at agreement with thy adversary while thou art in the way with him*, and *there will be peace from thy bones*, and when *my heart has rejoiced in the living God*, then *also my flesh shall rest in hope*.[36]

9. Therefore, my brother, *hold fast that which thou hast, that another may not take thy crown*.[37] In other words, cease not to desire what you formerly desired, and maintain unwavering your intention of coming to me. He whose power and favour enable us to achieve successfully what we dutifully desire will bring your devout exertions to the fruition for which you pray. For we know that for him who desires the good *all things proceed unto good*.[38]

But when I received your letter telling me of your illnesses, I, too, was ill. To me this was a most welcome proof of our harmony in all things, and I have put to the test in myself what Paul said and felt,[39] that the limbs of the one body share each other's pain. For I felt refreshed from the very fact that you wrote that you were restored to health, so that though set in different lands we felt the one spirit working in us, silently drawing together our separated bodies by harmonizing our identical ailments and recoveries.

10. So, my loving brother who are the better part of me in Christ, if your kindly mind has felt sadness on being informed of my affliction, lay it aside, because *the Lord chastising hath chastised me, but He hath not delivered me over to death*.[40] For we have been touched by the healing hand of the Almighty, nursed from our immediate sickness to entertain hopes of good health, and we have lightened each other's afflictions by exchanging consolation.

Indeed, the very fact that we shared this suffering afforded us a great and sweet solace, because it seemed that this conjunction of our pains would scarcely have occurred without the Lord's will, since not even a sparrow falls to the ground without His command.[41] And likewise our return to health began at the same time, whether because each of us was relieved by the solace of the other, or because the Lord who makes us one and who joins all His people in indivisible spirit refused to allow even the states of our body to differ from each other.

11. But it was not merely my own illness which has delayed my couriers. For our dear Vigilantius[42] came down with an attack of fever here in Campania both before he reached me and after his arrival. As a friend he shared my sickness with his own pains, for he was a limb of the same body. The catechumen accompanying Vigilantius, however, who was not yet a limb of our body, did not feel my wounds; he remained healthy and unafflicted by my weakness because his flesh was still estranged and could not experience the pain of the body which was not yet his.[43] Only when our dear Vigilantius was able to begin to improve did I at last decide to send you a reply. I confess that both Vigilantius and his catechumen have long been anxious to go. But to rush off before regaining his strength would have been rash for Vigilantius, because he was not equal to it, and for his healthy companion it would have been a dereliction of duty. So against their wishes I detained them both by refusing to write, since I could not keep them willingly by my advice.

12. So, as I mentioned earlier, I have recovered from the sickness, the pain of which we have both endured. My

recovery was partly the result of the prayers of holy and
dear friends, but chiefly because the Lord looked with
greater kindness on those dear to you.

But I am still drained and weak. Yet Paul bids us to exult
in this state; for he proclaims that weakness made him
strong, because when the flesh which wars on the spirit
is broken by ill health, it cannot with its strength crippled
so easily take by storm the power of the spirit.[44] So my
bodily weakness advances growth in the spirit, which rejoices at damage to the flesh, is delighted by the suffering
of the substance which it hates, and thrives on the sickness
of the body which is in thrall.

With this bodily weakness, but with the healthy and
thriving love which I abundantly feel for you through
the Lord Jesus, I send you this letter to console you. Meanwhile I get like consolation from having yours, until I can
lay eyes on you in accordance with your promise. I never
cease to hope for this from the Lord.

13. There are many things which ought to entice you
to me, and to remove you for a short time from your
native land. Above all there is the love for peace and the
avoidance of that jealousy which burns most fiercely when
one's gaze and person dwell in close intercourse with rivals.
In short, our remoteness from Rome quenches the fires of
those jealous clerics of the capital, and *all the iniquity*
there *stops her mouth.*[45] For my absence from Rome has
withdrawn the tinder, and the flame of hatreds grows
sluggish and cold and does not dare break into utterance;
but envy gnashes her teeth, blushes in the consciousness of
her wickedness, and cannot easily find a place to ignite the
torches of her spiteful intention.[46]

But the peace of God, which surpasseth all understand-

ing,[47] abounds in the hearts of very many men, and the whole of Campania reverences the work achieved through me by God our Saviour. Even in Rome, among the very clergy who alone seem to regard me as a stumbling block, there are few who are aroused by envy's tooth. But I say thanks be to God who has allowed even this most wretched sinner of His to say: *They have hated me without cause.*[48] My attitude has been: *Even with them that hate my peace I am peaceable in mind*, for *if any man wish to be contentious, we have no such custom.*[49] But scarcely a whisper permeates here of those who are said to hate me and to separate me from communion with their holy presence. I shut it from my ears, which are enclosed with a hedge of thorns,[50] as if it were a cold wind or the troublesome buzzing of an idle gnat.

14. But your couriers, who are my fellow servants, will be able more fully to reveal to you how little I am deprived of the Lord's kindness by the Pope of Rome's haughty refusal to see me. In the few days they have been here they have witnessed how unremitting and zealous are the services performed for me by my brother monks, by bishops, clerics, and even laymen during the whole period of my illness. I can boast before you my friend that by the grace of the Lord, whose work and gift this also has been, almost every bishop from the whole of Campania has thought it his duty to visit me. Those incapacitated by sickness or unavoidably detained have been represented by their clergy and their letters. Even bishops from Africa sent a courier to visit me a second time at the beginning of the summer.[51] Since this is so, you must realise how much you ought to hasten to visit my lowly person, so that in some degree you may remove an occasion of sin

from those who seek such an occasion, and make pilgrim-
age abroad to increase the grace of charity in you, whilst
you still lodge in the body and are a pilgrim from Christ;[52]
for the Truth Itself attests that *no prophet is accepted in
his own country.*[53]

15. I confess, however, that though nothing could give
me greater pleasure than your presence here, my longing
for your coming has been more ardently fired because you
have promised to bring here many spiritual brothers with
you.[54] Will that time, I wonder, ever come, will that day
fiinally dawn,[55] when I may welcome the arrival of you,
my brother, with an attendant train of God's chosen, in
the bosom of Felix,[56] the lord of my house, who will then
be our common patron? Will the time come when in
Felix's presence we may together give public thanks to the
Lord for granting the favour which I seek through the
saint's prayers, when I can embrace you all together and
in turn, and deserve to say to you as you sing in concert
with me: *This is clearly the day which the Lord hath
made; let us be glad and rejoice therein,* because *it is good
and pleasant to dwell together in unity?*[57] Then shall I set
you in the monastery not merely as a lodger of the martyr
who lies close by, but also as a husbandman in his garden;
but without payment, because you have already received
your penny from the father of the household,[58] in addition
to the pence which the Lord also generously paid to the
innkeeper to tend your wounds,[59] so that healed by the oil
of mercy and the wine of grace you might be a more useful
labourer in the Lord's vineyard with your body restored to
health.

16. Already I seem to see my modest garden better culti-
vated with the arrival in your company of the Lord's

labourers and fellow workers. It is not difficult to assess how easily the work of lighter cultivation will be performed by those whom Christ has chosen for His vineyard and has not allowed to stand doing nothing for God in the empty marketplace of this world.[60]

Already, too, in imagination I picture the joys of the house after our holy kiss of greeting. Drunk with the spirit of love, we shall unite our sober rejoicing over modest cups, and we shall celebrate our loving feast *not with the leaven of wickedness, but with the unleavened bread of sincerity, playing to the Lord with hymns and spiritual canticles, singing with tongues and hearts to God, giving thanks to the Father through Jesus Christ for all that we do in word and deed in His Son's name. He maketh men of one manner to dwell in a house,*[61] and I hope He will make us dwell together in Him. For *He hath made both one; lifted up from the earth He has drawn all things to Himself;*[62] humbled, He had brought peace to all things[63] by reconciling the world to God. When He has filled with joy my mouth at the presence of your loving person, I shall say: *The Lord has done great things with us,* and in our overflowing joy *we shall bless you out of the house of the Lord,* for you who *have come in the name of the Lord are blessed*[64] before Him. Receive the chalice of salvation, and eat the bread of the blessed in the kingdom of God.[65] For in the presence of the Lord Jesus you are our satisfaction and our joy.

17. So dare to tear yourself away, relying not on your own resources and strength, but depending and leaning on Christ. For *His rod and staff comfort us*[66] and sustain and guide us. He who bears our sicknesses, who has shouldered our weaknesses, who strengthens the weary and

steadies shaking knees, *will make thy way blameless* and harmless; *He will gird thee with strength* and *make thy feet like the feet of a hart* so that *thou rejoicest as a giant to run the way.*[67] No weakness of fearful flesh can hinder you, for you advance not by the flesh but by the spirit. For we who are slaves to Christ make our bodies serve and our minds govern,[68] so that the flesh receives its orders and accompanies our will which is guided by Christ our Maker. The body derives steadfastness from the mind's courage, and the servant obeys in accordance with the disposition of the master. So *power is made perfect in infirmity,*[69] whilst the soul serves God with the support of the tamed flesh, and performs the tasks of strength by employing its weakness.

18. So *set out, proceed prosperously, and the right hand of God shall conduct thee wonderfully. His mercy and grace shall go before thy face.*[70] Should you be ill when you leave your house, you will gain strength on the journey. For *they that hope in the Lord shall renew their strength, they shall take wings as eagles.*[71] If then your heart is eager on the way, *thy youth shall be renewed like the eagle's; thou shalt run and not be weary, thou shalt walk and not faint.*[72] No staff or purse or wallet shall weigh you down; shoes or two coats shall not hinder you.[73] Stripped of the bonds of flesh you can set your foot as though on holy ground; with your loins girt and your belt not weighed down with money, you will hasten on your road with speed, for the Passover of the Lord and the work of Christ must be performed within a short time.[74] *The God of our salvation will make our journey prosperous to us.* For you *every valley will be filled out, and every hill made low, so that the rough ways of uneven ground may*

become level, so that nowhere on the way *may you dash your foot against a stone. For He has given His angels charge over you, to keep you in all your ways.*[75] *The Lord is thy keeper,*[76] and He will surround you with the shield of His peace, shining on you *with the light of His countenance* and *shading you with the shadows of His wings,* so that *the sun shall not burn thee by day nor the moon by night.*[77] Everywhere will He guard and bless your entrances and departures, so that in every place you may find the Son of peace and your peace may come on all who receive you.[78]

19. But if when setting out you chance to weep when you reflect that you are tearing yourself away from friends or familiar places, your momentary sadness will be turned into eternal joy. The Psalm says: *Going, they went and wept, casting their seeds, but coming, they shall come with joyfulness, carrying their sheaves.*[79] In the same way if you weep in coming, you will rejoice on your return, and you will reap with joy what you sowed with tears. *The grace of our Lord Jesus Christ and the charity of God the Father and the communication of the Holy Ghost be with the whole of your house.*[80] That house is not made by hands, for you are the living temple of the Lord *built upon the foundation of the apostles*[81] in Christ God.

My loving, revered, most beloved and sorely missed friend, I ask that our holy mother,[82] who is in Christ your fellow heir in the respect of which she is worthy, be greeted in my name. My fellow servant[83] in the Lord hails you as her brother with the respectful love which she feels for you. Greet with great deference in my name the whole of your holy brotherhood, which I am confident acts in harmony with you. All who are with me in the Lord send their greeting, amongst them Proforus, restored from the Jews to Christ,[84] who loves the Lord, feels affection for you whom he has found in Christ, and longs to see you.

20. In writing the heading of this letter I was afraid to imitate your love for me which excels all others, for I thought it safer to write what was true. So in the future, as the servant of Christ and as one summoned to freedom, be sure not to sign yourself as the servant of a man, of a brother, and of a fellow slave of lesser account than you. For it is a sin of flattery, not a proof of humility, to bestow on any man, let alone a most wretched sinner like me, the distinction due to the Lord alone, the one Master on earth. It is enough to have *charity from a pure heart and an unfeigned faith; what is over and above is of evil.*[85]

I beg you, my brother, in the Lord's name to view my presumption towards you *with the spirit of revelation,*[86] otherwise I must fear that you will be offended by such a prating letter. But the grace won by charity, *which endureth all things,*[87] ought to be increased when it is merited in that situation which usually causes disgust when no charity tempers the loathing. For when I am dictating and wholly concentrating on you, I speak as if we were face to face after a long separation, and I forget to limit the words which I inflict on you.

21. I send you some Campanian bread as a blessing[88] from our store, relying on your merits before the Lord so much that I believe that the bread must reach you with its full grace. Though you are already filled with richer morsels from the Lord's table, deign to receive this bread in the name of the Lord and convert it into a blessing.

In case you think that wheaten bread is a gift which carries my practice of humility too far, I send you a platter made of boxwood to attest my riches. You must take it as a gift of my spiritual longing for you, and regard it as an example to follow if you are not yet using wood as a substitute for silver.

If you have any dark oil,[89] send it to me in the vessels which I have entrusted to my sons the couriers. For I love earthenware vases, because they are related to us through Adam and we bear the treasure of the Lord entrusted to us in such vessels.[90]

22. Since I trust that I have the highest claim to your affection, I also make this request. If my freedmen, slaves, and brothers fail me and your supervision becomes necessary, please arrange that the vintage wine, which I believe I still possess at Narbo, be sent to me. My holy brother, do not fear the financial loss if you make me your debtor in money as in other things. For *all my people are gone aside and are become impious together, and those of the household are become a man's enemies.*[91]

LETTER 6

To Augustine[1]

The sinners Paulinus and Therasia send their greetings to the Lord Augustine, their holy and loving brother.

1. My loving brother in Christ the Lord, I have for long known of you in your holy and dutiful labours, though you were unaware of it, and I have beheld and embraced you, though we are apart, with my whole heart. I have hastened also to address you by letter with words of friendship and brotherhood. I believe that my words have reached you by the hand and grace of the Lord. But since the courier whom I sent before winter to greet you and those others equally dear to God still lingers on the way, I could no longer postpone my duty or restrain my most eager desire to hear from you. So now I have written what will be a second letter if my earlier one has deserved to arrive, or a first one if the other has unfortunately failed to reach your hands.

2. But do not, *my spiritual brother who judges all things,*[2] assess my love for you merely by my courtesy or the frequency of my letters. For the Lord, *the one same God who worketh everywhere His love in His actions,*[3] is my witness that ever since I have known you through your writings against the Manicheans,[4] through the kindness of the venerable bishops Aurelius and Alypius,[5] my love for you has become so rooted in me that I seem not to be embarking on a new friendship, but rather to be

taking up again a long-standing intimacy. In short, however unformed the language of this letter, I write with
mature affection and seem to be meeting you a second
time in the spirit through the inner man.

Nor is it surprising that we are together though apart,
and acquainted though unknown to each other, for we
are members of the one body, we have the one Head, we
are steeped in the one grace, we live on the one Bread,
we tread the same path, we dwell in the same house.[6] In
short, all that we are,[7] in all the hope and faith in which
we now stand as we strive for the future, is one in the
spirit and body of the Lord; and if we break away from
this unity, we are nothing.

3. How unimportant, then, is the fact that our physical
separation begrudges us merely the reward which is a
feast for eyes seeking transient joys! Yet in men of the
spirit even bodily graces ought not to be called transient,
for the resurrection will bestow immortality also on our
bodies. This is what we presume to believe, however
unworthy we are, through the power of Christ and the
goodness of God the Father. So I pray that the grace of
God through our Lord Jesus Christ may confer the further
blessing of seeing your countenance also in the flesh. Not
only would great joy be given to me in my longing, but the
light of my understanding would be increased, and my
poverty would be enriched by your wealth.

Yet you can confer this kindness on me even at a distance, especially at this time. For my loving and most dear
sons in the Lord, Romanus and Agilis,[8] whom I commend
to you in God's name with the rest of us, will be returning[9]
once their work of charity is completed. I pray that in this
work they may enjoy the special regard of your charity.

For you know what lofty promises the Most High makes to the brother who helps his brother.[10] You can safely employ these men if you wish to repay me with any gift for the favour which has been bestowed on you.[11] For I want you to believe that we have *one heart and one soul*[12] in the Lord.

May the grace of God abide as now with you forever, my loving and revered brother in Christ the Lord. I cherish you and long to see you.

Greet on my behalf all the holy men in Christ who must surely attend on you. Commend me to all these holy men, that with you they may deign to pray for me.

LETTER 7

To Romanianus[1]

Paulinus and Therasia send greetings to their brother the lord Romanianus,[2] truly worthy of praise and recognition.

1. You knew with what anticipation I was awaiting the return of my brothers[3] from Africa. They returned yesterday, bringing with them letters most eagerly awaited from Aurelius, Alypius, Augustine, Profuturus, and Severus, all holy and most beloved men and now all bishops as well.[4] I am therefore so delighted at getting this up-to-date news from all these distinguished and saintly men that I have hastened to tell you of my joy. So now that I have passed on the happy news you may share with me this joy, so long awaited during your anxious journeying. If you have already received this information from those revered and most beloved men by the arrival of other ships, hear it a second time from me, and rejoice again with redoubled delight. But if this message from me comes as the first you have heard, take pleasure that by Christ's gift I have won such great affection in your country that whatever God's providence achieves there (as Scripture says, *He is wonderful in His saints*)[5] I am the first or among the first to know.

2. I do not mean we should rejoice merely because Augustine has been raised to the episcopate, but also because the churches of Africa so merited God's care that they heard the words of heaven from Augustine's mouth.

His advance to the higher grace of the Lord's gift was irregular, for he has been consecrated not to succeed the bishop in his see but to join him. For Augustine is co-adjutor of the church at Hippo whilst Valerius is still alive.[6] How happy is the old man! He never stained his most chaste mind with envious hatred, and now he obtains from the Most High a reward worthy of his heart's peace. For he has deserved to obtain as colleague the one who he prayed would follow him only in the priesthood. Could this have been credible before it occurred? But we can apply the words of the Gospel to this work of the Almighty as well: *With men this is difficult, but with God all things are possible.*[7] So let us rejoice and be glad in Him *who alone doth wonderful things, who maketh men of one manner to dwell in a house.*[8] For He has looked with kindness on our lowliness and visited His people with good;[9] *He hath raised up an horn in the house of David His servant,*[10] and has now exalted the horn of His church amongst His chosen people, so that in accord with His promise spoken through the prophet He may *break the horns of sinners,*[11] that is, those of the Donatists and the Manicheans.[12]

3. I pray that this trumpet of the Lord, which He now sounds through the person of Augustine, may strike the ears of our son Licentius[13] in such a way that he will listen with the ear by which Christ enters and from which the enemy does not bear away God's seed.[14] Then indeed will Augustine see himself as a most eminent bishop of Christ; for then will he know that his prayers, too, are granted by the Most High, if he brings to birth in Christ as a son worthy of himself the boy whom in his literary studies he has made worthy of you. For I should like you to believe

that on this occasion, too, he has written to me with most fervent and loving care about Licentius. I trust in the almighty Christ that the spiritual prayers of Augustine will prevail over the desires of the flesh of our youthful son. Believe me, he will be worsted even against his will, he will be worsted by the faith of his most dutiful father, he will be prevented from winning an impious victory, should he prefer the triumph that brings his destruction to the defeat that wins salvation.

So that this dutiful letter should not seem empty of brotherly kindness, I send to you and our son Licentius five loaves from the rations of my campaign for Christ, in readiness for which I serve my daily duty for meagre sustenance. For I long to join him closely to me in the one grace, and so I could not deprive him of my blessing. But let me address a few words to him separately, so that he may not claim that what I have told you about him was not communicated to him; for Aeschinus is informed of what Micio hears.[15] But why should I speak in the language of foreigners, since our own store is adequate for all things, and to speak the language of strangers is not the act of a sane mind?[16] Our head is sane and sound by the grace of God, for our head is Christ.

My prayer and desire are that you may have a long and healthy life, and that you and your entire house may always be blessed. I send my respects, my brother; you are deservedly worthy of the greatest honour and affection.

LETTER 8

To Licentius[1]

Paulinus greets his most dear son Licentius.[2]

1. Hear, then, my son, the law of your father, in other words, the faith of Augustine, and do not reject the instruction of your mother.[3] For not only has the fatherly regard of Augustine a claim on you, since he held you on his knee when you were small, but he has also from your early years reared you in the first milk of worldly wisdom. Now he sees that whilst your body is mature in age, you are still a crying baby in the cradle of the spirit, you have not yet begun to speak the word of God, and you have scarcely taken your first footsteps in Christ, creeping along with tottering footsteps. So he is anxious to give you suck and nourishment from the breasts of the spirit as well, if only you will allow his teaching to guide you as a mother's hand or nurse's arm guides an unsteady child.

But if you heed and follow him (to entice you again with the words of Solomon), *you will have a crown of grace added to your head.*[4] Then indeed you will be fashioned consul and high priest, not in the phantom of a dream, but in reality; Christ will fill out the empty prospects of an unsubstantial career with the substantial accomplishments of His work. For Licentius will be truly a pontifex and truly a consul, if you hug the footsteps of Augustine, which are the teachings of the prophets and apostles, as blessed Eliseus followed the consecrated Elias

and the young Timothy followed the glorious apostle
Paul.[5] Like them, tread the ways of God in close attend-
ance on your master, so that you may learn both by perfection of heart to deserve the priesthood, and to help
nations to salvation with magisterial words.

2. But this is enough of advice and exhortation. For I
think that you, dear Licentius, can be roused to follow
Christ by a few words and by modest efforts; for through
the spirit and words of the venerable Augustine you have
been fired from boyhood towards the study of truth and
wisdom, which are in reality both Christ, and towards the
highest point of every good. But if Augustine could not
prevail on you in your own interests, what can I achieve
at this much later date, endowed as I am with none of his
riches? But I trust in his persuasive powers and in your
refined disposition, and have hopes that fuller and greater
results have been achieved in you than remain to be
achieved, so I have dared to open my mouth for two
reasons—first, that I may with due charity be compared
with Augustine in my anxious regard for you, and
secondly, that I may be numbered among those who care
for your salvation, even after my affection has been tested.
For I know that the prize for accomplishing perfection in
you is to go chiefly to Augustine.

3. My son, I am afraid that with the harsh tone of my
rash words I may offend your ears, and that through your
ears I may afflict your mind also with boredom for me.
But I have remembered your letter[6] in which I discovered
that you were acquainted with poetic measures, a pursuit
which I, too, was far from disdaining at your age. So if
I have hurt your mind in any way, by recalling your letter
I have devised a remedy to soothe it. I should like to lead

you to the Lord, the inventor of every kind of harmony,[7] by the metres of poetry. Please listen, and do not neglect the cause of your salvation residing in my words, but willingly show a reverent interest, and respect for your father, even if you despise my speech. For in it is lodged the name of Christ, *which is above all names*,[8] and makes such reverence due to it that a believer cannot despise it.

So[9] now break loose from delay and the confining bonds of the world, and do not fear the gentle yoke of the tranquil Lord. Our present life has a fine appearance, but only vacillating minds admire it; the wise spirit does not regard it with awe. Now Rome with evil persuasion tempts you with her manifold impressions, and, sadly, Rome can seduce even the strong. But I pray, my son, that your father Augustine may always outweigh all the enticements of the capital. If you keep your eye on him and lock him in your heart whilst surrounded by the dangers of this insecure life, you will be safe.

But this advice I shall repeat again and again: Avoid the slippery dangers of exacting state service.[10] Position has an inviting title, but it brings evil slavery and a wretched end. He who now delights in desiring it, later repents of having desired it. It is pleasant to mount the summit, but fearsome to descend from it; if you stumble, your fall from the top of the citadel will be worse. Do false blessings now delight you? Does ambition bear you off on every breeze? Does the bubble reputation hold you in her brittle grasp? But when the belt of office, purchased and worn, redounds to your great harm, and breaks your spirit with the barren toil it entails, you will vainly and too late reproach your idle hopes, and desire to loose the bonds which you are now tying. Then will you vainly recall your father Augus-

tine, and grieve that you despised his truthful warnings. So
if, my dear boy, you are wise and dutiful, hear and embrace
the words and advice of your aged elders.

"Why do you draw back your neck untamed from the
yoke? My burden is light, My yoke is sweet." So speaks
the fatherly voice of Christ.[11] Put your belief in God, place
your head beneath the yoke, surrender your mouth to the
soft muzzle,[12] bend and submit your shoulders to the light
weight. You can do this now while you are free, whilst
no bonds of marital care or high position tie your hands.
This is the goodly freedom, to serve Christ and to live in
Him beyond all else. He who surrenders to Christ the Lord
only is no slave to human lords, to vices, or to proud kings.
Do not regard as free the nobles whom you watch borne
aloft before the awestruck populace; as you see, their freedom seems so great to them that they disdain to bow their
heads to God. Yet, in the eyes of many, such men are
wretched, slaves even to their slaves, buying maidservants
to be ruled by them. Those who have endured eunuchs
and huge courts, those who voluntarily but wretchedly
put up with Rome[13] know how great a price is paid in
sweat and loss of honour for the distinction of a palace-
cloak or a Roman office.

Even the ruler who reaches an unrivalled height of
power is not freed from subservience. For after proudly
boasting his dominion over the whole city, he is a slave to
demons if he worships images. Good grief! Is it for such
men, Licentius, that you linger in Rome? Is it to please
them that you spurn Christ's kingdom? Do you repeatedly
address as lords and greet with bowed head men whom
you see as slaves of wood and stone? They worship gold
and silver under the name of gods; their religion is what

diseased greed loves. I pray that men who do not love
Augustine should love these men, and that those who wish
to cultivate them should not worship Christ. It was because
an undivided mind is pleasing to God that He said we cannot serve two masters.[14] There is one faith, one God,[15]
one Christ from the Father; and service to the one Lord
cannot be divided. For the gulf between the things and
commands of Christ and those of Caesar is as great as that
between heaven and earth. Be raised from the earth now,
while the spirit governs these limbs;[16] attain in mind the
vault of heaven, for the flesh does not impede or delay
you. Become dead now to the works of the body,[17] and
ponder with serene mind the blessings of the life of heaven.
Though confined by the body, you are spirit if with a
sense of duty you now conquer and destroy the work of
the flesh.

My dear boy, I have written these words with the
prompting of faithful love. If you hear them, God will bear
you up. Believe that I have become for you a second
Augustine; take us both as your father with the same filial
regard. If you spurn us, you will be torn from us both with
greater grief. But if you listen to us, you will be a pledge
of affection to us both. Two fathers have lavished happy
care and sweat on you; it is a great distinction for you to
have brought joy to two fathers.

But in coupling myself with Augustine, I do not boast
of being his equal in merit, but compare myself with him
only in love for you. For what water can I pour upon you
from my modest stream? Without me you have two rivers
to cleanse you. There is your brother Alypius and your
master Augustine; one is your kinsman and the other
fathered your talent. What, Licentius? Do you thrive with

so distinguished a brother and teacher, and yet hesitate with
the wings you have to make for the stars? Whatever you
do, you will not be abandoned to the world, for yours is a
soul owed to Christ, and the world cannot hope to win
you as its friend. Though your mind is on marriage and
high distinctions, you must now restore yourself to your
former lord. I am confident that two just men will prevail
over a single sinner, and that the prayers of your brothers
will banish your desires. Return, then, to the fold; the two
priests bid you return, the one your father in exhortation,
the other your brother in blood. They bring you back to
your own possessions, for now you aspire to alien ones; this
rather is your kingdom, to which your dear ones hold fast.
Come back to it, devote your admiration to it, and do not
waste your time on alien matters. If you reject your own
possessions, will anyone give you another's? You will not
be your own master, but despatched to distant lands, you
will be exiled (a sad thought) from the affections of your
own heart.

This is enough for a worried father to sing to his son.
My wishes and fears for you are the same as for myself.
If you harken to my words, the recording page will one
day bring you life; but if you reject them, it will witness
your rejection.

My dearest son, I pray that Christ will keep you un-
harmed and make you His servant forever. I pray that you
will live, but for God; for to live for the world is an act of
death, whilst living for God is the true life.

LETTER 9

To Amandus[1]

To the holy Amandus, truly loving and rightly beloved.

1. So far as I can see, you shout from the housetops the words I whisper into your ear.[2] In your excessive affection for me, in the abundant pleasure which I your foolish brother afford you, you do not hesitate to recommend even to the ear of our holy and venerable father the brash and ignorant words with which I dare to slight you rather than him. For how otherwise could he have regarded me as a suitable person from whom to beg by letter a message worthy of his own spirit? Trusting your feelings rather than your judgment, you must have persuaded him that the Lord had opened my mouth too amongst the dumb and the infants,[3] whose glory the Almighty effects. So Delphinus bids me produce words seasoned with the salt of the spirit[4]—his salt, for he remembers that he sprinkled me with the salt of his word.[5] This he continues to do, for all his letters to me are spiritual seasoning. For he, too, is *the salt of the earth*,[6] redolent of the living savour of the apostles' teaching. But I fear that I have not admitted his salt into my insipid heart, and that my mind knows not *wherewith it shall be seasoned* so that it may taste the sweetness of the Lord,[7] if the taste of Delphinus could fade from it and his force be blunted.

2. Who has been able to rouse me as I murmured: *There is a lion outside, and murderers in the streets?*[8] I am

not roused with the eagerness of the mystical bee[9] or by
the example of the clever ant[10] to take thought for my life
and to do useful tasks; but *I sleep a little, I slumber a little,
I fold my hands over my heart to rest a little, and poverty
meanwhile comes to me like a good runner.*[11] And Christ,
who *being rich became poor that through His poverty He
might enrich us*[12] who are truly poor, saw me obstinately
persisting in my need and rightly pronounced: *What profit
is there in my blood, whilst I go down to corruption?*[13]

Yet I pray that even as I speak these words, I may be
roused by the very judgment of my conscience and the
laments of my own words, so that however late in the
day I may be able to say: *Now have I begun, this is the
change of the right hand of the Most High.*[14] But we are
slothful bellies, and therefore *my soul cleaves to the pave-
ment,* although you have for long been bidding it *arise
from the dead that it may attain to Christ.*[15]

It is true that by the intervention of your faith, through
the sacrament of grace, both of you have established Christ
as Lord in the barque of my heart. But through my idle
slumbering, Christ is asleep within me.[16] You must both
awake Him that He may arise to animate my soul and
enjoin silence on the tempestuous gales of my earthly
thoughts, calming with the peace of His word the troubled
waters of my senses. Then a chaste peace will govern my
heart; the spirit of truth will be the helmsman and the
Word of God my oarsman, and I shall be guided to the
harbour of my desire.[17]

3. For what hope have I save the Lord Jesus, who is able
to save me from pusillanimity of spirit and a storm?[18] He
can accede to your prayers that *my flight be not in the
winter or on the Sabbath,*[19] which symbolises the time

when spiritual works are idle and good works barren. For the Sabbath is a day of idleness, and winter is barren of growth. So at the dictate of the spirit, not of the flesh, we must abstain from all servile work, which is the life of sin.[20] It is surrender to this which marks the real slave *who does not abide in the house.*[21] We keep not the Sabbath which the soul of the Lord cannot endure, but that in which God finds rest, seeking quiet in the lowly hearts of His fearful servants. No storm of winter will afflict our flight or with its cold restrain our indolent feet from free departure, provided that *rejoicing in hope and in spirit fervent*[22] we keep our hands open with the refreshment of mercy and not closed with the chill of greed, and provided that the secret onset of our last hour find us covered and clad in the saving armour of faithful works,[23] so we may be able to stand *before the face of His cold,*[24] the cold of Him who desires us now to make ourselves ready through fear of His command so that He may find us worthy of acquittal on the day of anger.[25]

4. So now in your kindness pray that *I may apprehend wherein I am also apprehended,* and, as I strive for the reward of my heavenly calling, forget what lies behind.[26] Pray that I may in spirit set my hand to the plough of the cross, not gazing at completed furrows but looking forward to what remains to be ploughed,[27] until I reach the mountains to which *I have lifted up my eyes, so that help may come to me from the Lord, who is wonderful in His saints.*[28] The saints are the mountains of God, to whom I shall be advanced by the good works of a faithful soul. If I walk worthily in the pure way of truth, then the Lord Himself, *who is the way and the truth,* will make *my feet like the feet of harts, and set me on high places.*[29] For the

Psalmist says that *the high hills are a refuge for the harts,
the rock for the urchins.*[30] If by bounding over wickedness
with the speed of harts we flee from Nemrod the hunter
who, in the words of Scripture, was *a hunter against the
Lord,*[31] if with the help of Christ and deeds of devotion we
climb the heights of the virtues through the teaching of the
prophets and the apostles, who are the mountains, the
fruitful mountains,[32] of God, then we shall look down as
from a lofty cliff on the empty shadows of the transient
world and cry out in a voice of exultation: *I will extol
Thee, O Lord, for Thou hast lifted me above them that
rise up against me, and my eye hath looked down upon
my enemies.*[33] On these high mountains I shall be moulded
in mental humility, and by salutary schooling my limbs
shall be protected on all sides, as if by bristles. So I shall
become like a hedgehog, one of those whose tiny bodies
are protected by sharp armour, defended by natural darts
against the hostile teeth of dogs and hands of men. But
those who humble themselves through fear of God and
are armed by the grace of humility itself have *as refuge the
rock* which is Christ,[34] whose words are our protective or
offensive darts against the devil. For by His words *we
hedge in our ears from wicked tongues,*[35] and impale the
hostile vices in our hearts. So by spiritual devotion and
upright faith I shall become both hedgehog and hart, if
only humble and lowly like these smaller beasts I hide in
Christ as in the rock of refuge, and protected by the word
and spirit of truth show prickly opposition to both the
devil and the enticements of this world.

5. As for the larger beasts with speed of foot and horns
raised high, I shall rival them only if I keep my feet firmly
planted in the way of the Lord and my steps are not di-

verted from His path.[36] I must use such speed of foot, too, to avoid sins and the wicked infections of this world. The Catholic faith, the head of my salvation, I must keep both adorned and armed with the horns of good works, whether to resist hostile hunters or to be your greatest *joy and crown*,[37] laurelled with deeds pleasing to God.

I am planted in Christ, and am Christ's daily toil.[38] For I know well that every day you pray that there may be accomplished in me that blessed *change of the right hand of the Most High*, so that I can truly say: *My heart and my flesh hath fainted away: Thou art the God of my heart and the God that is my portion forever.*[39] For when my corporeal heart fails, destroyed by the growth of the spiritual heart,[40] God will deign to be the God of my heart. It will be then that I shall dare to call myself also *your portion in the land of the living*,[41] once I have been able to say to the Lord, when I am *renewed in the spirit of my mind*[42] in accordance with Christ and fashioned to the heavenly exemplar: *Thou art the God of my heart and the God that is my portion forever.*[43]

LETTER 10

To Delphinus[1]

Paulinus greets Delphinus,[2] his most blessed lord above all others, and his father forever in Christ the Lord.

1. I have received the letter testifying to your holy love in which you bid me append to the letters I send you something beyond the demands of courtesy, some discourse on the Scriptures to unfold to you the treasures of my heart. But the rule of piety enjoins, and our master Paul teaches, that rather *parents should lay up treasure for their children.*[3] Yet you, who were appointed my father by the Lord and in the Lord, have always laid up good treasure and never cease to do so.

It was from your hands that I received the talent of saving grace, which must not be buried in the earth or left twisted in a handkerchief. It must be invested with the money-lenders, so that by them the sum may be multiplied with abundant interest,[4] or at the right moment it must be allotted to those who sell the oil which the wise must buy to prepare their torches for the coming of the Bridegroom.[5]

But over and above this talent, you continually lay up treasure for me in another way, for you ask that, in addition to the grace which has been granted me through you, some of the treasures of the Lord be assigned to me. I only pray that I may obtain all that you can persuade the Lord to let me have. It is surely because of this awareness of and confidence in your petitions on my behalf, that you ask (or rather, ask back) from me some spiritual message worthy of your seed which lies within me. For in your faith you believe that your petitions, past and present, on my behalf have been granted; and now you long to experience, by the proof of words, the outcome of your unremitting prayers for the fecundity of my heart and mouth. For *out of the abundance of the heart the mouth speaketh*,[6] and the flavour of the mind is savoured in speech.

2. So it is right that your holy person seeks due repayment of what is lodged with me and awaits the budding of its own seed. But I am barren land; what can I do? I have brought forth thistles not wheat, thorns not grapes.[7] With what harvest can I repay you? Aware, then, that I am a blighted harvest or a barren tree, I cannot do justice even to the filial love I owe you. I can only simulate dutiful words in my letters, and in my shameful embarrassment at my sloth conceal my ignoble feelings from your heart. Knowing your boundless love for me, I fear that I may grieve your heart by deceiving its expectation, for it takes pleasure in hopeful anticipation of my future. I fear that you may be forced to say or to write to me: *"I planted you as a fruitful vineyard, but you have turned into the bitterness of an alien vine.*[8] I hoped that you would bring forth grapes, but you have brought forth thorns.[9] If only those poor thorns were useful to afford a barrier for pious ears against a wicked tongue, to defend the faith in a vigilant heart as crops in a walled field![10] But like a rough buckthorn[11] you have brought forth thorns which I feel are useless and harmful and which choke the Word.[12] Piercing men's hearts with thoughts still bent on the flesh, they turn them to tribulation."

3. Do you ask, then, most dutiful father, if there is still something which you can do and which you have not already done for me? For truly *you have planted me in the house of the Lord;*[13] and after planting me you enclosed me with the seal of salvation, so that I might be protected from the onslaught of the wild boar and the cropping of the fierce wild ass.[14] And you dug in it a press,[15] so that from your vine I might pour forth for you a vintage sweet through your kindly intercourse.

Yet you can still imitate the man who from the master of the vineyard sought a respite for the barren fig tree, and who by his pledge postponed the destruction threatening the useless tree.[16] In the same way, then, may your diligent and fatherly love intervene on my behalf, and ask that the axe which is set at the roots of unproductive trees[17] be laid off, so that the kindly master may allow a trial-period even if only for a year. Pledge your zealous care on my behalf to the Master of the house; promise Him your unremitting prayers, which will be as the basket of fertilising dung of which the evangelist speaks.[18] With this I pray that the soil of my heart may be enriched, that the crops of your sowing may be nourished, or that the tree which you have planted may obtain the sap of your fertility, so that on the day of examination, on which sower and reaper will equally rejoice, you may set me also amongst your company in the bosom of the Father. He nourishes the seeds of those who water them, and He brings to fruition the toil of those who cultivate them. Then you may seek from Him the reward for your cultivation, when you have offered Him in my person not the dead wood which He orders to be cut off and burned, but the wheat which He deigns to gather into His barn.[19]

LETTER 11

To Severus[1]

Paulinus greets his loving brother Severus.

1. Through you above all I experience what I apprehend through Jesus Christ our Lord and God. I joyfully find, through the gift and word of God, that *nothing can be compared to a faithful friend* and that *grace abounds on the tongue of the good man.*[2] For the consolation of your love is *like the medicine of life,* and your *words are as a honeycomb.*[3] *As cold water to thirsty souls, so is good tidings from a far country*[4] to me when it concerns you. Though this news with its evidence you are well and with its expression of your love *makes my bones fat,*[5] the joy and pleasure it creates are greater because it is brought and delivered by your servants who are my sons in the Lord. So I have obtained not only a letter from you but what one might call an outer part of your person.

What shall I render to my Lord for this grace in addition to *all that he has rendered to me?*[6] For through this grace He has joined you to me not only as a most beloved friend in our earlier life in the world,[7] but also as an inseparable companion and partner in the spiritual brotherhood of His affairs. This I account a gift beyond price.

2. Christ said: *Who is My mother or who are My brethren?*[8] Surely not those who *are born of the will of the flesh* and of intercourse in sleep, but those *born of God*[9] through the Wisdom of God which is Christ. Abid-

ing in Himself He renews all things, giving men *power to be made the sons of God*[10] and coheirs of His kingdom. He took the form of our lowly bodies *to shape us to the body of His glory*,[11] to tear us from our native land and our kin and to bear us off to share His fortune and to become His offspring.[12] By this gift He has deigned to create us for Himself, and to link us with the chain of His love. To replace that physical friendship in which we realise He had already prepared us for this covenant, He has advanced us to permanent kinship through a higher love. For the charity of Christ is that *which never falleth away*,[13] for it flows down from God and abides in Him, investing with its own immortality every man in whom it rests. This is the charity that knows not pride and is free from guile, knows no malice[14] and imitates God, not in spiritual pride, but in the spirit of meekness and rivalry in reverent love. For our Lord, as we know by experience and as He Himself bore witness, is sweet and *meek and humble of heart*.[15]

3. You who are born of Him as my brother outstrip by your immediate help and eternal fellowship all the affection shown to me by my kin of the flesh, for you are my brother sprung from a better Father than are those joined to me by flesh and blood alone. For where now are my blood brothers? Where are my former friendships and the companionship of old? I have vanished from all such men and *am become a stranger to my brethren, and an alien to the sons of my mother*.[16] *My friends and former neighbours now stand afar off*.[17] They pass me like a river racing by or a wave passing over me. Perhaps they are troubled in my regard and are ashamed to come to me; as Scripture says, those who were near stand afar off, and those who were afar come near.[18] *Instead of thy fathers, sons are born*

to thee.[19] So by the Lord's doing you replace my parents, brothers, and friends, because you show the anxious care of parents, the loving worry of a brother, and the diligent, total loyalty of a true friend. You flood me with all your inner kindness, continually sending me letters and soothing me with the sweetest consolations.

4. You could not be satisfied with a fresh visit by letter at every opportunity, but you must also send your servants, choosing them as couriers not merely from your own retainers but also from your holy sons, those blessed offspring who afford you joy in the Lord. Through their eyes you seek to see me, and through their lips, to touch me. *How beautiful to me are the feet of those who bring good tidings.*[20] For they tell me about you and bring word which sets my heart at rest when they announce the works of the Lord which you perform by God's word, or your writings composed by the spirit of the Word.

What riches of ours could afford gifts so precious, what kinship could offer consolations so sweet? Without thinking of the promises for eternity which God in His generosity pledges,[21] I readily note how preferable are the rewards already paid here in this world to the possessions I have put aside. For I ask you, what loss of loving-kindness does an unnatural father or indifferent brother or unmindful friend impose on me, when love under all these titles and pledges of affection or ties of friendship is abundantly requited by you alone? I need not mention the considerable number of those who resemble you in their attitude towards God and to me, both in our own region and even in areas unknown,[22] whose boundless affection is conferred upon me to replace my fatherland, parents, and inheritance through the kindness of a compensating God. If I reckon the blessings obtained from you alone, I shall find that in you all my gifts have been repaid with greater generosity and at higher cost.

No brother can redeem, nor shall man redeem,[23] says the Psalm, and we can likewise say: The world does not love us, but Christ does. Man is indifferent, but God loves. *A man's enemies shall be they of his own household*,[24] but equally a man's friends are those of the household of God. True, I had brothers, friends, and neighbours who were good and great. But God decided that they were not for me, and chose to grant me you as inseparable brother and most beloved neighbour, so that I may worthily love you as myself. For with you I have one heart and one soul in Christ.[25]

5. So when I spoke briefly just now of the love of many friends of the spirit being equal with yours, I spoke in a wholly unsuitable and unworthy manner, for in no other person can I obtain the grace which I obtain through you. It is true that like you they deign to love the Lord's grace in my lowly person. But in your person I have been granted a unique gift; that intimate friendship of our earlier life, when we still loved the things which we now reject in Christ, marked us out for each other in the love of Christ. Yet it was through that earlier close intimacy that we advanced towards the connexion by which through God's intervention we are now tied. So by loving each other with faith even on that path of unbelief we learnt to love also spiritually. For we always loved each other so scrupulously that no affection could be added to our mutual love except the charity of Christ, which alone transcends every feeling and affection.[26]

So we ought to thank the good Lord still more earnestly,

for He has deigned to look with pity on our lowliness;[27] for finding us together in the field, He drew us forth together as twins from the womb of flesh, and together adopted us. For, as you wrote, we are indeed *two in the field*, but I presume to say that through the goodness and omnipotence of God *one of us has been taken*,[28] yet neither of us is left. For each of us was two, since our flesh rebelled from and was at variance with the spirit, and there was no peace within us since the outer man was at war with the inner.[29] But now, through the kindness of Him *who hath made both one*,[30] we two are one, because in both of us there is a single spirit, and we are not separate since we belong to one body. However, as I have said, we share this with all our brothers in Christ. But in you I find a uniquely pleasant cause for rejoicing, because it was through my friendship with you that I obtained the most blessed gift of God. So not even when our paths divided did we separate, a loss which we both sometimes experience, as you will acknowledge, in the case of many of our dearest ones.

6. You, then, are truly my father, my brother, and my neighbour, since you achieve in me as in yourself the will of God and the fulfilment of the Law.[31] You love me as yourself, you are my friend in the love of Christ and my true brother in the rebirth achieved by God. Since you see and acknowledge this, why do you oppress me and malign yourself by saying: *We were two in the field and one of us has been taken?*[32] Let us not show ingratitude to God, who has taken not one of us, but both of us as one. We were two when we were united with our former brothers; but we have separated from them because of our attitude to life, because we are called one not merely because we are one body, but also because we, though more

than one, are of one mind. This is what the same passage of Matthew makes sufficiently clear when it suggests that the *two in the field* are not two men but two peoples, as the Gentiles who believed and the Jews who remained behind show. The two women grinding at the mill,[33] one of whom was taken as was one man from the field, portray in my opinion the synagogue and the Church.[34] For in the entire course of Sacred Scripture the only allegorical representation is that of the distinction between believers and unbelievers throughout mankind, or that of the creation of the two forms of being in the nature of every man.[35]

So, my brother, because we have always been close to each other in one heart as we are now in Christ, we have been either taken together or left together. We have been taken, however, not through our own merit, but through the grace of God, *whose gifts and calling are without repentance.*[36] We have been taken not because our works gave us preference, but because our right disposition showed its faith.[37] By this we were as one fired with love for Him, as was shown by the same decision we reached and the identical time of our conversion.[38] We must also glory and rejoice in Him who justifies wicked men because of their faith, and *giveth food to all flesh*[39]—not the food which decays, but that prepared to be eternal sustenance, which is digested by the soul that performs God's works and by the Catholic Church. For it is the body of the true Bread *which cometh down from heaven*[40] and gives the food of life to those who thirst after justice. It does not fatten the flesh, but it strengthens the human heart. The more this Bread is eaten, the more we hunger for it; the more we drink of this Fountain, the more we thirst for it.[41] To eat this Bread forever, let us grind in the mill of this world the good wheat, which is the faithful performance of obedience and *charity from a pure heart and an unfeigned faith.*[42]

7. Since you abound in this grace and strength, you grind good grain for God, and you show yourself a worthy food for His feast *with the unleavened bread of sincerity and truth.*[43] Whoever performs His wishes[44] and becomes one of His limbs, is His food. For God Himself says that *he who is joined to God becomes one spirit.*[45] We achieve this *if we bear the image of the heavenly* with the same watchfulness and care *as we have borne the image of the earthly.*[46] It is by imitating him who imitated Christ that we shall attain to imitation of God; *for we are the good odour of Christ unto God,* if we show Him *a living sacrifice with reasonable service.*[47] Thus we can offer to Him from our innermost being the pure flour sifted by the mill of a clean heart. Erecting a chaste altar in our breasts, we can sacrifice the animals which the Law enjoins us to slay for our wrongdoing.[48] We can slay a goat by excising our sins, in which is the stench of death. We can kill a bull by abandoning our pride. We can sacrifice a sheep if we expel effeminacy and idleness by the heat of our love and our burning spirit. We can offer within ourselves a lamb, if our lives are spotless, and a steer, if we become as children strangers to wickedness, so that we can reproduce the purity of the lamb by our chastity and the stupidity of the steer by our simplicity.[49] I know that you are offering to God a sacrifice of this kind in the temple of your body, in the sanctuary of your heart, in the sacrifice of your flesh and the dedication of your soul. You sacrifice a bull when you bend low your proud head in

reverent humility and strike it with the fear of God. You sacrifice a kid when in pursuit of justice you cut out all the works of your evil nature. You slay a sheep when you sedulously perform and eagerly ponder the law and will of God, felling your idleness and sloth as easily as a weak ewe, and with the pincers of the heavenly word tearing off the obstructing attachments of this life. They are like a fleece[50] which is useful to the shearer but a burden on him who carries them.

Christ has caught us with the pincers of the two Testaments and holds us fast with them. He strips us of the wool of our worldly baggage; or alternatively He tears off the fleece from our bodily sins, which are, so to speak, the diseased and feeble bodies of sheep. He spins it out into the yarn of the Church, and interweaves it as the embroidering of His garments to clothe His body, which He covers by the works of those who believe in Him. For when *we put on the Lord Christ*,[51] we are in turn put on by Him.

8. This Shepherd has, I think, now shorn you and set your fleece in His courtyard and sprinkled it with the dew of heaven.[52] For there is poured into your mouth and over your face, like a river streaming from the fountains of Israel, or, as Scripture says, like a channel flowing in abundance from Paradise,[53] the grace which teaches me that *the Lord has come down on you like rain upon the fleece*,[54] and has given you water from the well of Jacob,[55] because you, too, from amongst the children of Israel have drawn near to the Lord and shown Him your face. If, then, you have been shorn, you realise that you have obtained a double benefit. For relieved of your weight in the heat of this world, you crop the pasture of the Word

which is sprinkled with the dew of morning gladness, and you are not parched by the heat of the devil at noonday, because you find rest beneath the shadow of the Lord's wings.[56] Meanwhile from your own wool a shirt is being spun for you to clothe you on that wintry day, so that you can stand firm before its arctic face, if only when robbed of your body you are not found naked of good works.

Then in His turn Christ will make Himself a sheep for you, the Lamb that *was led to the slaughter* for us, *and was dumb before His shearer*,[57] allowing His fleece, which are the spoils of His flesh, to be torn from Him. For He laid down His soul and body for us, and for us He regained them.[58] He is priest, victim, lamb, and shepherd. As shepherd, He died for His sheep; as lamb, He was killed for His shepherds, for the Lord Himself is the sacrificial victim of all priests.[59] Offering Himself to the Father to win back all mankind, He was the victim which His priesthood offered, and the priest who offered Himself as victim. To Him now, as the one Lord of all, each new creature is a sacrifice, and the priests themselves are victims. If we now offer ourselves to be shorn with that silent humility and patience in which He offered Himself for us, He will take on Himself the burdens of our fleeces, and will not disdain to carry the wool of His sheep. For He condescends to bring back to the fold on His shoulders the sheep which He has called back from sin.[60]

9. And since *He has no need of our goods*,[61] but we have need of all of His, He shows goodness to us merely for our own good. He takes from us the things which are really His, but He does not wish to keep them as His, so that He takes them and credits us with them as though they were ours. Yet we possess nothing except what has

been given to us,[62] and we could not even exist without
His nod. So when we come into this world bearing
nothing, He allots to us temporal possessions as if they
were a fleece to be shorn. He does this not to weigh down
with baggage those whom He orders to be born free of it,
but to provide us with the opportunity for virtue to win
merit, and to allow us to show proof of our faith and devotion to God who is our true Father and Lord. This
proof we can give if we have abundance of what is sweet
and dear to us, for we can put God first and win a great
reward by indifference to our possessions.[63] Through the
boundless goodness of God, these possessions, though we
did not bring them with us into the world and cannot take
them out again,[64] are so ordered as to be transformed for
the better by obedience to His commands, and changed
from temporal into eternal benefits. For the things which
we neither brought with us nor can take away because
of the limits of our humanity and the transitory nature of
this world,[65] we transform into a blessed form of merchan-
dise through the work of Almighty God, and not only
take it with us but send it on already flowering[66] into the
bosom of the Lord.

10. I think that this is the reason for the commandment
that the lazy workman should not eat bread.[67] The bread
Paul mentions is not the food that perishes,[68] but that by
which we live and attain true life. For as Scripture says,
each man shall eat of his own fruits and live by the work
of his own hands.[69] Each man's work is precisely the
bread, the true Bread, the living Christ which the lazy
workman cannot eat. For this is our Pasch[70] which we are
ordered to eat with all haste in marching dress, girt up
and strongly shod, without laying down our sticks[71] which

are the unremitting good works on which we lean. For *the time is short* and it is expedient for us *to be without solicitude because of the pressing necessity*,[72] as Paul says, so that we may be found ready, and when the Lord knocks we may not be afraid to open the door for fear of suffering merited punishment, guiltily aware of our sleep or indifference.[73] It will avail us nothing if none the less we are preserved for death after death, so that we pay the just penalty of indifference and impiety, if we prefer to serve a master other than our own and are caught red-handed intent on the world's business rather than Christ's, and so do not open to the Lord when He knocks, but rather are dragged unwilling to the Father.

We are, then, forewarned to work and pray for our souls at a seasonable time.[74] The seasonable time is now. We are ushered into the present limits of time to seek for the true life by means of this short and transitory one. The plain or field of this life is the world we live in,[75] or man himself. He is sent into the world *from which one is taken*[76] when he has subjected the flesh to the spirit and, as I have said, made the two one. For in each of us, according to Paul,[77] there are two minds and two laws. By their grinding within us, the flour is made either acceptable to God or doomed to rejection.

11. But your words, as eloquent as they are chaste, bear witness that you have conquered the law of the members[78] and the outer corrupt man, that you are preparing a pure paste, and that unleavened bread without yeast is being got ready for Christ.[79] You would not have been privileged to tell of Martin if you had not made your mouth worthy of such sacred praise by means of a pure heart.[80] So you are a man blessed before the Lord, since you have re-

counted, in language as apposite as your love is righteous, the history of this great priest who is most clearly a Confessor of the Church. He, too, is blessed as he deserves, for he has merited an historian worthy of his faith and life; he is destined for heavenly glory by his merits, and for fame amongst men by your writing. And these words of yours are your fleece, helping to cover with a most welcome garment our Lord Jesus, whose limbs[81] they cover with fine adornment, and they deck out with the bloom of your talent. The Lamb will in His turn clothe you with His fleece on the day of retribution, investing your mortal frame with His own immortality.[82]

12. Only remember me and turn your gaze on me, refusing to look back[83] but still mindful of your friend. For you are sure to obtain a greater harvest than I because you are a cleverer husbandman, and as a swifter runner you will outstrip my slow progress in attaining *the prize of the supernatural vocation.*[84] For through weakness of mind rather than of body I follow far behind you. Yet it is only distance which separates us, not different roads. My weak, inferior hand drives the same millstone as yours. I am your partner on the mill. But my crop is inferior to yours, because I grind cockle mixed with the wheat.[85] I need your prayers to ensure that all may be transformed for the harvest; by your prayers I hope to escape both my riches and my poverty, for both redound to my harm, since I am poor in righteousness and rich in sin.

I should indeed believe that I was rich in goodness if I were now as poor as you believe. But let me in this matter briefly examine your own person from your words, in which you are inconsistent. Though I do not possess the virtues you attribute to me, you none the less thought it right, whilst imputing to me by your words the virtues of others, to praise those virtues. How, then, can you admit that you recoil from the poverty which you claim to admire? You believe I have been granted the virtue which you claim you desire but cannot achieve, of *being content, having food and wherewith to be covered*, of not being solicitous for the morrow.[86] Why, then, do you think that the constraint of poverty will compel me to cease inviting you, when I cannot fail to long for you? Or why, if you really follow Him who said: *Take up thy cross and come, follow Me*,[87] do you show such a weak and unsure face to Christ that you fear to come to the friend whose qualities you proclaim? How else do you think that you should follow Christ except by the law which He taught and the image which He projected? Yet when He came unto His own, He had no place in His domain to lay His head.[88]

13. Imitate Christ's imitator.[89] Live as one dead. Crucify yourself to the world and the world to you,[90] dying every day by faith in the word and living by the word of faith. For *not in bread alone doth man live*,[91] and especially the Christian, of whom in particular it is written that he lives by faith.[92]

Paul did not say "by bread," did he? Why, then, do you fear hunger here if you have faith? Your bread is within you. If you feast on God's word, you will not long for *meat for the belly; for God shall destroy both*[93] as He establishes Himself within us, provided that we base ourselves on His love and do not set our house on the sand[94] of vacillating doubt. We surely believe in Him, and both of us have sworn allegiance to Him who said: *Be not solicitous for tomorrow. Sufficient for the day is the evil*

thereof. Seek ye first the kingdom and His justice, and
all these things shall be added unto you.[95] If you believe
in Him, why do you fear hunger because of the poverty
of the brother who you know has preferred poverty to
riches because he has confidence in those words of Scripture? Do you think that he who trusts in this world has
greater abundance than he who trusts in God? Or that he
who feasts on his own preoccupations is richer than he
who feasts on God's? What possessions can the wretch
have who does not possess himself? For he who puts greater
hopes in himself than in God does not possess himself; he
is indeed dead who fears that if he trusts and entrusts himself wholly to God he is not alive.

So I pray that this was a friendly jest of yours rather
than feeble faith when you expressed your belief that I
should soon be so poor I would not dare to invite you any
more. I confess I prefer nothing more than the blessing of
this great freedom, for this circumcision of the heart is
the fullest perfection.[96] But if your faith in Christ, your
admiration for the divine virtues in a man, and your zeal
to imitate a man who lives in God are genuine, how could
you not seek me out all the more through hearing that I
was grown more perfect? Unless perhaps you were to
confess openly that you do not inwardly believe what your
lips proclaim. But you are convicted of fleeing from the
sinner, not the poor man, in me, because you so often visit
the most blessed Martin, and you would certainly never
have longed to see him if you had feared physical hunger.[97]

14. I shall certainly never cease to long for your
presence and to invite you here, for the growth of love,
which is the fulfilment of the law,[98] is the greatest necessity
in the growth of spiritual works.

Come to me, if possible with all haste. I have nothing except Christ; come and see if I have nothing when I have Him who has everything. For I have not abandoned Hebromagus[99] in order to win a little garden, as you suggest. Rather I have preferred to my inheritance and to my fatherland the garden of Paradise. For my truer home is my eternal one; my truer native land is my first country and chief dwelling. For if you believe in the kindness of Christ, in whom *by having nothing we possess all things,*[100] the muddy earth does not possess us even in this tiny plot with its soil full of thorns and toils. Yet would that there were no dirt from sin clinging to me!

If you believe, as you proclaim, that this life of dedication is good, and if you believe that I am committed to it, as you say in your letter, and yet you are rather slow in longing for my presence, then you are sinning not against me, who am always a sinner unworthy of your sight, but against the Lord Himself, if you think that I shall cease to have sustenance for this mortal life once I have begun to possess God.

LETTER 12

To Amandus[1]

Paulinus greets the holy Amandus, truly worthy of veneration and greatly loved.

1. I confess that I admire the saintly kindness and patience of your love. After the wordy letters, more irksome than pleasing, which I am wont to send to you, you still feel a longing for, rather than weariness towards, my letters, for you urge me to write epistles one after another, and at even greater length. You rouse me by the pleasure I get from your correspondence, in which *charity from a pure heart, and an unfeigned faith with the unleavened bread of truth*[2] tells of your holy affection, and awakens mine in turn from the depths of my heart.

What, then, am I to do? Shall I obey you and write profuse letters? But *thou hast no need of my goods,*[3] and it is juster that I should be enriched by you, because a rich man ought to give to the poor *that there may be an equality.*[4] And should I not consult my own interests more, and *set a guard to my mouth* so that I may avoid the danger of sin caused by a multitude of words?[5] On the other hand, I fear that I may be indicted for disobedience, and my sin may perhaps be greater if I wrong you by disobeying you than if I fail to write through fear for myself.

2. So I pray that the Lord grant by His power that I may open my mouth to you, and that He direct the light of His word before my feet, so that the darkness of my

stupidity may be enlightened as the day.[6] May He who opened the mouth of the ass to speak the language of men loosen my tongue to speak a good word.[7] For I am one of those stones or beasts which were being foreshadowed when the ass spoke on that occasion, showing that the dumb obstinacy and stupidity of the members of its breed would burst into speech if God loosed their tongues.[8] If you like, let us protract this letter to describe precisely this grace of God, for all our words should be concerned with the commands and praises of the Most High; all our speech and all our life ought to be expended on Him with unceasing expression of gratitude, for by His work and gift we speak and have life.

For He made us, and not we ourselves. The Lord Himself, I say, *made us.*[9] And He also renews us, for in all that He has done and said through His saints from the beginning, He has strained to achieve the mystery of our salvation, which is the renewal of man. For the just Abel was immediately replaced by the God-sent birth of Seth,[10] who resembled his father, fashioned with similar countenance in the image of God. So the stream of righteousness descended from the original fount and seeped through the rest; and though the deluge intervened, the seed of mankind thus destroyed survived in one just man.[11] For the mystery of the one Redeemer was already at work on that occasion, in order that the restoration might be achieved through one man, since the sin had occurred through many.[12] But as the human race again flourished, righteousness relapsed. As nations increased, so did their sins; and so a second one was chosen to be called the father of faith,[13] so that both the promise of the kingdom and the seed of the eternal King should come forth from him, and so that the wickedness of man should not merit the destruction of the race a second time. This seed, multiplied by the faith of the Gentiles, was embodied in Christ. He appeared to the patriarchs, was foreshadowed by the Law, spoke through the prophets before His coming, and then came to fulfill the Law and the prophets, so that by His grace He might apply the remedy which the Law in its working had been unable to supply.[14]

3. For by now sin had so penetrated the whole body, the entire human race, that neither poultice nor bandage could help the weak and wounded.[15] The strength of vices had so grown that the disease was more powerful than the medicines and had driven out every remedy supplied by human aid. So He came, He who will also come again, fashioning Himself to our lowly bodies so that He might fashion us to the body of His glory;[16] for only the craftsman is master of his own trade, and only the potter has dominion over his clay.[17] The Lord of all, He who had made all men, deigned to descend to our world and to take us up in His body, so that with the same skill or power with which He had made us, He could form us anew. He came, however, not with the high bearing of the Lord He was, but with the appearance of the slave He was not.[18] He who is the strength of God, Lord of armies, helper and protector of all men, *was become as a man without help.*[19] He *who was free amongst the dead*[20] died for those who were to be freed. He who justifies the wicked through faith *was counted amongst the evildoers.*[21] The Lamb who *taketh away the sins of the world* was *led as a sheep to the slaughter.*[22] He who bestows eternity suffered death.

4. But to apprehend this great design and gift we have

the light of Him who *enlightens us from the everlasting hills*,[23] so that we may look upon them with raised eyes. We have discovered them anew by the same paths by which we once fell, by the second tree and the second virgin.[24] But we are not to be cast down a second time through pride, but rather to return through humility. For the King of glory and the Lord of majesty *emptied Himself, taking the form of a servant;*[25] but He concealed His hidden greatness by visible lowliness so that He could raise us—we who are externally nurtured but inwardly oppressed by that chronic disease of arrogance so wilfully assumed—to His sublime nature by adopting our lowliness within Himself.

The good Lord has worked and still works daily that we may achieve the glory of being fashioned as God, as long as we follow the example of our fashioning here in Christ. We know that through the control of the Most High our nature has been so ordered that by His grace we can advance beyond ourselves, if we remain mindful of ourselves and stick to our own path. We are prepared for this due moderation by the prophetic words in the Book of Numbers: *We will not turn aside, neither to the right hand nor to the left; we will go the king's highway.*[26] Christ is this way for us, Mediator between God and men,[27] guiding us between heavenly and human things, leading us to His kingdom by the royal road, so that humble in heart but exalted in deeds[28] we may be sustained from the perils of the left, the sins which drag us to death, and rescued by the law of humility from the peril on the right, which is haughty presumption. Thus we may keep to the saving mean, so that we do not cast our eyes on the ground and be like beasts *which have no understanding*, or seek things which are too high for us and detain our thoughts in vanity.[29] Therefore, *not minding high things but consenting to the humble,* let us measure ourselves *according to the measure of the rule which the Lord hath measured to us,* so that we may be straitened in ourselves and enlarged in the Lord,[30] not like the philosophers of this world whose wisdom the Lord has censured and destroyed and shut out by the foolishness of our preaching.[31] *They have argued to hide their snares,*[32] says the Psalm, because the whole technique of philosophers seeks to hide the light of truth by maintaining falsehoods, to wean minds from the truth and enmesh them in the nooses of empty controversies, to deceive them with clever tricks and beguile them with dissimulation of words.[33]

5. But after *a light rose up in darkness,* which was *the merciful and compassionate and just* Lord, *they have set their mouth against heaven* in vain.[34] Though they have no knowledge even of earthly things or of their own nature, they "survey the quarters of the sky"[35] and seek a godless God.[36] So *they have searched and failed in their search,* and *the arrows of children have become their wounds.*[37] For the Lord *has caught the wise in their own craftiness* and confounded them *out of the mouths of infants and sucklings,* and He has established *His kingdom not by words but by power.*[38] So even I, the smallest of the small, the neediest of the needy, the most speechless of the children of the Lord, dare to burst out in His praise and give thanks to the highest Lord. For He has revealed the mystery of His lofty love, which He had buried in the treasures of His wisdom, to His tiny children, and hidden it from the worldly-wise,[39] so that this world could not glory in the vanity of her wise ones which raised an obscur-

ing cloud and caused the world not to recognise the wisdom of God. But Jesus our Peace, who came *to make both one* and to bring equality to everything, has *destroyed the strong and chosen the weak things*, spurned the wise things and adopted the foolish, so that there might be *an equality*.[40] No one could claim anything as his own, since it was necessary for every man to boast in the Lord,[41] as each attains salvation and wisdom only by God's gift. So let us rejoice yet tremble in God our Lord, who is humble of heart and lofty in majesty, feeling within ourselves the same humility as Christ's.[42] For, as I have said, He bestowed the grace of salvation on us by taking lowly shape, so that we who had deserved to fall because of our spirit of arrogance should learn to rise again in humility of heart.

6. But the good Lord, by His Crucifixion and Resurrection, sought not only the annihilation of death in us and the renewal of our immortality,[43] but also the fashioning of this present life by which we obtain the merit to pave the way for possession of the eternal life of blessedness. What was the mysterious design of the Lord's love which caused Him to be nailed to the cross? Paul gives us the answer. It was to break down the wall of the rampart, to destroy enmities, to sack the ambition of this world, and by leading captivity captive to triumph over the entire power of the Enemy.[44] He took into His flesh, says Paul, *the likeness of sinful flesh*.[45] Note he does not say "the likeness of flesh"—for God is the Truth for all men, and *the Word was made flesh*[46] truly and physically—but rather *the likeness of sinful flesh*. Thus He who committed no sin through His own impregnable and invulnerable nature, became a sinner, as Scripture says, in that He took and played the part of a sinner in the form of a servant.

He was made a curse for us so that He might redeem us from the curse of the law.[47] He condemned sin by means of sin,[48] for by deigning to assume the flesh of Adam He removed the cause of sin still alive in the flesh of Adam. He destroyed the wall of the rampart, which is sin, standing between God and ourselves, and *made both one.*[49] This He did not only that the faith of the Jews and the Gentiles might coalesce in Christ, but also that the nature of each of us believers might become harmonious. The discord previously present in us, because the consciousness of the flesh was at war with the feeling of the spirit, was dissolved by the peace of faith. For now the old war, in which the law of sin struggled with the law of God,[50] is wiped out in Christ, for the spirit which serves God governs by faith the soul subjected to it, and the flesh in turn becomes the servant of the soul, accompanying it, as it serves God, in every duty of obedience.

7. So it is that through the Passion and Resurrection of the Lord we are not merely equipped for hope and faith in our resurrection. We also come to realise that we are dead not only when we are released from the flesh, but also when we voluntarily retire from this world, so that by faith we become dead to this world and alive to God. For a life which loves the world is death for the soul. Hence Paul says to us: *Mortify your members upon the earth.*[51] He bears witness that he himself dies every day, *bruising his body, forgetting the things which are behind, and stretching forth himself to those that are before.*[52] Here Paul teaches both humility and loftiness, because the body cannot be afflicted without a humble spirit, and the soul cannot rise to heavenly things without mortification of the limbs. Yet we must preserve due measure in such

humility, so that we bow low only through fear of God to the one Lord. *The Lord thy God thou shalt adore, and Him only shalt thou serve*[53] whose service is freedom. For he who submits to God alone is subject to none, whereas he who wishes to free himself from righteousness is the slave of all the lowest spirits or other creatures, or of his own vices and desires.

There are such things as saintly pride and wicked humility. For that pride is justified which is arrogant towards this world, holds it in contempt, and refrains from enjoying all its great, sweet, and beautiful possessions, because of absorption with heavenly things and subjection to God's commands. And on the other side, that humility is condemned which is complaisant to men not from faith but from mental cowardice,[54] which cares more for popularity with men than for salvation. It is the servant of lies, the enemy of truth, a stranger to freedom, a subject of injustice; it mixes water with wine, weakening the wine of truth with the water of flattery.[55] I think it is humility of this kind which is specifically attacked and condemned by these words of Scripture: *Woe to you that call evil good, that proclaim the sweet for those who are bitter, and righteousness for the wicked.*[56] These men, as you know, are also cursed by the truth uttered by Solomon.[57]

8. The blessed Psalmist in a short but wholly magisterial Psalm shapes us to the appropriate measure of control over ourselves when he asserts the merit of humility in his prayers: *Lord, my heart is not exalted, nor are my eyes lofty. Neither have I walked in great matters, nor in wonderful things above me.* But then, having asked God to look with favour on his humility of heart, he says: *If I was not humbly minded but exalted my soul, as a child*

that is weaned is towards his mother, so you will reward my soul.[58] So he asks for a reward because his feelings have not been humble, but rather his soul was exalted. Surely the utterance of the prophet will seem inconsistent unless we make the same mental distinctions as were made in his heart and spirit in such a way as to be harmonised. For through fear of God he spoke fittingly and humbly, and he offered, as he himself states, *an afflicted spirit and a humbled heart as a sacrifice to God.*[59] Yet retaining unimpaired the humility of his heart, he also exalted his soul with no feelings of humility, because his wisdom was in no earthly things and his mind was fixed on God, considering that his only good was *to adhere to God and to put his hope in God.*[60]

So, too, Paul, when he teaches us humility and says that in this above all we should be eager to imitate Christ, states: *For let this mind be in you which was also in Christ Jesus, who thought it not robbery to be equal with God, but emptied Himself, taking the form of a servant.*[61] Yet Paul, too, challenges us to raise our souls to the heavenly and divine when he says: *Seek the things which are above, where Christ is at the right hand and in the glory of God the Father.*[62]

9. Let us, then, hold fast to this rule of both humility and exaltation. Each is sinful if misused, as I have said, but each wins grace if we follow the course we are taught. Let us keep them both with appropriate order and measure, humbling our hearts before God and also exalting our souls to the Lord in dutiful love. Let us fear nothing save Him, let us love nothing beyond Him. Let us subject our necks only to His yoke, which is sweet, and to His burden, which is light,[63] so that in freedom we may be borne over

every yoke of the Enemy's power to the realms of heaven. The yoke of our Lord is sweet and His burden is light, because He raises us from the lowly things of earth to the heights of the heavenly kingdom. For all that is light makes for the heights, and soaring aloft is borne onwards by the speed of its slender form.

10. But the weight of sin, opposed to this grace, pushes us downward and drives us to hell. The prophet attests the weight of this burden when he groans and cries: *My iniquities are gone over my head, and as a heavy burden are become heavy upon me.*[64] But thanks be to the Lord Jesus our God, who is able *to deliver us from the body of this death, according to the multitude of His mercies*[65] and the riches of His goodness. With these He outnumbers our numerous sins, and *saves them that trust in Him.*[66] I believe that you keep vigil and pray before Him on my behalf; for I know that you have fought for Him since boyhood, that nurtured by Holy Scripture you have not been corrupted by any stigma of intercourse with the world or the flesh, and so you have found grace in the sight of the Highest and can intercede on my behalf. For I have been snatched late from the forest of the world into the flock or chariot of the Lord; *evils without number are multiplied above the hairs of my head,*[67] and I am unworthy to have my name oppress the ears of God, lest your lips also become unclean by naming me and your mouth have to be touched with a blazing coal.[68] Yet with the humility or the trust of the ancient prophet you can say: *Lord, forgive them, or strike me out of thy book.*[69] The prophet, who shared conversation with God, did not neglect his salvation or show arrogance to the Lord when he dared to say these words with the skill of a deep-laid

design. The just Lord was threatening His sinning people with the death they deserved, but the prophet presented Him with the offer of his own destruction instead. Doubtless he trusted in God's love and justice, and was sure that His mercy would spare even the unjust, since His justice cannot destroy the just.

11. On my account, then, bind the highest Lord to this proviso, that since He cannot delete you from His book He should receive the unjust under the veil of His just. For since *greater is he that is in you than he that is in the world*,[70] so the righteousness which defends sinners is stronger than the wickedness which wars on the pleas of holy men. I should like to continue this topic, so far as I can, but my paper is running out and I fear that I weary you. So I am compelled to set a limit to my words and to end this letter. Please forgive my rashness in all this, and send me a reply so that I may receive consolation and instruction from your letter.

12. Now I commend Sanemarius,[71] the bearer of this letter, in a special way to your affection, that you may arrange things as I have requested of the holy bishop my father.[72] For I have given him his freedom in the Lord and made him my fellow servant. But let him serve you in the house of the Lord, and let his services be utilised in tending the monument of my parents, so that by holy slavery he may deserve to obtain stable freedom under your protection. Arrange with our brother, the holy priest Exsuperius, that Sanemarius be given a plot of ground on which to maintain himself on the church estate.

I also ask you to ensure that the bishop sends on my letter to my son Daducius by the hand of a faithful and keen fellow servant, even if he is now in Gaul.[73] If

Delphinus is unwilling to take up the time of a cleric, please send someone from Portus Alingonis[74] with letters written by you to support mine. For you will realise from the letter I have sent him that the situation is worthy of your intervention. But there is particular need of swift action, so that a most holy priest, so venerable because of his years and his life, who is enduring the violence which I have described, should be freed as soon as possible from the exile of a stranger's house.[75]

LETTER 13

To Pammachius[1]

Paulinus sends greetings to his most beloved brother Pammachius, truly worthy of praise and veneration.

1. Hitherto, my most beloved and venerable brother in Christ the Lord, I have with fitting humility observed *the time to keep silence,* and likewise now with the necessary charity I recognise that it is *the time to speak.*[2] I have just heard, in a letter from my holy brother Olympius,[3] the dear friend of both of us, the news of your sorrow, which was as unexpected as it was unhoped for. Even if personal feelings of love were silent, yet the charity of Christ who is our Lord and God (for we are joined in Him and through Him as the limbs of a single body) would not permit me to withhold my share in your grief and my duty to speak. For the Lord God, who is our Mentor not only in our way of life but also in devoted love, has taught us, through that heavenly vessel whom He chose,[4] *to rejoice with them that rejoice, to weep with them that weep,*[5] to show sympathy towards each other and *bear each other's burdens,*[6] so that by mutual consolation we might strengthen our common faith and warm our wearied hearts. To this service of consolation God has granted so great a gift that He has promised that he who performs it will be exalted as a great city; for He announced through His prophet that *a brother that is helped by a brother will be raised like a great city.*[7] This is doubtless because

117

brotherly sympathy fortifies the struggling soul, and like a wall resists the various buffets on the oppressed mind.

2. But in case you regard my delay in this duty of charity as blameworthy rather than courteous, please believe that I wrote as soon as I heard the news. And clearly it is not because I neglected you that I have heard so late, since geographical remoteness and my vocation defend me on this charge. In my sequestered and silent life I can see only an occasional passerby, and I desire to question only those holy brothers who are dear to me. But even in my silence I have always thought of you, and now that charity seemed to demand it I have released and sent you by this letter the love locked in my heart.

Writing was the only way by which I could make the journey to your holy and loving person. I could not put the same limits on my mind as on my body; for the flesh is always weak and refused to be transported too far in winter, whereas the spirit, always more willing,[8] flew to you in fervent longing, so that though I did not embrace you in person I was able to do so in mind.[9] So *I ran in the thirst*[10] of my desires to you, my loving and revered brother in Christ, and if you in turn mentally look at me, you will see and feel that I am wholly with you. If it is true that we see and hear better by our feelings, I am certainly with you in the better part of me. For it is in mind that I have come to you. Wherever we are present bodily but not in mind, we cannot prove that we are really there, since in the absence of our mind there is only the empty appearance of the body. So I have sealed and discharged this duty of friendship, and through my faith I have made it fitting for me to visit you by a spiritual journey. I ask that I may deserve the same favour of you in turn. Regard me with the eyes of the mind. Welcome me, and look on me as I speak, as if I were standing next to you and talking face to face, sharing your grievous distress at the thought of the end we must all meet, or congratulating your patient observance of the hope of faith. For a man's words are the mirror of his mind. Indeed, the very word of God establishes that *from the abundance of the heart the mouth speaketh,* and the treasure of the heart is revealed by speech.[11] Therefore, take to yourself my mind, as it is shaped in this letter, in the truth by which we stand in Christ.

Please do not measure our friendship in terms of time. For ours is not that worldly friendship which is born more often of hope than of faith, but the spiritual friendship sprung from the fatherhood of God and joined through the hidden kinship of spirits. So it is not the experience of years by which it grows in love, and it does not depend on and expect proof. Rather it should be strong and great at its very birth, like a true daughter of truth; for since it arises through Christ, it overflows at the very start.

3. Therefore, I embrace you in this love, and reverence you as Christ's member. I love you as my fellow member. For those who have one faith must have one mind also, and those who have one God have a single spirit. So, since our bodies are one in the harness of belief, how can our hearts be divided as we bear with each other? I speak the truth and no lie when I say that in reflecting on your emotions I feel my own heart torn by your sighs, and the limbs which truly belong to both of us pierced by the pain of your wound.

Yet the thought of your prudence and faith revives me as

much as my concern at your grief troubles me. In short, I confess that I have been doubtful whether to write sad words expressive of my love for you, or to write words which congratulate you on your faith. For I have heard not only of my holy sister being called to God, but also of your devoted piety in Christ. For the father of the household who prompted this letter has told me of your wise, holy, and true love for your wife,[12] since unlike most men you accompanied her to burial with her tribute of tears, and unlike those deprived of Christian hope, without empty pomp and honour. Instead, you first fittingly performed the proper rites for her dear body, sprinkling and bedewing it with affectionate and copious tears of love, and then in more religious fashion you honoured her burial by attending her with remedies which bring salvation and works which live—in other words, with almsgiving.[13]

4. So I shall first praise the work of devotion which you have performed. For Holy Scripture shows that this, too, is pleasing to God, when it says: *My son, shed tears over the dead, and begin to lament as if thou hadst suffered some great harm, and neglect not his burial.*[14] In short, our patriarchs provide a precedent for this religious act as well. For the father of faith mourned his wife Sara, the mother of our calling,[15] not because he had any doubt that she would be reunited to him, but because he missed her when she went before him. For how could the father of faith, the first man to hear the blessed promise, doubt the resurrection? Yet mindful of his human nature, he did not neglect the care of the body because the soul was safe, but he bought a field for the burial and laid his dead wife in a costly grave.[16] By so doing he also taught us what pro-

vision men should make on this earth. For he who at God's word had left his country and kindred,[17] and had bought none of the vast territories traversed by different tribes, but was a stranger to every land, bought only a field for a grave, an eternal and no transient possession, land not for greed but for peace.

Jacob, too, honoured the much beloved and eagerly awaited Rachel with a famous tomb and inscription, so that this pious duty might lighten his present sorrow and be a witness to posterity. And yet with prophetic mind he marked that spot with the inscription of his wife's death, foreseeing that at the birth of the Gospel the Law must fall into disuse. By this mystery the wife of the patriarch, who lived in many places as an image of the Church, died there, I think, to symbolise the death of the synagogue, having brought forth in labour the son of grief in that place[18] where the end of the Law was to be announced in the childbirth of the Virgin. *For the end of the law is Christ.*[19]

Tobias, too, teaches us that conscientious burial brings hope sacred and sanctified, for by putting this duty first he was especially justified by the Lord and praised by the voice of the archangel for preferring the burial of a poor man to his dinner.[20] For neglecting his stomach because he was attentive to his soul, he preferred his body rather than his spirit to go unnourished, so that he might provide for us an example of preferring bodily fasting so as to attain the soul's repletion.

So the duty of burial is good, and so are the tears of love with which father Abraham buried the mother of our pledge. Good, too, are the tears of affection which Joseph duly bestowed on his father.[21] Good are the tears in prayer with which David watered his bed night after night.[22]

But why should I proclaim the tears of holy men, when Jesus, too, wept for a friend? He deigned also to experience this suffering, which is a part of our unhappiness, so that He might weep over a dead man, and with human weakness mourn him whom He was to revive with divine strength.[23] But in that one man the merciful and pitying Lord bewailed the universal condition of the human race, and washed us with those tears with which He mourned for our sins.

5. Your tears, my brother, were holy and dutiful like theirs, because they flowed with the same love. They lamented a wife worthy of your chaste couch, not because you have doubts about the resurrection, but because of your longings of love. *For the grace of a woman wins glory from her husband*[24] when she is in his embrace, and wins his longing when she is taken before him. As she always was, so shall she be *a crown for her husband for ever*, and *her lamp shall not be put out*.[25] For, as Scripture says, *she has put out her hand to useful things, she has opened her mouth to wisdom*, and *she has rendered her husband good*.[26] She has crowned you with fame and honour, so that she might share your joy in your final days. Hence she is more worthy of tears than of lamentation; it is better that you should long for her continually than grieve for her. For though the very thought of her merits provokes bitter sadness in her surviving husband (for a just person who dies will leave regret behind), yet to the believer it provides abundant consolation, *for the memory of the just man is immortal*.[27] And do not, holy brother, feel a sharper stab of pain because she died young, for the word of God affords consolation for this very

eventuality. *For the just man, if he be prevented with death, will live in rest.*[28]

6. The same Wisdom in the words that follow proves to you that she was also old, so that she may not seem to have died at all before her time: *Venerable old age is not that of long time nor counted by the number of years. For the understanding of a man is grey hairs, and a spotless life is old age.*[29] Let us be thankful, then, for her rightful summons and her death at a ripe age; for though she was young in the bloom of years, she had grown grey in the holiness of her character, adorning a girl's years with the merits of old age. Thus those very causes which inflame your heart's wound can bring you a greater consolation. Though you do not now have this holy woman as wife, you did so in the past. The loss of a mortal woman you share with all, but few share with you the former possession of so excellent a wife. So I am not surprised that she did not linger in the world, but was summoned more quickly to Christ. For *her soul pleased God*, and, therefore, in the words of Scripture, *He hastened to bring her out of the midst of iniquities*, lest *our wickedness should alter our understanding.*[30] For it is written that *the whole of this world is lying in wickedness*, and *evil communications often corrupt good manners*, and *he that toucheth pitch shall be defiled with it.*[31] It was fear of this that made one holy man afraid of delay, and anxious about how long his old age lingered, and he begged God to make known to him his end and the number of his days; and since he realised that his time had been prolonged (for the Spirit by which he prophesied revealed it to him), he groaned and said: *Woe is me that my sojourning is prolonged!*[32] He bore witness that the reason for his groaning

and fear was that *he was dwelling amongst the tents of Cedar*,[33] that is, in the darkness of the world. For Cedar in Hebrew means the same as *obscuritas* in Latin.[34]

7. Finally, David himself, when his two sons whose merits were so different were lost to him, exemplified this mysterious truth. He wept for his beloved son when this son was ill, but not when this son was dead, since he knew that the child had passed to the happiness of eternal peace.[35] But he wept for the dead Absalom,[36] whom he had made his enemy, because as prophet he was aware of God's justice. He had no hope that this impious son would obtain rest, and he knew that the blessing of resurrection was not owed to one who had killed his brother.[37] But, as I say, he wept for the first child when it was sick, and put off his royal garments for black clothing, and supported his prayers to God with fasting and goat hair and ashes. But when death brought his son's sickness to an end, he made the end of the child's life the end of his grief, once the material cause of his worry vanished. So the son was freed from his body, and the father from his grief. David simultaneously laid aside his sadness and his garments, took food, put on again his royal apparel, and anointed his head which was foul with dust. When his servants, astonished at this unusual manifestation of parental love, asked the reason for David's grief before his deprivation and his joy after it, he replied: *I shall go to him rather, but he shall not return to me.*[38]

8. I think that this king and prophet has given us sufficient instruction on the anxiety which we are to assume after our loved ones have gone. We are to concern ourselves with the journey by which we ourselves follow, rather than with the journey of them who have already

gone before us and arrived. It is a loving act to show
sadness when our dear ones are torn from us, but it is a
holy act to be joyful through hope and trust in the promises
of God, and to say to one's troubled soul: *Why art thou
sad, O my soul, and why dost thou trouble me? Shall he
that sleepeth rise again no more?*[39]

Thankful joy is more acceptable to God than long and
querulous grief. We learn by David's example not to shed
superfluous tears. Tears bestowed on the dead are especially
vain—they do nothing for the one whom God has taken,
and they oppress the one left behind. So David wept while
his son lived, but was joyful when the son was dead; for
whilst the child breathed the father could by prayers and
tears still obtain a respite from death, but once the child
had been summoned by God it was David's duty to be
thankful, as indeed he was—for the will of God is undoubtedly superior to our wishes.

9. So let us perform the duties of love without breach-
ing our faith, and prefer the joys of faith without damage
to our love. Granted our love may weep for a time, but
our faith must ever rejoice. We should long for those who
have been sent before us, but we should not lose hope of
gaining them back. For *ours is the God of the living and
not of the dead,* and Paul says that the dead are asleep in
Christ.[40] You are to understand from the word "sleep"
that death is not permanent. For one who sleeps is later
roused and arises. So in our love for our dear ones, let us
show the longing of intimate friendship, but let us console
ourselves by that confidence in the resurrection which is
afforded by our faith.

10. Accordingly, my dearest brother, you must follow
the authority of these heavenly words and examples, not

only in the shedding of loving tears, but also in restraining them. For it is written: *All things have their season.*[41] The time for weeping is surely past, and now it is the time for joy, for the Lord is at hand.

Divine Scripture, which allows us to prolong our tears as though to disperse our grief, enjoins also a limit to them at a fixed time. It says that *the bitterness of grief is to be borne for a single day.*[42] What riches God's goodness affords! With what loving care for us He makes this stipulation! He does not begrudge our ready love, but He is aware of our weakness and restrains any immoderation; so He commands us to prolong our tears over the dead, but restricts our bitter weeping to a single day. He allows us to weep the tears which dissolve our grief and relieve our souls, but He cuts short the sorrow which oppresses our minds with uncontrolled and unreasonable torture, and which our frailty cannot longer endure. But God in His love explains this more fully with words of His own. For in the same passage He added: *and comfort thyself at the proper time in thy sadness, for of sadness hasteneth death, and it shall overwhelm thy power. For only the sorrow that is according to God achieveth salvation.*[43] On the other hand, as Paul says, *the sorrow of the flesh,* which is of man and so springs from weakness, *worketh death.*[44] Though the two authors are different, Scripture speaks in harmony through both holy men with the spirit and word of God. For real death lies in one's strength being overshadowed. Now if *Christ is the power of God*[45] and our life, you see the truth of the statement that death hastens on through the grief by which our power is overwhelmed, and the whole man is, as Paul says, *swallowed up with overgreat sorrow*[46] as if by some whirlpool of hell.

But thanks be to God, because this grief of yours and this fear of mine are balanced by my awareness of your strength and wisdom, the light from which is too abundant in you to be buried in the darkness of grief. Rather, your strength conceals your sadness and swallows up death itself and the onset of baneful grief. It is not in mere words that I attribute this power to you; this is no guess I make about it. Your actions witness this in you, and it is experience of them which compels me to speak.

11. I intend to pass now to the proclamation of your deeds, to the mention of your religious acts springing from your holy tears. You discharged what was due to both parts of your wife; you shed tears for her body and lavished alms for her soul. As a son of light really aware of truth, you shed tears where you knew there was death, but performed good works where you believe there is life. So upon the empty you bestow empty things, but on the living, living things.

In the basilica of the apostle you gathered together a crowd of poor people, the patrons of our souls, those from the whole of Rome deserving of alms. I myself feast on the splendid scene of this great work of yours. For I seem to behold all those pious swarms of the wretched populace, the nurslings of God's affection, thronging in great lines deep into the huge basilica of the renowned Peter, through that venerable colonnade smiling afar with azure front, so that all the precincts are thronged—inside the basilica, before the gates of the atrium, and on the whole level area before the steps.[47] I see the gathering being divided amongst separate tables, and all the people being filled with abundance of food, so that before their eyes there appears the plenty bestowed by the Gospel's blessing and the picture of those crowds whom Christ, the true Bread and the Fish of living water, filled with five loaves and two fishes.[48] He did not act in His normal manner and produce plants which would grow to be food for men; but by a new gift He brought forth food already prepared for them. For by divine provision a hidden hand served a visible feast, pouring out bodily nourishment with spiritual abundance; from a source of bread and flesh which cannot be named it brought physical repletion and spiritual refreshment to peoples hungering for faith, inspiring hope in the races still unfed. With hidden increase it swelled the foodstuffs, supplied abundance of what was to be consumed, and proffered extra fragments to the diners, so that the food grew bigger in the hands or mouths of those who ate it. They experienced abundance of food, but they did not see the masticated food return from their mouths, nor did they see it being lifted as it approached their teeth.[49]

12. Taking your precedent from the action of the Lord, you ordered the crowd to sit on the ground. For we read that Jesus, too, commanded them to recline on the earth.[50] Indeed the Lord Himself was and is in you, because no man performs Christ's works without His aid. By His gift and blessing you received for yourself abundance of bread in His name and, like the disciples who received from Him blessed bread to distribute, you apportioned it to the countless mouths of the poor. They ate and were filled, and all filled their baskets from the abundant bread remaining. But you gathered together all the excess of spiritual fragments, apostolic faith from the twelve baskets, and spiritual grace from the seven,[51] for Christ worked equal miracles with your bread. At your feast He changed your material bread into heavenly food, and prepared it to give you

eternal fulness. For at the feast of Christ, clothed in a
wedding garment you will deservedly recline with our
fathers, Abraham, Isaac, and Jacob,[52] since here on earth
Christ reclines with you amongst His poor, and in you
the Son of man has a place to lay His head.[53]

13. It is still pleasant even now to linger in visualising
and praising this great work, for we are praising not the
acts of a man but those of God performed through a man.
How joyful to God and to His holy angels was the show
you put on from your abundant store, as the saying is, a
holy and no profane exhibitor! With what pleasure did
you delight the apostle himself when you packed the
whole of his basilica with dense crowds of the needy!
They stood where, under its lofty roof, the huge basilica[54]
extends far beneath the central ceiling, and glittering afar
from the apostle's tomb[55] arrests the eyes and delights the
hearts of those who enter; or where under the same imposing roof it extends sideways with twin colonnades on
each side; or where the gleaming atrium merges with the
projecting entrance, in which a cupola roofed with solid
bronze adorns and shades a fountain spouting forth water
to tend our hands and faces,[56] and encloses the jets of
water with four columns which lend it a mystical appearance.[57] Such adornment is proper to the entrance of a
church, so that the performance of the mystery of salvation within may be marked by a worthy construction
without. For the one faith of the Gospel sustains with its
fourfold support the temple of our body; and since the
grace by which we are reborn flows from that Gospel, and
Christ by whom we live is revealed in it, it is sure that *a
fountain of water springing up unto life eternal*[58] is born
there in us on the four columns of life. It waters us within

and engenders heat inside us, but only if we can say, or deserve to feel, that we have *our heart burning within us in the way*,[59] enflamed by Christ as He walks along with us.

14. What a happy sight, then, you have afforded to God, to the angels of peace, and to all the spirits of the saints! First of all, you showed your veneration for Peter, whose faith and memory you have celebrated with such repeated offerings of your wealth; for you first offered to God pure libations as a sacred sacrifice,[60] with the most welcome commemoration of the apostle himself. Then with appropriate generosity, with pure heart and lowly spirit, you offered a most acceptable sacrifice to Christ, *in whose tabernacle you have offered up a sacrifice of true jubilation*, by refreshing and feeding those who with many blessings *offered to God the sacrifice of praise*.[61] With what happy din did our city then resound, when you poured forth the entrails of your mercy by feeding and clothing the poor! You transformed the pallid bodies of the needy, watered the dry throats of the thirsty, clothed the trembling limbs of the shivering, and brought them from their prison so that their countenances were meet for God's blessing.[62]

But as you cherished those bodies in need, your good works redounded to your advantage, for you have nurtured your spirit with God's reward and refreshed the soul of your blessed wife. For Christ's hand poured over her the gifts you expended on the poor, as at the blink of an eye that earthly food was transformed into heavenly nourishment. All the money which you cheerfully gave and untiringly allotted, pouring it from your laden hand into the twin palms of the recipients, was immediately deposited in the bosom of the rejoicing Lord by angels who intercepted it in flight, and it was restored to you to be so counted that your reward and revenue might be thirtyfold.[63] To your reward were added not merely riches, but also the graces of blessings; for that cry and prayer of the poor, by which through your gift they blessed God, were accounted to your justice. For the voices of the poor are readily directed to the ear of God; as Scripture says: *The prayer of the poor man pierceth the clouds.*[64]

15. Rome, you would not need to fear those earnest threats in the Apocalypse[65] if the entertainments provided by your senators were always such as this! Noblemen such as this in Rome would be truly noble. Our holy fathers Abraham, Isaac, and Jacob would welcome them to their fatherly bosoms; the prophets, apostles, and martyrs who compose the heavenly senate would acknowledge them as their own; and when they had doffed their togas, polluted with no foul and unchaste blood, Christ would clothe them in the royal stole of promised light and inscribe their names in the white book, the book of eternal life. Those riches would be rich indeed, for on them would feed no bloody cruelty of ancient dragon but the boundless goodness of the saving God, if only what is wickedly spent on purchasing and feeding beasts or gladiators were spent on our own salvation, and if only life were dearer to us than death. But through greed and distorted generosity we have been niggardly to God, who is our defender, and lavish towards the devil, who is our enemy. We consider our loss our gain and our gain our loss; we show no desire to redeem our lives even with frugal outlay, but we extravagantly buy death instead of life. Our condition would be blessed if we were afraid to displease, or sought to please, God as much as men, if we feared the commands of Christ as

much as the hissing of the mob, and if the praise which God pronounces were bought for the price we pay for the applause of the common herd.

16. *Blessed are you who have not drawn near to such counsel*, who win praise *not in the chair of pestilence*[66] but in the home of the apostle and the throng of the Church, that is, in Christ's theatre, where the spectators on the benches are not hostile, but approving, and where God Himself looks on. Your spectacles you exhibit for the Church; you are not a candidate in the arena seeking vainglory, but rather eternal praise. You purchase no gladiators or beasts, but the means by which you can destroy the real gladiators, who are the princes of this darkness, and can overcome the real beasts, the full strength of the devil, and *trample underfoot* with impunity *the lion and the dragon*.[67]

Happy are you, by whom the name of the Lord shall be blessed. You have your seed in Sion and your servants in Jerusalem, that they may in turn *receive you into everlasting dwellings*.[68] You shall not fear being assigned to the abode of the rich man who was engulfed by deserved fire in Tartarus, that is, in the lower depths and outer darkness of hell, and who begged to be sprinkled with water if only from the tip of the finger of the poor man whom he had despised in this life. Father Abraham justly replied to him: *Son, remember that thou didst receive good things in thy lifetime, and Lazarus evil things; but now he is comforted, and thou art tormented.*[69]

17. So I believe that the rich should tremble at such interchange of punishment and delight. For here on earth they think only of themselves. Steeped in vices, they either brood on their hidden wealth without allotting a portion

to the poor, or they wickedly squander it and lack all merit, even at the cost of necessary punishment for eternity. For in their love of luxury they have reckoned themselves so cheap that they are convicted of accounting a single day's feasting more precious than their entire eternal life. So they shall not share the heavenly blessings of the poor for all eternity because the poor never saw their earthly goods in this life.

And more grievously parched will be the tongues of those who now find the infirmities of the poor disgusting or objects of scorn, for their disgust and wit brings death upon them as they pass by,[70] leaving their neighbours' wounds to be licked by dogs. I say "neighbours," for by nature all men are neighbours of each other. Would it not be more apposite, I ask you, to call such rich men dogs, men who have not even imitated dogs in tending and licking men, and who order their brothers, their true-born brothers who share nature with them as their mother, to be thrust out from barred doors and even to be driven away with savage lashes when they seek their fill merely from the crumbs falling from the rich man's table?[71] So I believe that the rich man in hell described by the Gospel, he who cried out that his whole person was being wretchedly tortured in the flame of the fiery whirlpool, asked for refreshment only for his tongue because doubtless his tongue burned the most fiercely, since he had sinned against Lazarus, who had lain at his gate abandoned to the dogs, most often with his proud and greedy mouth. For this reason Scripture elsewhere warns us *to set a watch before our mouths*, for Wisdom teaches us through Solomon that *death and life are in the power of the tongue*. And in another place it tells us that *by thy words thou shalt be justified, or by thy words thou shalt be condemned.*[72]

18. So, my loving brother in Christ, since you are fearful of that rich man's punishment and share the abode of Lazarus, since your mouth abounds in blessings, since your riches are the paps of the poor, since your house is Christ's and you do not allow a beggar to lie before your gate as you feast, but rather joyfully admit him to your house to eat with you or to fill himself as you fast, your poverty happily lies in absence of sins, and your blessed wealth lies in your virtues. You, too, shall be rightly numbered amongst the poor who possess the kingdom of heaven,[73] and amongst those rich who possess *a city of strength*,[74] for you are rich in God's spirit and poor in your own. For God loves rich men of this kind in company with His poor; He hymns them in His sacred writings and ennobles them with the authority of His immortal pages.

19. Please reflect on the fact that the names of the rich whose crimes or punishments have been attested in the Scriptures have not been divulged. This is doubtless because they were unworthy to be named by the word of God, since the wickedness of their lives erased them or their greed destroyed them. This was how God had foretold of them through His prophet: *Nor will I be mindful of their names by my lips.*[75] By His lips He means the two Testaments of immortal words, which are rightly called the lips of God's mouth, because they are part of Him and are opened by God's word alone, and through them *God kisses us with the kiss of His mouth.*[76] So God's justice did not wish these lips to be sullied with the names of the wicked.

That is why the name of the rich man whose vanity and

greed are exemplified is not revealed. His life was already over, but he was thinking of expensive feasting as though it had just begun. But he was told: *Thou fool, this night thy soul is required of thee; and whose shall those things be which thou hast provided?*[77] Likewise the name of the rich man in hell is not known; and we realise that this is not accidental, because the poor man's name is given. Again, we are not given the name of the rich man of whose blindness we read; he boasted that he had fulfilled the Law, but through love of his riches he turned aside from the condition of attaining perfection. For, as Scripture says, *he had many possessions,*[78] and accordingly there followed that well-known saying[79] which would have shut the kingdom of heaven to almost every rich man, if God, the only Good, had not exacted from His omnipotence the gift of enriching the wealthy with the will of poor men.

So these rich are hateful to God and expunged from record, for they preferred the transient to the eternal and thought it better to trust this life rather than God. Thus they provide food for worms and booty for thieves, and *do not know*, as Scripture says, *for whom they lay up treasure,*[80] for they do not wish to realise to whom they owe their treasures. It is right for them not to know who will obtain what they relinquish, because they do not know who bestowed their possessions on them. *For what hast thou, man, that thou hast not received? And since thou hast received, why dost thou glory as if thou hadst not received it?*[81] Why do you show arrogance to God regarding the gifts that are His? The names of such rich men, my brother, are not written in the Gospel, because they are not contained in the book of life.[82]

20. In short, you should know that it is not riches but men's use of them which is blameworthy or acceptable to God. To realise this, read how the holy fathers Abraham and Job became dear to God by use of their wealth.[83] Indeed, in that Gospel in which the rich man in hell who despised Lazarus goes unnamed, we note that the rich Joseph of Arimathea is cited by name.[84] For *blessed is he with special understanding concerning the needy and the poor*,[85] who honoured the body of Christ with loving service and did not fear to approach the judge on behalf of the Lord's battered body. So at the burial of the Lord there was this rich man who with love met the cost of an expensive burial robe and a new tomb. With these names will the holy page enrol you; it is the lot of such rich men as these that you will share, for your spirit's resources, as well as your wealth, are equal to theirs. For what they had they did not employ for themselves, but *no one called anything his own*,[86] and they considered that "all humanity was their concern,"[87] like that former multitude which was first in faith, *who had one heart and one soul and all things in common*.[88]

Observe the reason for this. It will be easy for you to realise that it is a murderous crime to despise the poor on our own judgment, for no act of God has set them apart from us. How, then, can we shut out from our small dwellings those whom God has enclosed with us in the single house of this world? How can we disdain to make them associates in the enjoyment of earthly possessions, when however unwillingly we have them as partners in the unity of our divine origin? It was by clinging to this truth that Abraham became dear to God. By observing it, Lot escaped from Sodom. By following it, Job triumphed over the devil.[89]

21. Let us also, then, open our homes to our brothers, whether after the fashion of the fathers just mentioned we fear the danger of rejecting an angel when we repulse men, or whether we hope to deserve to have angels as our guests as we assist the passage of every stranger with ready kindness. For when our father Abraham entertained strangers, he received Christ the Lord and His angels; in his hospitable tent he saw that day which in the Gospel the Saviour reveals in Abraham's presence.[90]

It was for the abuse of guests that the Sodomites were condemned, and Lot obtained immunity chiefly for his goodwill in putting his guests before his daughters.[91] In this he showed no negligence of duty, but perfect duty; for it was not by holding his daughters cheap that he gained his reward. No, before his family duty he put the justice of love, which is fear of God. It was precisely the command and spirit of love that he obeyed when he welcomed his guests, and his purpose fulfilled already on that occasion the perfection of faith, by which we are told: *Every one that hath left brethren or sisters or mother or sons or daughters for my name's sake shall receive an hundredfold, and shall possess life everlasting.*[92] It was the perfection of this purpose, or the purpose of this perfection, which already at the beginning of the world freed Lot in his justice from the fire which ravaged five cities.[93] In return for the hospitality of his house, he deserved to receive, as a gift from God, a great city[94] as a home. For he alone had been dutiful and chaste in that incestuous and wicked city; and he transcended his sense of duty with holiness and did not hesitate to purchase, so far as in him lay, the chastity of his guests at the price of his daughters' virginity.

Again, Job, who was the silver tested in the fire of the Lord,[95] attests that he was always *an eye to the blind and a foot to the lame*,[96] and he demands and obtains a reward for these works in the very struggle of his temptation. He is robbed of the wealth of his inheritance, not of his spirit. He cannot be wounded in heart, and he commits no sin by his lips. Stripped of the ambition of wealth, he is armed with the virtue of patience. Bereft of his children, but not of the light of his heart, he embraces the sons of his purpose, which are the works of justice, and he cries: *Naked came I out of my mother's womb, and naked must I return into the earth. We brought nothing into this world, and certainly we can carry nothing out.*[97] But because he had not lost his spiritual resources, he got back his temporal riches as well as a reward for his patience. He was enriched threefold, because he had been proved and purified sevenfold. For, as Scripture says, *he had eaten the labours of his fruits*[98] by toiling in dutiful works, and therefore he ate the fruits of his labours by recovering the rewards for his works even in this world.[99]

22. Your destiny is with rich men like these. For you have been mindful that the God of Abraham, Lot, and Job is the source of your riches. You are free from greed, because you are a slave to justice. You employ the mammon of iniquity in the proper way.[100] You are the master, not the slave, of your money, because you are possessed by Christ, *who has led captivity captive*.[101] Therefore, glory in the Lord, for flesh and blood have not revealed to you the wisdom of this foresight,[102] but Christ Himself

who is the true light and the wisdom of God.[103] By this wisdom you are aware that Christ is given food, drink, covering, and visitation in the person of every man in need and poverty.[104] You are as those whom *the Lord will deliver in the evil day*[105] because of this kindly service which I have just mentioned.

23. *May the Lord Himself preserve you and give you life and make you blessed, and help you now on your bed of sorrow.*[106] May He *turn your* dutiful *mourning into holy joy;* may He *cut the sackcloth*[107] of your grief and restore to you the joy of His salvation. May He *strengthen you with a perfect spirit,* and *make firm your arms like a brazen bow*[108] in prayers and almsgiving. May He *make your feet like the feet of harts,*[109] so that you may be swift to flee from the devil and follow Christ, so that you may implant your steps with the twin hooves of the Old and New Testaments, and *be steadfast in the way of the Lord.*[110] May your feet be *saved from falling* and your *eyes from tears* by the hand of the Lord, so that with your blessed wife you may *please the Lord forever in the land of the living.*[111]

It will be done unto you according to your faith, for *the Lord is faithful in His words,* and *He will be mindful of this thy sacrifice* forever, and *thy whole burnt-offering shall be made fat.*[112] You yourself He will receive as a living victim to be for Him an odour of sweetness.[113] He will repay your loan on that day on which the Debtor, who is richer than His creditors, will restore to each with abundant interest the money they have lodged. The day of repayment is not far off, for *the countries are white already with the coming harvest.*[114]

24. Meanwhile you are to ponder happily and promise

yourself the wealth you must regain. You will console your mind much more fruitfully by faith in the future life than by words from me or anyone else. For it is no small pleasure for believers mentally to anticipate in sweet reflexion the blessings promised to the faithful, and to walk already in imagination the paths of paradise. A farmer takes pleasure in his cornfields in admiring the prospect of the harvest, whilst awaiting from the harvest the fruits of his labour; the eager desire of his prayers more easily bears the time of the delay if he feasts his eyes whilst hoping for what is to come. How much more pleasure can we obtain! For though we are sinners, we are faithful servants. We have been ordered to sow[115] our scattered seed, not in the dubious reliability of the earth, but in the unchangeable truth of God. We hope for what Truth Itself has promised.

25. For we do not guess at the afterlife from human opinions, the fictitious dreams of poets, or the images of philosophers, but we draw our faith in actuality from the very fount of truth. And who could have greater knowledge of things divine than God Himself, who is aware of His own works and laws? We shall not tell lying doctrines of souls passing into other bodies so that men become beasts, or of souls surviving utterly without bodies, or of souls dying in the body.[116] Let those who do not possess the prophets of truth delude themselves with the lies of poets. Let those who are not enlightened by the testimonies of the apostles be blinded by the mistaken beliefs of philosophers. Let those who have no hope console themselves in despair, saying: *Our time is as the passing of a shadow, and there is no going back of our end; for it is fast sealed, and no man returneth.*[117] For blinded by the

darkness of their wickedness and unbelief, they cannot
say: *I believe to see the good things of the Lord in the light
of the living.*[118] But we have no need of such desperate
remedies, for we have Truth Itself. This Truth, which is
God and the word of God, has promised by Its teaching,
and proved by Its rising again, the resurrection of the flesh
unto eternal life. For the Son of God Himself, through
whom all things exist and without whom there is nothing,
has testified: *I am the resurrection; he that believeth in Me,
although he be dead shall live; and every one that liveth
and believeth in Me shall not die forever.*[119] So that He
should not maintain this solely by words, He ratified it by
example. He showed to His disciples His own person, in
whom all men are taken up, raised from the dead, and He
instilled in them belief in His risen flesh when He said to
Thomas: *Put in thy finger hither and see My hands; and
bring hither thy hand and put it in My side; and be not
faithless but believing, for a spirit hath not flesh and bones
as you see Me to have.*[120]

26. Since we have these testimonies, these proofs and
this light of faith, under what circumstances will we be
able to throw doubt on the resurrection, which we have
heard from God's word, which we have seen with the
eyes and felt with the hands of the apostles?[121] Moreover,
we are so closely bound and united to God through Christ
that we possess the Holy Spirit whom God gave to us as
an earnest on this earth, and we have the flesh of Christ
as our pledge in God.[122] For over the boundless space
which separates things mortal and divine He has established His mediation like a bridge to connect the two,[123]
so that by this path the earthly may be joined with the
heavenly, once the celestial incorruption has permeated

our corrupt nature, once immortality, in the words of Scripture,[124] has swallowed up our mortality, and our life, victorious in Christ and from Christ, has conquered and absorbed death.

We cannot doubt the truth of this blessing, though we can doubt if our merit deserves to obtain it. But let us carry out Christ's commands that we may obtain Christ's promises. His truth is with us; let not our faith fail Him. He is the Life, the Way, the Gate for all men.[125] To no one does He close His kingdom, and He allows us to make entry by force.[126]

27. Advance to your goal, that *you may apprehend wherein you are apprehended.*[127] Struggle along the narrow path,[128] that you may attain the glorious possession of your eternal heritage. In your wife you have now a great pledge in Christ, one who will make efforts to win support for you. In heaven she is obtaining for you as much grace as the wealth which you accumulate for her on earth; for, as I have said, you do not honour her with vain grief, but rather you heap up for her the gifts of life in which she now takes pleasure. Already she enjoys the fruit of your work for her, whereas her gift to you is still newly sown.

28. She now obtains honour through your deserving deeds. Now she feasts on your bread and is enriched by your wealth. She is dressed *in gilded clothing, surrounded by variety,*[129] and bathed in precious light. She needs no refreshment from the tip of another's finger,[130] for she is sprinkled with the water from her own fingers, that is, from the works of your right hand. You did not enrich her when she married you with a marriage portion as large as the wealth you pour on her now in her rest. For in life

she could enjoy only a fraction of your gifts, since she took pleasure only in the finery she could wear. But now, however great your gifts, with her wealth of understanding she will possess them all with the pleasures of all her senses. She is blessed, for her influence with Christ is boundless; her head is ringed by a many-decked crown of glittering jewels, not interwoven with the blooms of others but gleaming with the lights that are her own. Her soul is truly precious to the Lord, for three pearls lend it such worth. For she is the wife of faith, the sister of virginity, and the daughter of perfection, since Paula is her mother, Eustochium her sister, and you her husband.[131]

LETTER 14

To Delphinus[1]

Paulinus greets his most blessed father Delphinus, ever revered and greatly longed for.

1. I was delighted by your letter, written and brought to me by Cardamas.[2] For the words announcing your good health were like the oil of joy *making fat my bones;*[3] filled with joy I cried: *The Lord hath done great things for me,* for He has visited me *on the bed of your sorrow,* and I rose up when you became well and I sang a hymn to my Lord, saying that *He had delivered my eyes from tears.*[4]

He has postponed your attainment of a crown, but held you back to help me, so that through your easing of my burdens with your earnest prayers and by your going before me on my journeys I might be lightened and *run after the odour of the Lord's ointments.*[5] This sweet-smelling fragrance I find in your holy person, and though I do not deserve to obtain it, I pursue it in my affection for you; for I hope that by reason of the inseparable bond of your love I am to be drawn along and by your guidance reach the place which you will attain by your own efforts. For *your sickness is not unto death but for the glory of God,*[6] so that it may impart perfection to your strength, and strength to my weakness. Many exemplars of the Lord's holy people drawn from the patriarchs strengthen me in my refusal to be anxious about you.

2. The fathers of faith themselves, in addition to their

other physical trials, also perfected their spiritual strength
when the eyes of their bodies were heavy[7] and their flesh
was frail, in that prophetic old age in which they gained
inner light and already foresaw the eternity of the world
and the interconnexion of all ages. So, too, blessed Job
was tried so that he might be put to the test; he wrestled
to conquer, was humbled to be exalted, wept to win joy.[8]
And what of the Holy of Holies Himself? Did He not
conquer when condemned, and by falling into death rise
unto glory? When the brave suffer in weakness, it is for
the weak a stimulus to strength; for the strong man is
weakened so that the weak may be strengthened and, by
imitation of the strong, learn to prevail in the fight. So, too,
the just man is punished that the unjust may be reformed.

3. So the bodily sickness of holy men achieves a double
function. First, their own spiritual strength is given practice. Second, *he who prospereth in his way*,[9] and who
through the powers of his unimpaired health tauntingly
says: *I have sinned and what harm hath befallen me?*[10]
does not dare to flatter himself on his physical well-being.
He is perhaps induced by fear of God's power to amend
his ways and seek righteousness, for because of his wicked
deeds he justifiably fears the avenging hand of the heavenly
Lord, which he sees is harsh even to the just. For if men
like you scarcely escape the scourge of punishment, *where
shall the ungodly sinner* like me *appear?*[11]

But I believe that your recent physical suffering has
endured harsher blows than usual for good reason. You
have been troubled long by burning fevers, and now by
colds in the head, so that when you lie happily at rest in
the Lord you can say: *We have passed through fire and
water, and Thou hast brought us into a refreshment.*[12] So

I was overjoyed at that mercy with which God looked kindly on my lowliness, so that I gained a reward for my intense anxiety when you showed the same amount of anxiety and relief about me as I showed for you.

And I received a further gift of divine grace in the same letter, the news that the business concerning the house of the holy priest Basilius, which was on my mind, has been settled by your action in accordance with my wish.[13]

4. I pray that the whole of the blessing for this act may descend on your head, and may blossom there to be interwoven with and to enhance your crown. Through it the Lord has been blessed not only by those who benefited from this kindness, but also by almost the whole of Capua. The thronged church of that city shared the joy of its priest and offered praise to God for helping the poor man in his need and humbling the proud hearts of the rich. As a result, even those rich may have hope of an eternal dwelling in *the city of habitation*,[14] for they have been accounted worthy of the enlightenment of good understanding through the agency of your words. This has led them to undertake the proper restoration of that mean dwelling, and so they have prepared for themselves an eternal lodging in the heavenly dwelling[15] of that holy pauper in their midst, by whom they will be welcomed in turn.

LETTER 15

To Amandus[1]

Paulinus greets his brother Amandus, rightly revered and dearly beloved.

1.With loving joy and *blessings of sweetness*[2] I have welcomed Cardamas[3] bringing me news wholly good, a letter informing me of your good health. It *rejoiced my heart* and was *sweeter than honey and the honeycomb;*[4] its sweetness was like oil penetrating my heart. *The bones that had been humbled rejoiced,* and in a joyful voice I said to the Lord: *We have received Thy mercy, O God,* with which *Thou hast delivered the poor from the mighty, and the lowly from the hand of him that is stronger.*[5]

Reasons for rejoicing thronged into my heart from every side—the arrival of your letter, the proof that you were thinking of me, the news that my prayer was granted and you are well, the news that my lord and father is recovered from his serious and lengthy illness. I rejoiced equally for both of you. For the same affliction had oppressed you both, Delphinus in body and you in heart; and the same visitation which brought him God's help *on his bed of sorrow* brought you likewise the refinement of relief on your couch of sympathetic suffering.[6] Yet my love for you both pricked me when I thought of his sickness and your concern, because during the time of your affliction I was perhaps in good health and even in good spirits. But thanks be to God, who softens the guilt of ignorance, and

147

who has not treated me as I deserved. For He has allowed thankfulness to precede my grief, deigning so to dispose events that I heard of your relapse into sickness by the same message as I heard of your restoration to health.

2. What shall I say of that good work which your holy person has achieved? You have enhanced your kindness to me here and now, as much as the abundance of your eternal reward. I speak of the business of the holy priest Basilius,[7] *whose mourning thou hast turned into joy,* and *whose old age* you have settled *in abundant mercy.*[8] *The voice of rejoicing and of salvation is in his tabernacle,*[9] and unceasingly and with the harmonious rejoicing of the Church he joyfully blesses the Lord in company with his whole house. For the Lord has *regarded his lowliness,* and *has bound up his bruises,* and has covered with confusion those who *rejoiced at his evils; He has cut the sackcloth* of Basilius, and *encompassed him with the strength of gladness.*[10]

3. So now, on behalf of those brothers of mine of whom I had asked you to make the request,[11] I beseech your loving-kindness to give them more than the customary affection, and if they happen to have come to Bordeaux as they often do, to give them in person my thanks from the depth of my heart and feelings. Or if the chance to see them is slow in coming, please send them at the earliest moment the thanks due to them and the blessing on their work that they deserve, so that they may know and realise how acceptable a sacrifice they have given to God because of the obedience of their faith.[12] With that obedience they were prevailed upon to accede to the prayer I made through you, and by so doing they gave me immediate joy through their devotion, but for their own salvation they

can look forward to eternal benefit. True, their acknowl-
edgment of justice, in ordering that that which belonged to
another should be given back,[13] was only doing what was
right. Yet they deserve abundant gratitude for their attitude of good will, for they *could have transgressed, and
did not*.[14] They preferred to do what was fitting rather
than what was open to them. They deigned to obey me
with such pure and wholly committed hearts that no one
can dispute the kindness they have done. For they made
no difficulties, and they ordered the holy priest's house to
be restored to him, though he could not prove that it was
his. The result was that if he could not take possession
through legal ownership, he was able to have it as a gift
from them. But the favour granted by their holy generosity
has not gone for nothing. For that most holy man, on
whose behalf the Lord arranged your intervention because
of his merits, thanks and praises them as though he has received a gift which was not due to him. But I have put off
replying to these brothers of mine at the moment, because
there will be more suitable opportunities of writing directly to them wherever they are, for their servants make
journeys quite frequently from Campania.[15]

4. I confess that I owe a considerable favour to your
kindness regarding Cardamas himself, who I hear has not
merely advanced to the ministry but is also making spiritual
progress. For when he came here during Lent, and I received him with the brotherly love owed a cleric, he did
not evade the daily fasting.[16] He joined us for the evening
meal and did not shudder at our poor board. More remarkable still, he was satisfied with the available drink,[17] so that
I realised that in your holy presence he has reformed, and
is being schooled by Paul,[18] drinking wine in moderation,

not in full measure, rejoicing his heart and not distending his stomach. I saw that he was drunk with sobriety,[19] full of spiritual intoxication and uttering a hymn[20] to God, whom he invokes repeatedly, not only aloud, but also with silent heart. He hears the Lord's will with the ear of faith, recounts it with holy eloquence, and fulfils it with energetic purpose. *Blessed be the Lord who doth wonderful things, who turned the rock into pools of water,*[21] and made Cardamas a cleric, as I have seen, and sober, as I have believed.[22] For when the Easter feast reinstated the days when the midday meal is taken,[23] he began to murmur to me about noon: "*My throat is dried up like a potsherd, and my tongue hath cleaved to my jaws.*[24] *My soul*—and my belly—*has grown faint, and my bones have cleaved to my flesh* with hunger and thirst."[25] I made reply to him. "My son, *in thy humiliation keep patience, let not the lusts of the belly take hold of thee,* for *not in bread alone doth man live, but in every word of God.*"[26] But he was *like a deaf man and did not hear,* and *like deaf asps he stopped his ears*[27] to my words, but in vain. At lunchtime he longed to fill his stomach, and no one gave him even a husk[28] until the day faded into evening. Then, after the hymn was sung,[29] however melancholy his abstention from lunch had made him, he became reconciled to me when refreshed by dinner.

But lest I appear by further joking to do injustice to his serious manners, which now take more joy in drops from a cup than from the flowing bowl of drunkenness, I shall speak seriously of his welfare. He states that his wife is feeble and therefore unable to help herself. If this is indeed the case, I ask that some small property be afforded her.

LETTER 16

To Jovius[1]

Paulinus greets his brother Jovius.[2]

1. Since my sons Posthumianus and Theridius[3] are returning home from Campania, which they visited for my sake, I considered it would be a betrayal of duty and affection not to write to you, dear friend. My motive is not merely to avoid the impression of losing interest in our mutual regard because you are strangely forgetful of me. I am much more concerned not to be thought of as misjudging your outlook on God and therefore refraining from sending you greetings through pious messengers, as if you were distasteful to consecrated men. For I love the opportunity of writing to you on all topics.

I am told that you are certainly eager to be called Christian, and that you also approve my committed way of life out of love for me. So welcome these messengers with pleasure. Do not approve of them because of my letter, but of my letter because of them. For their holiness made them have scruples about returning to their native land without visiting you, or about visiting you with no letter from me.

It struck me, then, that the attitude of these couriers fitted in with my making some reply to that earlier letter of yours. That was your answer to the letter of mine in which I hymned the manifest kindness which the power and supervision of God had bestowed on us through the elements. You surely remember that your letter afforded me a cause for thankful reply. I urged you not to ascribe God's blessing to chance, not to think that the silver of that holy commerce⁴ had, after the loss of its guardian, been preserved amongst stormy gales and greedy sailors by chance rather than by divine power. For the ship was cast up on that very shore where the townsfolk were friends of mine, and where you had a family estate, so our property was preserved in the safest possible haven.

2. But in your reply you were louder in complaint about the unkindness of the storm than in gratitude for the kindness of God. You attributed not only all the motions of the elements (in which only the hand of God can ensure the safety of men) but also our actions (which are guided by the power of the highest Lord, who directs and governs them in accordance with our merit) to the empty concepts of fate and fortune, as though they were powers equal to God.⁵

Do not think that by this argument you have indicted God. It was unjust of you to refuse to acknowledge the event as the kindness of God it was. You said that these happenings ought to be separated from the sphere of divine power, for evils are more appropriately attributed to chance than to God, and undoubtedly frequent human peril or loss is an evil. I note that you include in the catalogue of these evils storms which on land cause devastation in the fields or on sea cause the toils of shipwreck. This argument I perceive springs from those teachers who are haughty in their own wisdom and disdain to seek God's. They are exiles from the territory of truth, and advocates for their own beliefs. They have abandoned their minds to a great void, and, in the proved words of Scripture, have *become vain in their thoughts.*[6] They have represented God's works and plans according to their own judgments. They can believe that the sea or sky is governed and moved by chance, for they argue that this world has no ruler, or is ignored by a deity on holiday,[7] and so glides around at random; or that it was made by no creator, and so has no beginning or end. Physical nature, or the world of which we are each a part, does not endure because every structure can be broken down;[8] or, a more stupid suggestion, they posit that the world created itself,[9] as if anything could be the cause of its own birth and thus be creator and creature, workman and work—for clearly these differ as much in kind and condition as they do in name. Who indeed does not see that this physical world is controlled by a nonphysical force, that when the mind of the divine Spirit pours into and mingles with the great body of the universe which It created, the whole mass of creation is roused to life, ordered for employment, confined to its position, and organized for long life?

3. Since, then, it is clear that the objects of sight and touch need external help to remain as they are, there can be no doubt that they also needed outside help to be created. So we must admit that everything springs from God. And because only the impious can doubt that the world was created and finished by God, it must follow that the winds and all the parts of the created mass within the world—the entrails, if you like, of the body—are to be attributed to the control of no other. For the powers of all that God has created—that is, the material of every form of nature, with the great conflicts that rise between them —would allow themselves to be guided and restrained only by that nature and strength which is God, the single

Creator of all, the one Power which could create and order them, whose laws they must observe if they are to maintain their position. Now it is much more foolish to impugn any natural phenomenon and call it evil, for if all things come from God and He is good, assuredly all that God made is good. But if there be things in His secret edicts too lofty to be understood by our senses and thoughts, it is safer to believe that there are secret reasons for them rather than none, even if we cannot grasp and apprehend the logic of them. For we must have no doubt at all that all God's acts, however obscure to us, are planned.

4. So if God, who created the whole world, also guides it, where will chance, fate, and fortune govern a single created thing? If these powers depend, as some have it, on the motion and position of the stars,[10] then they obtain their power, which you regard as equal to God's, from tiny fires which are not only smaller than God but also smaller than the world itself—why, they adorn only a third of the world with the help of their ministering light!

It is certainly a mark of God's power to awake the elements, to rouse the violence of the winds in slumber or to restrain them when at full blast; and when storms rage, to deliver men to them or to rescue them. Since every creature subject to the one Creator lacks[11] this power, how can divine strength and power be accorded to abstractions lacking not only the name of creator but also the status of created thing? They are empty terms, not names of spirits or of bodies able to accomplish or give meaning to events; for "fortune" is the expression of a man in doubt, "fate" the utterance of a prophet,[12] "chance" the description of what falls out or happens. Yet through ignorance of God and lack of reason, men follow a long-standing error; with foolish imagination they endow these hollow names, as though they were also deities, with bodily form, and more foolishly still they accord them the honour due to gods. So images of Hope, Nemesis, Love, and even Madness are venerated. Opportunity is worshipped with shaven head,[13] and this Fortune of yours is fashioned as uneasily resting on a slippery ball.[14] By a lie of equal proportions the Fates are supposed to spin out human lives from a basket, or weigh them on scales. We must not impute such crazed ideas to the common folk. It is Plato who saves us from according too much admiration to philosophers, for even he insanely recounts it.[15] He says that the wool lies in the bosom of Necessity, an old woman, and that her three daughters are there singing in harmony, turning the spindle and joking over the threads. Plato thinks that by this wool-spinning they bring human affairs to an end, weaving the time allotted to each mortal. He so abused the ears of men with pride in his empty eloquence that he did not blush to insert such comic prattling of an old wives' tale in his writings in which he was bold enough to discuss the nature of God as if he were knowledgeable about it. But we must look to Plato only for his pleasant Attic style, not for any relevance in his pointless myth. Such books published only to charm the ear ought not to uproot the basis of our understanding.[16]

5. Rather we must heed the teaching of reason and truth. All that is around us, and of which we are a part, is God's achievement; all that guides and preserves us amidst the uncertainties of this frail and fleeting life is His gift. So we must attribute it to Him, and must not by

miscalculation regard anything as immune from His power; because whether we like it or not, He is the Creator and God of us as of all.

Such is His goodness, wisdom, and fount of reason that He has established all things according to reason, and created them in the form of His goodness. So let us devote all that we are to Him. Let us be keen to learn His pleasure and be eager to do it. Then, when our minds are cleansed, our gaze will be purer and we shall realise the truth that all that exists is from God, and the consequence that all the works of God are most beautiful, for that which has a good Creator cannot be evil. For everything in the world He has prepared for our enjoyment; He does everything for our profit, and He has created this universe in such a way that some elements are servants, some provide challenges, and some rule.[17] So by our reason we men are masters over physical and animal nature. But to avoid being enervated by the very freedom of our power, we are given useful trials by hostile elements—demonic spirits, or difficult tasks, or often the motions of the elements themselves—so that by being exercised by anxieties we may be whetted for the practice of wisdom and the fear of God.[18]

If we are untroubled by trials, we should be more thankful to the eternal Lord, but in fact we become indifferent. So Paul, the master of the Gentiles, says that it is by a secret design of God's love, and to the great advantage of mankind's salvation, that adversity replaces prosperity, and certain barriers like illnesses, financial losses, and dangers oppose our progress. For affliction achieves strength of patience, and patience begets proof of faith and bestows the reward of glory.[19] This reward virtue certainly cannot win unless she conquers, and she will not have the opportunity of victory unless she first struggles with some difficulty.

6. Though I wish that you would now put classical literature second to the Sacred Scriptures both in your judgment of their value and in your enthusiasm for them, yet even from such literature your wisdom of natural intelligence and education could have gained this lesson. For in it we read that the virtues of outstanding generals or philosophers attained brilliant and notable fame only by toils and dangers. So I am quite surprised that you have desired to obscure the clear truth of God's blessing, that you have called matters of chance that remarkable survival of the storm-tossed ship and the divine protection, revealed by manifest signs, of my property on land and sea, and that you have thrown away so great an opportunity to praise God.

Raise your mind to the height of wisdom! Seek Christ, the very tinder of the true light, who enlightens faithful souls and slips into chaste hearts! You have shown that you, too, realise this, though you put forward the excuse that you are still unfit for God and so are unable to receive Him; for you are obsessed by earthly matters and anxieties, and thus prevented from a higher vision of heavenly things by the clouds, as it were, which lie between. I only wish, however, that you could make this excuse with as much truth as eloquence. For the very abundance of your eloquence and knowledge proves that what is lacking is not so much sufficient leisure or ability as sufficient desire to read the sacred books. For it is not, I think, in sleep or by other work that you have gathered such riches of word or thought. Your breath is fragrant with the bouquets of all poets, your eloquence overflows with the rivers of all orators, and you are watered by the founts of philosophy. You are rich also in foreign letters, filling your Roman mouth from Athenian honeycombs. Tell me, to whom are you paying tribute when you are reading Cicero and Demosthenes from cover to cover? Or when you tire of being steeped in the common run of books, and turn again those pages already read of Xenophon and Plato, Cato and Varro, and many whose books you possess while I perhaps do not know even their names? You have freedom from duties to occupy yourself with these, but you are too busy paying tribute to them to learn of Christ, who is the wisdom of God. You have leisure to be a philosopher, but not to be a Christian.

Change your way of thinking, your style of eloquence! You need not abandon your inner philosophy if only you season it with faith and religion. When it is joined with them, employ it more wisely that you may be God's philosopher and God's poet, wise not in seeking God but in imitating Him, learned in manner of life rather than in tongue, yet with greatness of utterance equalling your deeds.

7. Be a Peripatetic for God and a Pythagorean as regards the world.[20] Preach the true wisdom that lies in Christ, and be finally silent towards what is vain. Avoid this destructive sweetness of empty literature as you would the Lotus-eaters, who made men forget their fatherland by the sweetness of their berries, or as you would the Sirens' songs, those melodies of baneful seduction.[21] And because we can make use of some features of such empty myths and one or two common clichés for truthful and serious discussion, let me say that not merely literature but all forms of worldly life are Lotus-eaters or Sirens. For the

noxious charm of pleasures makes us forgetful of our fatherland, for it blots out God, the common fatherland of all, from man's eyes; and the enticements of desires imitate the myth of the Sirens but bring a calamity that is real. What the Sirens are imagined to have been, enticing desires and alluring vices are in reality—inviting in appearance but poisonous to taste. Enjoyment of them is sinful, and the penalty is death. We must avoid them by being cleverer than Ulysses, blocking not only our ears but also our eyes and our mind, as it sails like a ship swiftly by, so that we may not be seduced by the delight that brings death and drawn on to the rocks of sin, be caught on the crags of death and suffer the shipwreck of our salvation.[22]

8. And I pray that we may escape, though naked, from the salt surge of the world, provided we remember now, whilst we float on physical frailty and treacherous possessions as on the untrustworthy structure of a leaking boat, to prepare for swimming by stripping ourselves of the wringing garments of our troublesome possessions, and to lay hold of the faith of salvation, on which we depend with Christ's strength under the standard of His cross, like a plank of refuge. So from our fluid possessions we may obtain solid hope, and from the harmful stuff of our desires we may snatch something conducive to innocence and salvation. In other words, by serving God and controlling our lusts we may limit our desires within the bounds of necessity; whilst keeping personal necessities we may refrain from seeking superfluous pomp, because we are warned to remember that we brought nothing into the world and can take nothing out.[23] This truth has such valid application that even those pagan philosophers who with loftier genius attained the outline of the very highest truth

felt that they could not devote themselves even to the investigation of wisdom, let alone the pursuit of it, unless they dumped the burden of their money, as though it were dung, even into the sea.[24]

9. But you must divide your possessions with God, and show gratitude to the highest Father for the kindness which one might say benefits both. Yet of all the gifts to you of inner ability or outward fortune, He asks of you in return only yourself. You and your family can keep all you possess, provided you take pains to admit that God bestows that on you as well. For we have nothing which we have not been given, because we came into this world unclothed, as I have said.[25]

Dedicate to God your powers of mind and all the resources of intellect and tongue; *offer to Him*, as Scripture says, *the sacrifice of praise*[26] with eloquent tongue and devoted heart. As soon as you concentrate your mind's eye on the sanctuary above, Truth will reveal Its face to you and unlock to you your own person, because it is by recognition of the divine truth that we also come to know ourselves. For how do you think that such perverse pride or indolence has become implanted in wretched men that they stop worshipping God, become slaves to evil spirits or to the elements subordinated to us, and reverence water, fire, stars, trees, and images, thus inflicting the most impious wrong on God's majesty? Whether it is demons or created things that they worship under God's name, they are exalting slaves; and so they deserve to be blinded with the darkness which, because they are unwilling to know the true God, afflicts them also with ignorance of themselves. Of such ignorance the man enlightened by faith is freed. He comes to recognise the order and measure of his own kind, and he realises that he is subject only to God, whose unity is marked by the Trinity which defies explanation, and that he is equal to all other creatures that have reason, and superior to those of mere physical parts.

10. If man is governed by this mean, he does not slip from the destiny of salvation or from the dignity of his nature. He becomes aware of the truth, a possessor of wisdom, a servant to righteousness, free from error, and master over the sins which condemn to slavery the soul that fails to serve God. That soul becomes an exile from its rightful condition, and dissipates itself on all the erroneous paths of its own or others' thoughts. It wanders amongst philosophers and snoops amongst soothsayers; it vacillates between hope and fear, its feelings always ambivalent as it weighs religion against superstition and impiety against religion. Then, exposed to every gust of any kind of belief, it loses all *fear of God, which is the beginning of wisdom;*[27] and so the feelings are dulled, and the soul knows not where to obtain understanding of life or to establish a judgment. After vainly wandering over all quarters of heaven and earth it becomes estranged from thought, and then it posits that the whole dynamic by which the world is driven resides in those empty concepts of chance and fate. "Its grip on the false and wicked matches its ignorance of the true."[28]

11. May your mind, which has been fired by the heavenly seed and now gives off divine heat, be guided by faith and directed to Christ, the very citadel of wisdom. You have a better chance of attaining the eloquence of the philosophers even in Christian studies, once you cease to love the wisdom hostile to truth. For it is preferable for you in your search to hold fast the things of God than to

search by disputing them. Abandon those who have always wallowed in the darkness of ignorance, detained in learned but interminable argumentation, enslaved in furious slanging with their own shadows, forever seeking wisdom but never finding it,[29] because, having no wish to believe in God, they do not deserve to know Him. Let it be enough for you to have taken from them your fluency of speech and verbal adornment, like spoils taken from enemy arms,[30] so that stripped of their errors and clothed in their eloquence you may adapt to the fulness of reality the sheen of eloquence used by empty wisdom to deceive. Thus you may adorn not the empty body of unreality but the full body of truth, and ponder thoughts which are not merely pleasing to human ears, but also of benefit to human minds.[31]

LETTER 17

To Severus[1]

Paulinus greets Severus.

1. I grow tired of inviting and awaiting you. I have now no prayers or words to say to add to the entreaties and letters so often and so vainly showered on you. Now that the hope of a meeting with each other is dashed, you have left but one avenue to our friendship; your words I repay with words, desiring to refresh my heart with these fruitless consolations if with no other. Yet you have begun to be sparing even with words, for now you write to me only "when opportunity offers."

For almost two years you have kept me in suspense, torturing me with the daily hope of seeing you. First I lived through the summer after our couriers' return to you, until winter closed in, believing that every day was to dawn on your arrival here. And since no information came about your being delayed, I consoled myself with the reflexion that you had not sent anyone because you were going to arrive yourself, however late in the day. Meanwhile this summer, too, was slipping away as I still flattered myself with this hope or belief. I set out for Rome for the revered feast of the apostles,[2] promising myself that I would meet you there during that obligatory but joyful commemoration. Your absence greatly diminished the pleasure of that anticipated hope, but did not extinguish it since I received your letter through the servant of my

163

most dear friend and brother Sabinus.—To begin with, I was surprised at his clothes and boots, which were most unlike a monk's; and his face was as ruddy as his cloak, for his cheeks betrayed no fine-drawn spirituality.[3] But finally I ascertained that the courier was not of our number. This I discovered when his master asked me to write you an answering letter. I also found that Sabinus and yourself are close relatives, so though he was a friend before, I embrace him now with redoubled affection.

2. I had no opportunity, however, of replying from Rome. I had only ten days to see the city, and saw nothing. The mornings I spent in prayerful vows, the reason for my visit, at the sacred tombs of the apostles and martyrs. Then, though I returned to my lodging, I was detained by countless meetings, some caused by friendship and some by duty. Since our gatherings scarcely broke up and gave me relaxation in the evening, I had to postpone my duty to you through lack of free time. Then after I returned home an unpleasant bodily illness caused further delay by severely afflicting me for many days. But He who is our Life and Resurrection visited my lowliness with good, and after His *chastising had chastised me, He did not deliver me over to death.*[4] *For many are the scourges of a sinner, but mercy shall encompass them that hope in the Lord.*[5] So I have been scourged as a sinner, but freed as one hoping in the mercy of Him who *healeth the broken of heart and bindeth up their bruises.*[6]

3. Now that I am recovering by the strength and mercy of God, I send this letter by the hand of Amachius, my dearest brother in the Lord, the subdeacon of my lord and father Delphinus. For his presence "offers an opportunity," and since he claims to be an intimate of yours I regard him

as a "most opportune"[7] person to entrust with my letter
to you. My greeting to you is as generous as my love for
you in the Lord and my continuing longing for you. For
not yet can I tear from my mind the hope by which I
anticipate seeing and embracing you (for God is good)
here in the house and the bosom of my lord Felix, our
common patron. I have witnessed your vows and enu-
merated your promises to him on all the occasions when, as
you recall, you stipulated them to me. If I have deceived
that witness to the truth, I do not think that for this offence
I should be put in the dock alone, for I had faith in my
pledges. Do you, my loving and most beloved brother,
ensure, I beg you, while there is still time, that you do not
appear to have given the lie to this great and holy confessor whose influence is so powerful with Christ.

4. How you can plead sickness rather than laziness or
exclusiveness, I do not know. For you could have visited
me and hastened back within a year. The effort would
have been only the same as you have repeatedly expended
on travelling in Gaul all these years, visiting Tours and
more distant places, often more than once, within the
same summer.

I am not envious; I praise your devotion to the Lord
more than your admiration and recognition of His servants.
I admit that Martin deservedly merits his visits. But I maintain that Felix is undeservedly and wrongfully mocked by
the empty promises of the man who honours Martin, or is
held in contempt by a dissembling which feels secure in
regarding a promise made as now annulled. The faith
which makes you hopeful of Christ's favour if you honour
Martin must also make you fearful of His displeasure
if you vex Felix. Yet perhaps your mind is more in-

trepid than mine, and your soul hardier, or strong in its awareness of your perfect love for Christ, so that you believe the sin with which you have afflicted my lord Felix (I pray that it is not so!) can be expiated and compensated for by your great and deserving merits of faith and good works. But though you promise yourself pardon and base your actions on faith because of the goodness shown to you by Felix, who derives it in abundance from Christ our God Himself, whose breath he is, I confess I am so fearful because of my fault of weakness, or so excessively devoted to you, that on your behalf I fear even what is secure. I want you to have abundance of Christ's grace through every saint, but I should not like you to encounter a stumbling block, especially not in the saint in whom God's love is notable and outstanding. I know that my Lord Felix, too, abounds with fatherly love through the riches of God's goodness, but I beg you to increase your love and fear for him as he shows greater goodness and kindness. Such fear will win you a great reward, and your greater anxiety will be the cause of your greater safety. In other words, you should fear to offend him, who is most dear to God, accordingly as he readily deigns to pardon you. For it is the greater impiety to insult one who refuses to take offence; he who does not look to be avenged is more heavily avenged by the Lord.

I beg you, weigh this matter in the disposition of the faith we share, and see whether you should confidently excuse yourself, or whether in your weakness you should have misgivings. For our Lord is everywhere close to us, and says: *In every place, even as you address Me, I am there.*[8] He also says: *All things are possible to him that believeth.*[9]

LETTER 18

To Victricius[1]

Paulinus greets Victricius,[2] ever his most blessed and revered father.

1. Suddenly and unexpectedly God has granted me a chance which I had sought for some time in vain. An opportunity of writing to your venerable and holy person has presented itself to me through one of the household of the faith, one specially chosen to be jointly our brother in the Lord. For at Rome on the crowded occasion of the birthday of the apostles I happened to meet our brother the blessed deacon Paschasius.[3]

Apart from the pleasure of our brotherly comradeship in the sacred ministry, I received him all the more respectfully and lovingly because I discovered that he belonged, body and spirit, to the clergy under your holy protection. But I must confess that I put pressure on him. He was eager to return from Rome to your sacred person. And although I approved the dutiful haste shown in this most justified longing, I embraced him out of love for you and bore him off to Nola. I hoped that through his visit my humble hospice there would be blessed by a breath of your spirit, and that by looking at and embracing Paschasius I would enjoy for a longer time what was virtually a part of your gracious presence. His unassuming manners, humble heart, gentle spirit, faith in the truth, and conversation spiced with wit on every topic proved that he was the pupil of your teaching and the companion of your journey.

So be indulgent to our brother for my sake, or to me for his. For whether his lingering is rebuked or my presumption censured, both faults will be excused in your eyes by the charity of the Lord. It was this charity of the Lord which either forced Paschasius to obey me, or else made me not fear to take possession of him and to keep him as if I had rights to him. For not with stubborn arrogance but *with a pure heart and an unfeigned faith*[4] I believed that what is yours is mine; and I had no doubt that you in your turn would believe that he was not absent from you during the time you knew he was with me. For even if actual distance separates our bodies, we are joined by the Spirit of the Lord, in which we live and abide, and which everywhere overflows, so that we have the limbs of one body, one heart, and one soul in the one God.

2. So I looked in the mirror of the spirit and thought of your regard for me and, in turn, of my intimacy with you because of the love my heart bears you; so in keeping our brother here, I have claimed your affection as being kindly disposed to me. The grace of the Lord, which has been given to you in abundance, has ensured that you are loved in the limbs of your body and in the hem of your garment. However, I lost many days of his stay here because the Lord in His mercy afflicted me, and I was racked with bodily sickness for my spiritual betterment. But God, who *comforteth the humble* and who *healeth the broken of heart*,[5] has comforted me with the presence of my brother the blessed Paschasius. His presence brought me refreshment of the spirit, and also bodily recovery. For a good friend is a cure for the heart,[6] and when two are happily joined together, Christ stands between them.[7]

3. But Paschasius has not merely shared the affliction and pain of my illness; he has also for long been exhausted by the very serious sickness of our most dear son Ursus, whom he had as an inseparable companion in his travels. In this matter I have observed Paschasius' faith and abounding love in the Lord. For the more bodily pain Ursus endured, the more torment Paschasius suffered in spirit. So the Lord looked kindly on Ursus because of Paschasius' humility,[8] and pressed on him another kindness. When Ursus was on the point of death, he obtained salvation from his peril through the faith and hard work of Paschasius. The Lord decided to try out on Ursus the power which our most beloved confessor Felix, lord of our house, exercises before Him. For when Ursus had been born through the hand of Paschasius, by being baptised on his bed, he returned to consciousness. Through the prayers of the saint, the Lord restored him to our brother Paschasius as also to the anxious longing of our church and more especially yours, for undoubtedly He always watches over you in the persons of your children wherever they are. The Lord, too, will now preserve him. May He bring him safe and sound, free from sin and a servant of justice,[9] into your sight. I have no doubt that Ursus, too, if he merits his return to you, will achieve great progress in faith, in step with Paschasius and with yourself, the master of both.

4. Tychicus, your dearest brother and faithful minister in the Lord, in praise not so much of you as of God's working in you, has told me of the great light which the Lord has caused to blaze forth through you in regions which were hitherto dark. For He who *bringeth up clouds from the end of the earth*[10] has brought you, too, up from

the end of the earth to enlighten His people, and He has made bright lightning to produce the fertilising rain. Just as once in *the land of Zabulon and of Nephthali*, and in *the way of the sea beyond the Jordan of Galilee, those who dwelt in the region of the shadow of death beheld a great light*,[11] so now in the land of the Morini at the edge of the world[12] battered by a deafening ocean with its wild waves; the people of those distant races, dwelling in hidden places by the sandy *way of the sea beyond the Jordan* before *the wilderness* there *grew fat*,[13] now rejoice in the light which through your saintly person has risen before them from the Lord. Now that Christ has entered them they have abandoned their harshness of heart.

Where once barbarian strangers or native brigands dwelt in deserted, equally hazardous areas of forest and shore, now cities, towns, islands, and woods with churches and monasteries crowded with people and harmonious in peace, are thronged by revered, angelic choruses of saintly men. Admittedly this is being achieved throughout the peoples of Gaul[14] and all over the world by Christ, who travels the globe *seeking such as are worthy of Him, and through nations conveyeth Himself into holy souls*, and *sheweth Himself cheerfully in the ways* of righteousness, and *meeteth with all providence*[15] those who love Him. Yet on this most distant stretch of Nervian shore,[16] on which the faith of truth had previously blown with feeble breath, leaving it for you her chosen vessel and no other, she first shone more brightly in you, grew warm with more fiery ardour, drew nearer, and chose someone in whom she could make her name holy there, so that by his name her *sound might go forth into all the earth*,[17] even where the sun sets.[18]

5. In short, I am told that Rouen,[19] which was only slightly known even in neighbouring districts, is now being mentioned with respect even in distant provinces. It is meriting God's praise and being counted amongst cities notable for consecrated places.

And deservedly so, for your deserving sanctity has transformed Rouen into the entire appearance of Jerusalem, as it is famed in the East, even including the presence of the apostles, who compare your city, not known to them before, to their own abode both for the love of holy spirits there and for the results achieved by God's working. And they have found with you a most suitable lodging for themselves. Clearly these friends of God, the leaders of the true people of Israel (that is, *the people approaching to Him*),[20] take delight in lingering in your city and aiding you in your work. In Rouen, in company with the holy angels, they are charmed by the unceasing praise, day and night, of Christ the Lord. In Rouen, through the most loving hearts of the servants of the faith, they are assigned welcome rest and friendly lodging by hosts of kindly virtues. In Rouen they take pleasure in the most chaste hearts and voices of your sheep in the daily harmony of those who *sing wisely*[21] in the crowded churches and remote monasteries. Now unviolated virginity gives them lodging within the temples of holy bodies, so that it may make them hosts ready to give Christ rest in chaste hearts. The impregnable chastity of widows slaving day and night in holy tasks and dutiful service fills them with equal pleasure. So does the conduct of married couples subject to God who secretly live as brother and sister;[22] with continual prayers such couples invite Christ, who is overjoyed by their actions, to visit what is now not a conjugal bed

but a couch of brotherhood. They unite with Him and
His saints in turn; joined in chaste love with the spirits of
these heavenly visitors, they enjoy the intercourse of
chastity. For now they are newly fashioned through the
bowels of mercy,[23] and find their rest amongst the sons
of filial love and righteousness. Amongst all the sons whom
you instruct, they show affection for you, loving Christ
in you. Thus in your city above all they perform the virtues of God, which is their power in Christ, and so bear
witness that you are their partner.

6. Grace and glory be to Him who does not abandon
the works of His hands, and who *will have all men to be
saved and to come to the knowledge of the truth.*[24] Hastening over the whole world *with the feet that bring good
tidings,*[25] He wished to make you, too, a splendid foot to
bear His word, so that in you He could *rejoice as a giant
to run the way.*[26] He has deigned to make *your feet shod
for the preparation of the gospel of His peace,* so that by
means of you also He might *walk upon the asp and the
basilisk, and trample underfoot the lion and the dragon.*[27]
And so that so glorious a lantern should not lie hidden
under the bushel of silence, by raising you to an apostolic
see He has set you, so to speak, on a lofty candlestick, so
that you might shine throughout the whole house for the
illumination of many.[28]

7. But by what paths did He lead you to the way of
His truth? He schooled you first in duties of the flesh
to lead you to the spiritual tasks of His virtue. He first
appointed as soldier one whom He later chose as bishop.
He allowed you to fight for Caesar so that you could learn
to fight for God, in order that whilst exercising your bodily
vigour in the work of the army, you could strengthen

yourself for spiritual battles, reinforcing your spirit to confess the faith and hardening your body for suffering.

Your subsequent abandonment of military service and your entry into the faith showed that divine providence had attached to you an important design. As soon as you were fired with love for Christ, the Lord Himself arranged a display of His activity. You marched on to the parade ground on the day designated for military assembly. You were clad in all the adornment of the armour of war which by then you had mentally rejected. All were admiring your most punctilious appearance and your awe-inspiring equipment, when suddenly the army gaped with surprise. You changed direction, altered your military oath of allegiance, and before the feet of your impious commanding officer you threw down the arms of blood to take up the arms of peace. Now that you were armed with Christ, you despised weapons of steel.

Straightaway the commander was roused to fury by the venom of the serpent of old. You were stretched out for scourging and beaten with huge sticks; but you were not conquered because you leaned on the wood of the Cross. Next your physical pain was redoubled. Your limbs, lacerated by great blows, were stretched out over sharp fragments of earthenware. But Christ gave you softer support, for His bosom was your bed and His right hand your pillow. So before your wounds were healed, you advanced eagerly and more bravely on a greater enemy, for you were restored by courage which was fired rather than broken by the pain of your wounds.

You were handed over to the commanding general,[29] but your triumph over this more powerful enemy was more glorious still. The clients of the devil did not dare to pile on further the torture which you had overcome, but they mooted the death penalty so that their defeats might end at any rate with the termination of your bodily life. But our *Lord who is strong and mighty and unconquered in battle*[30] shattered their hearts, however obstinate, with notable miracles. For on that journey on which you followed your assassin as a sacred victim, the executioner with menacing taunts laid a rash hand on your neck, stroking with a hand which sought to foreshadow the sword the spot where his blow would strike. But there and then his eyes were torn from him, and he was struck with blindness. What love Christ's indescribable goodness proffers to His own! He who begged pardon for those who crucified Him[31] did not let the slight to His confessor go unpunished; He who refused to have His Passion avenged[32] requited at once the insult to His witness. Yet this very anger is a mark of fatherly love, for one was blinded that many might be given light, and perhaps so that he who had lost physical sight should obtain mental insight.

Finally, there immediately followed a still greater sign. Those who performed the grim duty of guarding the condemned had refused your plea for the trifling kindness of loosening your bonds which were knotted too tightly and bit into your bones. But when before their eyes you addressed your prayers to Christ who is God, they saw the bonds without human agency drop away from your freed hands. They did not dare to fasten again what God had loosed, and so they fearfully rushed to the general, proclaiming the truth of God as if they were themselves confessors. He listened carefully, and believing the story he recounted it to his emperor with the soldiers' testimony.

His action then showed that his sudden change from anger to mercy should be counted among God's miracles. Though he had vowed to persecute Christ in your person, instead he praised Him in you. I believe that the Lord had at last filled him, as He had filled Saul,[33] with the Holy Spirit, for he loved you as if you were his David. He was sprinkled with the Lord's grace overflowing from the abundance of your faith, just as King Saul was affected after he set out to persecute the prophets. The official had come to punish the confessor, but retired himself confessing Christ. For he believed. Those whom he had previously savagely condemned as guilty, he praised as holy men and released. He who was eager to punish witnesses to the faith, himself bore witness to the truth.[34]

8. Why, then, should I marvel that you are so powerful in meritorious achievements, so rich in graces, when your commencement in the Christian virtues equalled what few attain at the completion of long labours? Am I to doubt your perfection even now, when you were perfect at the start? Am I to doubt whether you are to be duly crowned at the end of the race, when you have the crown at its beginning? *Who would give me wings like a dove?*[35] I would fly to you and take rest in the sight of your holy person, marvelling at and revering Christ the Lord present in your face. I would wash with my tears and wipe with my hair[36] your feet which are His; I would lick what one might call the traces of the Lord's Passion imprinted in your scars. *For sweeter are the wounds of a friend than the kisses of an enemy.*[37] *Woe is me*, a wretched sinner *of unclean lips*,[38] for this blessing was within my grasp and I did not seize it.

9. For you will graciously remember, I think, that I

once looked on your holy presence at Vienne,[39] when I
was entertained by my blessed father Martin, to whom
the Lord made you equal in rank though not at the same
age.[40] Though my knowledge of you derived from Martin
was small when we met, I embraced you with great affection, and revered your holy person with all the feeling I
could then muster. I commended eternally to you myself
and my dear ones, who were not there but who gazed
on you through my eyes, for Christ has joined us in one
body. Now I rejoice that I can at least boast of having seen
your face in the flesh. But I lament my unfortunate care-
lessness, because through ignorance I lost the chance of so
great a blessing. At that time I was shrouded not only in the
sins which still afflict me, but also in worldly cares, from
which God's kindness has now freed me; so in my ignorance I saw you only as the bishop you were on the
surface, and I had not the knowledge to recognise you
in your more splendid capacity as living martyr.

10. I beg you to remember me on that day when you
are accompanied by your countless retinue of good works
performed, decked out with the honours of the blessed,
and crowned with the adornment of glory, when angels
will hasten to meet you bearing the snowy wreaths of
consecrated bishops and the bright purple robes of confessors, when He who is the highest Refiner of His gold
and silver will welcome you as *silver tried by fire and gold
proved in the furnace*[41] of this world. The eternal King
will attach you like a precious pearl to His diadem. The
just Judge will acknowledge that He owes you a reward
for more than your own virtues when He sees the countless flocks of saintly men and women around you. For by
your daily teaching you bring them to birth for Him.

You are the exemplar of perfect virtue and faith before them all. Our brother Paschasius reveals this. In his gracious and kindly ways I have seen the outline, so to say, of your virtues and graces, like a reflection in a mirror.

You are indeed the blessed father of many blessed sons, the sower of a great harvest. By the fruitfulness of your soil you bring forth for God fruit which is a hundredfold and sixtyfold and thirtyfold;[42] and you will obtain in return equal measure from the varied fruits of your offspring. The Most High has named you among the greatest of His kingdom. He has allowed your words to equal your deeds, so that your teaching is part of your life, and your life part of your teaching.[43] And hence no disciple of yours dares excuse himself on the grounds that your command is difficult, for he is first bound by the example of your virtue.

LETTER 19

To Delphinus[1]

Paulinus greets the most blessed Delphinus, uniquely his lord and ever his father in Christ who is God.

1. I awaited the refreshment of your letter like a garden thirsting after rain, and *my soul was as earth without water,*[2] gasping inwardly for words from you. For almost two years had passed since, through the agency of our fellow servant Cardamas, you had relieved me with drops from your lips which, though few, were most sweet. Meanwhile I had given up hope of even the merest sprinkling of words from you, for after being on tenterhooks all the summer vainly waiting for Uranius,[3] who never came, I was reinforced in my belief that I would have to pass the winter without hearing a word from you.

And then *the merciful and gracious Lord, who giveth food to the hungry, comforteth the humble, and is able to grant our needs beyond our hopes,*[4] brought me the sudden return of Cardamas, for which I had prayed but had not dared to hope; and when through him *the voice of thy salutation sounded in my ears,* my heart *leaped for joy,* and *all my bones said: Lord, who is like to Thee? What am I,* poor lowly being, *that Thou art mindful of me and visitest me?*[5] *Lord, Thou hast blessed our land,* and *hast made us drink of the torrent of Thy pleasure.*[6] *My lips shall burst into a hymn, evening, morning, and noontide;*

*we will sing and hymn the Lord who giveth us good
things.*[7] For He sent *good tidings from a far country,*[8]
which informs me of the health of my most sweet and
dear father, and recounts to me his words. So my heart
was transformed from anxious sadness to untroubled joy.
My mind threw off its troubled thoughts on that day
which your letter made our holiday, and *we have rejoiced
for the days in which* your long silence *humbled us.*[9]

2. *So let us praise the Lord's mercies and offer to Him
the sacrifice of praise, for He hath satisfied the empty
soul*[10]—empty, that is, not because void of His grace
(which I attribute to His mercy), but because deprived
of the fulfilment of my desire, for it had long hungered
for the consolation of a letter from you, denied to me, as
I have said, for almost two years.

I pray that the Lord may not brand as sin the trans-
gression of those whose *iniquity has lied to itself*[11] and has
wasted my soul through long deprivation of the bread
from your mouth. Let them lodge where they will, for
they refuse to be where their preference should have in-
clined them. Let them do what they can, for they do not
do what is appropriate. The arrival of such people here
cannot rob me of any blessing, just as it could not have
bestowed one. I only pray that I may suffer no harm for
my sins, provided that they are driven far from me in
company with such neighbours, through the numerous
mercies of Him who *doth not reward us according to our
sins,* but *as a father hath compassion on his son, so hath
the Lord compassion on them that fear His name and hope
in His mercy.*[12] I am one of these, for in misery I long for
His coming through hope of His mercy, but as a sinner I

tremble at it for fear of His justice. But I pray that through
your prayers He may show kindness to your sons and
not enter into judgment with His evil servants,[13] amongst
whom I am the first, as I am the last amongst His good
ones.

Even the glory of having obtained you as the father of
my new birth in and from Christ I regard as adding to my
condemnation, for I have done nothing to deserve you as
my father, showing myself an unprofitable servant[14] and
a worthless son to the highest Lord. Even now I preserve
in my thorn-infested heart the barren hardness of the wild
olive, though the Lord in His kindness long ago tore me
away from the root of my kin; and I am now apparently
engrafted on your tree,[15] so that from it I might draw the
sap of your richness into the marrow of my soul and,
rooted on the path of peace in the spirit of meekness, I
might be recognised by my noble fruits as the seed of the
good olive.

3. But as it is I am bare of all my father's blessings because of my numerous vices. How, then, shall I frame my
excuse on the Day of Judgment, since I have not attained
your virtues and show no likeness to your stock, by which
your sons are recognised? Who will deliver me from the
wrath which is to come?[16] Who will rescue me from myself, so that cleansed of my sensual inclinations I may be
emptied of the cause of God's anger by the cleansing of
faith? For I feel within me the causes of eternal punishment, since the roots of thorns and thistles[17] still sprout in
my heart. The earlier shoots of my former life were like
the vines of Sodom, bearing grapes of gall as the bitter
proof of the life of the flesh; and my drunken mind spewed

forth angry malice with the venom of asps.[18]

But *He that is mighty hath done great things to me; He hath sent from heaven and delivered me.*[19] He has sent His mercy through you, and *renewed the face of my earth,*[20] and made me your planting for Him in His vineyard. Therefore, blessed and most revered father, you must speak to the Lord with continual anxiety and persistent prayer, that He may look down from heaven and *visit the vineyard which thy right hand has planted,*[21] so that I may adhere to the true Vine, and live as branches not to be lopped off for the fire but pruned to bear fruit. May He who is the Vine and our Life[22] direct me towards that whole rule of truth which is His teaching, *watering us from His upper rooms*[23] through your pure and devoted eloquence, as fiery as it is sweet. For your words are drops of that *free rain which God set aside for His inheritance.*[24] He came down on the fleece, that is, He silently approached and permeated the Virgin.[25] It is He in whose drops we find joy when He arises in us; He splashes my soul born anew with the first dew of His intimacy, so that He may *heal all my diseases,* for He is *the fountain of life* who *sent His word and healed us.*[26] He is the Word of God from whom springs *the free rain,*[27] for it was not the compulsion imposed on a subordinate but the assent of God's peer and the service of devoted love which made the Son, obedient to the Father, *humble Himself even to the death of the cross.*[28] As He had said through the prophet: *I will freely sacrifice to Thee.*[29] For the Lord is both priest and victim. He offered Himself for us, and by His own power both laid down and took up again His life. So this is *the free rain,* which voluntarily poured on the parched lands to

make the wilderness into rivers.[30] Paul tells us how that
rain became weak when he says: *He was crucified through
weakness.* And from the same source you know how it was
strengthened and established: *For He liveth by the power
of God.*[31]

4. Pray to this Lord until you win your entreaty, that
He may not allow my fleece, which He washed in the
water of renewal by your hands, to become once more
stained and foul by my sins, to revert to purple through
being stained by the dye of sins.[32] May the gift of His grace
mount guard in me through your praying vigils, and not
abandon the work of your hands in me until it comes to
maturity and achieves in me a harvest and a crown for
you, so that when you come with joyfulness on that day,
carrying your sheaves in laden arms,[33] you may be able to
count me also amongst your offspring and your harvest,
and to say: *Behold, Lord, I and the children whom Thou
hast given to me.*[34]

But now I am warned by fear of wearying you, and
also by fear of that sin which *does not flee from the multitude of words*,[35] to put a bridle on my mouth and to close
the door on my words, though the end of this letter is
long delayed. Let my conclusion be a commendation of
Cardamas. I felicitate him on being so rejuvenated by the
blessing of your hand that whereas previously the joking
of the mime's profession encouraged levity in him,[36] now
the seriousness of his role as exorcist[37] has instilled reverence. But I admired him and rejoiced the more because he
has given up his earlier habitual disposition in favour of
devoted service. He consistently dined at our poor board,
restricting himself to the measure of our diet and avoiding

neither our poor vegetarian dishes[38] nor our meagre cups. The emaciation of his body and pallor of his face can bear witness to this, unless a strenuous return journey encourages him to renew acquaintance with his former cups and refreshes his strength.

LETTER 20

To Delphinus[1]

Paulinus greets his father Delphinus, most blessed and deservedly revered.

1. I ought to have observed the teaching of Wisdom by imposing a yoke on my tongue and a bar on my words, and thus avoided redoubling the sin arising from my multitude of words and from wearying you.[2] But your boundless love makes me open my mouth to you, and I cannot restrain the affection welling from my heart within the bonds of a silent breast by barring the door to speech. So I address your revered self with a second letter.

It is true that the one reply I have written is so diffuse that it is enough to satiate you to the point of nausea. Yet one letter is not enough to write to you, for as you realise a very long time has elapsed between my receipt of your words and my answer. My soul gets some consolation, however slight, from the fact that while I am writing to your loving person, my whole mind is concentrated on your features and I suddenly forget you are not here. I prolong my words because I seem to be lingering in conversation with you face to face. Though this does not wholly quench the burning thirst of my longing for you (for that would hardly be right), yet it is relieved by my picturing your person and conversation with the inner eye. For though *my sojourning seems prolonged*[3] from the places where you dwell, yet my spirit is not separated

184

from your loving embrace. For *who, says* Scripture, *shall separate us from the love of Christ?*[4] If neither death nor life nor any creature does so,[5] how much less can physical absence, which cannot dislodge the presence of the spirit? For as the spirit is stronger than the flesh, so the fusion of minds is preferable to that of bodies; and the presence of the inner man is superior to the separation of the outer.

It is often pointless for people to meet if their minds are apart. *For it is not he is a Jew, who is so outwardly, nor is that circumcision which is outwardly in the flesh. But he is a Jew that is one inwardly, and the circumcision is in the spirit, not in the letter; whose praise is not of men but of God.*[6] So this law, which makes the circumcision of the heart more true than that of the flesh, and makes the presence of the spirit stronger than the fusion and union of the flesh, always unites us with each other. For though we are physically separated for a time, I always remain united with you in mind, and you in turn *dwell in my heart, to die together and to live together.*[7]

Of course, it is important for the anxieties and consolations of this love of ours to be made aware of each other's activities, so that the worry caused by our separation can be more easily borne if we are well informed about each other. So, as you ask, I tell you that by Christ's kindness I am well; for I know that in your affection you are greatly concerned about my entire welfare. I am well not in physical vigour, but in healthy frailty of body and poverty of spirit—not my spirit, but that of God, whose goodness I lack, steeped as I am in my own wickedness.

2. Cardamas, however, warned me that you have given instructions on this matter. He claims that I should also report on all that goes on at Nola in the Lord's service. So

your revered person should know that your holy brother
Anastasius,[8] Pope of Rome, is most affectionate to my
lowly person; for as soon as the opportunity presented
itself of offering me his love, he hastened not only to obtain my regard but also to lavish on me his most devoted
affection. Shortly after his consecration he sent letters
about me, full of piety, devotion, and peace, to the bishops
of Campania, so that he could reveal his own affection for
me and set the precedent of his kindness before others.
Next, when I attended the feast of the blessed apostles[9]
according to my regular custom, he welcomed me at Rome
with as much charm as honour. Subsequently, after the
lapse of some time, he was kind enough to invite me also to
the anniversary of his election, a privilege he normally
restricts to his fellow bishops. And he showed no rancour
when I excused myself. Instead, he welcomed the dutiful
letter I sent to represent me, and thus he welcomed me in
my absence with fatherly spirit. If only the Lord permits
me to revisit him at the time when I customarily go to
Rome, I hope that I shall elicit from him a letter to your
holy self, so that he may begin to commend me to you as
well.

3. The new bishop of Milan, Venerius,[10] previously
your son and now your brother, had already written to me
after his consecration. But because Cardamas reported
your additional instruction, I wrote to Venerius through
Cardamas, informing him that the time was ripe to write
to your blessed person and commend to your heart the
beginning of his episcopate, if he desired to acknowledge
this as a service of fitting devotion.

But I rejoice and glory in the Lord that you, who are
truly my good father and advocate of my salvation, are

both visibly and invisibly performing the work of that salvation for my house. Unseen, you build me up by praying that the kingdom of God may reside within me; and visibly you work for me in the construction of churches, allowing me a share in company with the centurion whose house merited a visit from Christ.[11] For He had heard the testimony of pious folk about the centurion's building of a synagogue, which is now the Church. I confess to your venerable and holy person that when I read that part of your letter in which you revealed that the new daughter of the Church at Portus Alingonis,[12] already fathered by you in the name of the Lord, had progressed to the day of dedication, my spirit so gloried in God our salvation that I seemed to be present amongst the throngs of those dedicating the new church, and I sang the words of prophetic joy from the Psalms: *Rejoice to God our helper. Take a psalm and bring hither the timbrel. Bring up sacrifices and come into the courts of the Lord; adore ye the Lord in His holy court.*[13] Or another hymn of the same prophet: *Arise, O Lord, into Thy resting-place, Thou and the ark which Thou hast sanctified. Let Thy priests be clothed with salvation; and let Thy saints rejoice. Let them appoint their day.*[14]

4. You have thought it right to tell me that there are some *on the side of him by whose envy death came into the world*, who *gnash their teeth and pine away.*[15] This does not surprise me. In Jerusalem, too, when the temple of God was being rebuilt, the Assyrians were jealous and often tried to hinder the building, as it rose again, with unfriendly attacks.[16] But because *He that is in us is greater than he that is in this world, the desire of the wicked shall perish,*[17] and ours shall be strengthened. For we *hope*

in the mercy of Him who never confounds *those who hope in Him.*[18] Only ensure in your holiness, as indeed you are doing, that a house based on and in Christ is built within me also; *for unless the Lord build the house, they have laboured in vain that build it.*[19] And unless this house is built on the rock which is Christ,[20] it will be unable to resist the winds of spiritual wickedness and the torrents of worldly temptations.

5. Pray that the Lord Jesus may come to my heart as His temple, that He may brandish the whip of His love, with which He chastises everyone whom He accepts as His son, and drive out from my inner thoughts, as if they were traders in the temple,[21] all the commerce and contagion of wickedness. May He drive forth from me the oxen, the dove-merchants, and the tables of the money-lenders,[22] so that I may be cleansed of all foulness and lust and may possess the pure simplicity of faith and charity. For the shadow of Christ remains in the place from which Caesar's currency is driven out. *Where there are no oxen, the crib is clean.*[23] Where no doves are sold, the faith is kept undefiled.

If we do not entrust ourselves to God, we sell ourselves to the devil. So our old man who bound himself to the design of the evil-counselling serpent is said to have been *sold under sin.*[24] In short, since he had been sold, he had need of a Redeemer, who bought us at a heavy price[25] so that we should no longer belong to the devil or to ourselves. He sought to transform us from the progeny of vipers to a royal and priestly race,[26] that we might become the blood of Him who first made our souls precious by trading His blood for them; for we had declined from the nobility of our original creation, and had become cheap by persistent sin. Then, with a love which knew no malice, He allowed us to become coheirs with Him and sons of God.[27] Let us rejoice and glory in Him who became *a refuge of the poor* that He might *humble the eyes of the proud*.[28] Let us show Him the temple and the sacrifice within us, cleansing ourselves if possible of the old leaven so that we may become unleavened bread,[29] and so that Christ who was sacrificed for us may feast within us.

6. May I remember that I was sundered from the womb of my land and my kin, and was made the son of Delphinus to become his *fish that pass through the paths of the sea*.[30] May I remember that you were made not only my father but also my Peter, because you cast your net down to draw me from the depths and bitter billows of this world, that I might become the prey of salvation, that I might be dead to the nature of my present life, and that I might live for the Lord towards whom I had been dead.

But if I am your fish, I must bear in my mouth a valuable stater[31] on which there shines not the head and inscription of Caesar,[32] but the living, life-giving image of the eternal King. That coin symbolises faith in the truth, which has left the impression of your teaching and the seal of your ring on the coin of my heart and the wax of my mind. For your teaching is *the silver tried by the fire, proved in the earth, refined seven times*.[33]

7. May the Lord grant my prayers, that I may be a coin of your mint, a fish of your net, a twig of your vine, a son of your chaste womb. For the sons of Delphinus shall be numbered amongst the sons of Aaron, though not those who *offered before the Lord strange fire* and were consumed by that divine flame which they had quenched in their own hearts.[34]

May the hearts of your sons burn not with the wicked fires of lusts and worldly allurements, but with the fire which the Lord came to kindle in us. Of that fire He says: *I am come to cast fire on the earth. And what will I, if it now be kindled?*[35] So I pray that no greed, or lust of the eyes, or baneful love of temporal goods blaze with polluting flame within me, for this is the fire which is *strange before the Lord.*[36] May our God Himself, who is *a consuming fire*, recognise His fire in me, so that I may say: *The Lord is my light and my salvation; whom shall I fear?*[37] This fire enlightens hearts and destroys sins, puts out the darkness which brings death upon us, and kindles life-giving light. If my lamps perpetually burn with this fire, I shall make bold to say: *Though I should walk in the midst of the shadow of death, I will fear no evils, for Thou art with me.*[38] Enlightened by this flame, fired by the heat of this blaze to thirst for the living water and to long for the Lord, I shall truly say: *As the hart longs for the fountains of water, so my soul longs for Thee, O God.*[39] For *with Thee is the fountain of life; and in Thy light we shall see light.*[40]

LETTER 21

To Amandus[1]

Paulinus greets the holy Amandus, rightly revered and greatly loved.

1. In the sacred history of the Kings[2] we marvel at Asael, the famed brother of Joab, so swift of foot and light over the ground that he competed with and rivalled hinds or goats in speed. And we are no less astonished when we read of that giant of foreign race who had grown beyond human measure even in the number of his members, for his hands had six fingers each, and each foot that many toes.[3] This made him stronger and swifter than other men. But the hands and strength of no enemies, however great they were, prevailed over David, who fought with God's hand and remained undefeated, for he was the representation of Christ. For the haughty pride of the devil, appearing in foreign giants, was cast down, and God's saving figure, overpowering in its humility, prevailed in us feeble men.

2. But I must get back to the main head of my letter, for I have started at the wrong end. I want to praise Cardamas, the Lord's courier, by these exemplars of swift men of old designated in the divine Law. So also the happy speed of the young apostle in the Gospel serves my purpose; for he raced to the Lord's tomb before Peter, whose desire to run was equally great, but whose speed was less because of his greater weight of years.[4] John raced there first, for he alone had rested on Christ's breast,[5] and so

he wished to be the first to see the resurrection of His body. So John drew into the depth of his heart these twin sources of his knowledge, and later, as the herald of Revelation and the Gospel, he disseminated them throughout the earth. His physical nimbleness of foot he later complemented with the beautiful measure of the Word, as he hastened through the whole inhabited world with the speed of the spirit.

3. John also lived the longest of the apostles, and he is said to have written his Gospel last, so that (as Paul, the chosen vessel, says of him) he might be a pillar to add strength to the Church's foundations.[6] He strengthens the authority of the earlier evangelists by harmonising his Gospel with theirs. He is the last evangelist chronologically, but he is the first to begin with the source of the Mystery, for he alone of the four rivers begins his course from the very highest and divine source, thundering forth from a lofty cloud: *In the beginning was the Word, and the Word was with God, and the Word was God.*[7] He rises higher than Moses, who with mental eye extends the boundaries of knowledge to the origin of the world and the beginnings of visible creatures.[8] He flies higher than the other evangelists, who begin the Gospel of the Resurrection with the human lineage of the Saviour, or from the prefiguring sacrifice of the Law, or from the prophetic proclamation of Christ's forerunner, John the Baptist.[9] He reached the very heavens and did not halt even at the angels, but mounting above archangels and all created beings—Virtues, Principalities, Dominations, Thrones[10]— he guided his course with lofty mind to the very Creator. Beginning with that indescribable begetting, he told of the Son who shares eternity, substance, omnipotence, and

creation with the Father. He beheld God in the divine Holy Spirit, for in the Spirit the divine Trinity is completed, and the single divinity of the Trinity is seen. For the Spirit of God, like His Word, is God. Both dwell in the one fount and flow forth from the single source which is the Father—the Son by being born, the Spirit by coming forth. They are undivided but distinct, because each keeps unimpaired the unique quality of His own Person.[11]

4. So the blessed John who reclined on the Lord's breast, and who drank in a perception deeper than that of all other creatures from the very heart of Wisdom who created all things, became drunk with the Holy Spirit who *searcheth even the deep things of God;*[12] and so he began his Gospel from the innermost, infinite beginning of all beginnings. By this one chapter all the mouths of the devil, barking in heretics, are closed. The tongue of Arius[13] is first cut off, but the blasphemy of Sabellius[14] is also made void. The unity of the Godhead in Father and Son, and their distinction as Persons, is expressed in one and the same statement of our fisherman.[15] By the same chapter Photinus, who crazily teaches that Christ had only a human beginning,[16] is rejected; Marcion, who distinguishes between the God of the Law and the God of the Gospel,[17] is annihilated; and the Manichee, who denies the true Creator and invents a false one,[18] is trodden underfoot, for he is confounded by the sentence appended there in that supercelestial Gospel. (I call it "supercelestial" because its beginning takes its source above all the heavens and before all ages.) He is confounded because he is told about the Word of God which is Itself God: *Through Him all things were made, and without Him was made nothing.*[19] Even whilst the Gnostic boasts in the empty title of his

false knowledge, diverting all the understanding of his distorted mind to ethereal images by lending spiritual shapes to bodily objects,[20] he is forced by John to believe in the flesh of Christ. John speaks of the Word which was with God and was God: *And the Word was made flesh.*[21] He was not, however, as certain other snakes are said to be hissing,[22] made flesh in such a way as to abandon His nature for ours, but whilst remaining what He was to begin to be for our sakes what He was not.

5. But I am carried along too far, and I abuse your loving-kindness in having no fear either of wearying you with my prolixity or of speaking error in your presence through stupidity. For I know that *whereas you yourself are wise, you gladly suffer your foolish son* out of that charity which *endureth all things and never falleth away.*[23]

However, I shall now tell myself to set *a guard on the ways of my mouth that I sin not with my tongue,*[24] and I shall briefly pass on to Cardamas, who is our Asael, for *you have made his feet as swift as a hind's.*[25] You have renewed his youth as an eagle's[26] by your abounding love, with which out of regard for my lowly person you welcomed him and set him in the courts of God's house. You did this so he might be more fully free in the eyes of man once he had begun to be Christ's freedman. By this devotion you have rejuvenated him not only in spirit but also in body. He, too, is filled with that heartfelt affection which you have for me. He conveys your longings to me, and in turn consoles mine for you; and he is able, in spite of the great distance lying between us, to make almost a regular routine of the journey to and fro, *keeping hard ways for the sake of the words of your lips.*[27] In fact I believe that from the very letters which he bears he obtains what

one might call the dove's wings[28] of your sanctity, and
from your words, the strength of foot to reach here. Yet
I felicitate him on that very grace by which he has set
himself to perform out of love this service of slavery in
freedom, journeying to and fro at his advanced age, and
preferring to spend his time of rest, in the retirement he
has deserved, in travelling hard rather than in sitting at
home. He refuses to set foot on *the paths of the slothful
which are strewn with thorns*[29] lest he be afflicted with
distress, pierced with the thorn of miserable anxiety
through the fruitless leisure of idleness. He takes delight
in the active life of fast journeys, so that the resourceless-
ness of the lazy may not confront him like a good runner
as he whiles away idle leisure.[30] But once he reaches here,
how great is the joy with which he steeps and fills my soul
with the splendid news of your good health! *It makes my
bones fat* and *the voice of rejoicing is heard in my taber-
nacles*, as my mind is refreshed by the consolation I prayed
for, and I say: *The Lord hath been mindful of us, and hath
blessed us*.[31]

6. *Let us be glad and rejoice in Him* who grants the
prayers which we make and *gives us our hearts' desire, for
He has prevented us with a blessing of sweetness*.[32] For
what blessing is now sweeter, what sweetness more pleasant
to us than the reward and consolation of love which is
given in fulness to me by your letter? In it I embrace
pledges, so to speak, of your voice and heart, for your
eloquence is the offspring of your soul; *for out of the
abundance of the heart the mouth speaketh*.[33] So I love
Cardamas as he comes with your words, and I commend
him as he departs with my own; for the old age which
toils for the needs and duties of love deserves rest in plenti-

ful mercy.[34] Moreover (and I admire this in him even more than the speed with which his gray hairs move) he has so progressed towards abstemious living since he assumed the title of exorcist that there was scarcely a day on which he shrank from dining with us. And though he obtained only the drops from small and occasional cups, with which he could scarcely wet the surface of his lips, he made no complaint of the wrong done to his empty stomach or dry throat.[35] He certainly showed himself to me in so edifying a light that I beheld a cleric worthy of universal praise and an exorcist whom evil spirits fear.

For the rest, brother, I commend to you Cardamas, all our community, and myself, so that you may in turn commend us to the Lord in earnest prayer. And so may we all be slaves in freedom to the eternal Lord, and by slavery in Christ attain the reward of eternal freedom.

LETTER 22

To Severus[1]

Paulinus greets his loving brother Severus.

1. The letter which you had sent by that unspiritual monk of ours was intercepted and brought here by a courier of truly spiritual life, our son Sorianus.[2] I came to realise that by this happening the Lord has bestowed a double favour. First, Sorianus (who had longed to meet me through the love spreading from your heart) did not arrive here without word from you; and secondly, your letter was not brought to me by Marracinus,[3] who by what I regard as divine motivation was ashamed to look me in the face, or else too lazy to protract his journey beyond Rome. So in the capital he entrusted your letter to the brother I have mentioned. He was glad to have the opportunity of shortening his journey as he had desired. Through this lucky chance he thought that he had consulted his interests by contravening your instructions—he did not have to pretend that he was a monk, as you had ordered, or look a monk in the face, as he would have had to in me. So let him keep his soldier's cloak and boots and cheeks to himself, for he feared to remove the first two and to transform the third.

2. I pray that only poor fellow servants, pale of face like ourselves, will come on first or subsequent visits—not proud men in embroidered garments, but humble ones in bristly clothes of goat's hair;[4] not bodyguards in fine mantles, but

men draped in rough cloaks,[5] fastened up not with a military belt but with a length of rope; men with hair not long and trimmed over a shameless brow,[6] but cut close to the skin in chaste ugliness, half-shorn irregularly, shaved off in front, leaving the brow naked.[7] Let them be unadorned, with the adornment of chastity, and let their appearance be suitably uncultivated, honourably contemptible. Spurning their natural physical attraction for inner adornment, they should even be eager to look disreputable, so that they may be chastely mean in appearance as long as they become honourable at heart and fit for salvation.

The appearance, disposition, and smell of such monks cause nausea in people for whom the odour of death is as the odour of life, who regard the bitter as sweet, the chaste as foul, the holy as hateful.[8] So it is right that we should pay them back, that their smell should be to us the odour of death, so that we do not cease to be the odour of Christ.[9] For why should they who regard our odour as lethal be rightly angry with us if in turn their odour of life stinks in our nostrils? Marracinus finds my fasting distasteful; I cannot bear his drunkenness. He avoids the breath of a monk when he speaks; I avoid the breath of a belching Thraso.[10] If my dry throat displeases him, I loathe his overloaded gullet. If my parched abstention annoys him, the gluttony of his belly annoys me. So I pray for visitors who are not drunk in the early morning but rather are still fasting at evening, who are not blown up with yesterday's wine but rather are abstemious with today's, who are not crazily tottering through the drunkenness of lust but rather are healthily impaired with virtuous vigils and are drunk

with sobriety, men who stagger not because of overin-
dulgence but rather because of a meagre diet.

3. I rejoice to have welcomed such a man bearing your
letter. I ask you to welcome him as if you had sent him to
me. For he, too, ought to be counted amongst those who
have come to me to represent your brotherly person. The
Lord entrusted him with your letter, though you did not
know it, in order that you might so esteem him. But I think
that you, too, will attribute to him that benefit of God's
kindness, for it was through him that you were saved from
having your letter brought to me by a man who did not
bear your physical appearance.

But to prevent your accusing me in turn before Marracinus, I wish Sorianus to be praised only by his leave. For
I believe that I have praised rather than censured Marracinus by mention of the things in which a man must
glory if he is ashamed to be or to appear to be a monk. To
put it briefly, you remember that in Virgil the Fury is
praised by what are normally accusations.[11]

Be sure not to blame me for quoting a reference from
a poet whom I do not now read, and for appearing to break
my resolution in this respect.[12] I bear witness that I have
done this by following the authority of your example, for
I remember your letter which ends: "Live happy, for your
destiny is already accomplished."[13] I remember too "the
Lar of the family" which you named to express your own
abode in reminiscence of the prologue of Plautus.[14]

NOTES

LIST OF ABBREVIATIONS

AB	Analecta Bollandiana (Brussels 1882–)
ACW	Ancient Christian Writers (Westminster, Md.-London 1946–)
Cavallera	F. Cavallera, *Saint Jérôme: Sa vie et son oeuvre.* 2 vols. (Louvain-Paris 1922)
CDT	Catholic Dictionary of Theology (London 1962–)
CSEL	Corpus scriptorum ecclesiasticorum latinorum (Vienna 1886–)
DB	Dictionnaire de la Bible (Paris 1895–1912; Suppl. 1926 ff.)
DHGE	Dictionnaire d'histoire et de géographie ecclésiastiques (Paris 1912–)
DTC	Dictionnaire de théologie catholique (Paris 1903–50)
Duchesne	L. Duchesne, *Les fastes épiscopaux de l'ancienne Gaule.* 3 vols. (2nd ed. Paris 1907–15)
Fabre *Chron.*	P. Fabre, *Essai sur la chronologie de l'oeuvre de saint Paulin de Nole* (Paris 1948)
Fabre *Paulin*	P. Fabre, *Saint Paulin de Nole et l'amitié chrétienne* (Paris 1949)
Jones	A. H. M. Jones, *The Later Roman Empire.* 3 vols. (Oxford 1964)
JRS	Journal of Roman Studies (London 1911–)
Lagrange	F. Lagrange, *Histoire de s. Paulin.* 2 vols. (2nd ed. Paris 1884)
MG	Patrologia graeca, ed. J. P. Migne (Paris 1857–66)
ML	Patrologia latina, ed. J. P. Migne (Paris 1844–55)
Quasten *Patr.*	J. Quasten, *Patrology.* 3 vols. thus far (Westminster, Md.-Utrecht-Antwerp): 1 (1950) *The Beginnings of Patristic Literature;* 2 (1955) *The Ante-Nicene Literature after Irenaeus;* 3 (1960) *The Golden Age of Greek Patristic*

	Literature from the Council of Nicaea to the Council of Chalcedon
RB	Revue bénédictine (Maredsous 1884–)
Reinelt	P. Reinelt, *Studien über die Briefe des heiligen Paulinus von Nola* (diss. Breslau 1904)
REL	Revue des études latines (Paris 1923–)
RHLR	Revue d'histoire et de littérature religieuses (Paris 1896–1907)

INTRODUCTION

[1] On the chronology of the letters, cf. P. Fabre, *Essai sur la chronologie de l'oeuvre de Saint Paulin de Nole* (Paris 1948); also P. Reinelt, *Studien über die Briefe des heiligen Paulinus von Nola* (diss. Breslau 1904).

[2] Cf. Letter 4.3 and n. 17 thereto.

[3] Cf. below, n. 13 to Letter 5. The biographical detail is ably summarised by P. Fabre, *Saint Paulin de Nole et l'amitié chrétienne* (Paris 1949) ch. 1.

[4] An outline of these events is, however, given by Paulinus in his *Carm.* 21.400 ff.

[5] But cf. below, n. 14 to Letter 5. For the date of departure, cf. n. 62 to Letter 1.

[6] The six prose letters in question are, in chronological order, Nos. 35, 36, 9, 10, 1, 2. For a discussion of the poems which form the correspondence between Ausonius and Paulinus, cf. P. de Labriolle, *Un épisode de la fin du paganisme. La correspondance d'Ausone et de Paulin de Nole* (Paris 1910).

[7] The quoted phrase is from S. Dill, *Roman Society in the Last Century of the Western Empire* (2nd ed. London 1899) 168; cf. also G. Boisser, *La fin du paganisme* 2 (Paris 1891) 77 ff.

[8] In the CSEL edition of Hartel, Letter 34 is in fact a sermon appended to Letter 33, and should not be counted as a separate letter. But Letter 25*, addressed to Crispinianus, should be counted separately from Letter 25.

[9] On the date of Paulinus' arrival at Nola, cf. below, n. 1 to Letter 1. The date of death is established by the eye-witness account of Uranius which may be found in ML 53.859–66.

[10] Cf. Letter 41.1.

[11] On Paulinus and Jerome and their correspondence, cf. P. Courcelle, "Paulin de Nole et Saint Jérôme," REL 25 (1947) 250–80. Three of the extant letters of St. Jerome (Nos. 53, 58, and 85) are addressed to Paulinus. Jerome (*Ep.* 58.11) characteristically told Paulinus to buckle down to serious work on the Scriptures.

[12] Cf. Letter 20.2.

[13] On Paulinus and Ambrose, cf. Fabre *Paulin* 30.

[14] Cf. Letter 20.3.

[15] Cf. Letter 3 and n. 13 thereto.

[16] On whom, cf. G. Bardy in DTC 14.2760–62; F. Mouret, *Sulpice Sévère à Primulac* (Paris 1907); P. Hylten, *Studien zu Sulpicius Severus* (Lund 1940); G. Boissier, *op. cit.* 2.62 ff.

[17] The text of this may be found in CSEL 1 (ed. Halm, Vienna 1864) and in Dübner-Lejay (Paris 1890). Cf. also E. Ch. Babut, *Saint Martin de Tours* (Paris 1912); H. Delehaye, "Saint Martin de Tours et Sulpice Sévère," AB 38 (1920) 5–136.

[18] Cf. below, n. 6 to Letter 1.

[19] Cf. Letter 27.3.

[20] The text is in CSEL 1. The other main extant work of Severus is his *Chronicle,* a sacred history of the world from the Creation to his own day. In connexion with this Severus requested chronological information from Paulinus, who (Letter 28.5) passed the query on to Rufinus.

[21] A.D. 395–404. The argument from silence suggests that Severus may have died shortly after 404. Gennadius dates his death in the reign of Arcadius (395–408).

[22] For an analysis of the correspondence between Paulinus and Severus, cf. Fabre *Paulin* 277 ff.

[23] Cf. Letter 14.2, where Delphinus' sickness is compared with that of patriarchs in their old age.

[24] Cf., e.g., Letters 9.1 and 10.1.

[25] Cf. Letter 20.2 f.

[26] On the letters to Delphinus and Amandus, cf. Fabre *Paulin* 277 ff.

[27] The evidence of Paulinus would, however, seem to allow greater precision about the date of Augustine's consecration as bishop; cf. below, n. 1 to Letter 7.

[28] Cf. Letter 45.4.

[29] On the correspondence with Augustine, which covers the period 395–417, cf. A. P. Muys, *De Briefwisseling van Paulinus v. Nola en Augustinus* (Hilversum 1941); Fabre *Paulin* 236 ff.

[30] Nos. 45 and 186 in the collection of Augustine's letters.

[31] Cf. Augustine, *Ep.* 31.

[32] P. R. L. Brown, "Aspects of the Christianisation of the Roman Aristocracy," JRS 51 (1961) 10.

[33] Cf. Letter 13.15.

[34] Cf. R. Meiggs, *Roman Ostia* (Oxford 1960) 403.

[35] Cf. Letters 27.5 and 40.6.

[36] Cf. Palladius, *Historia Lausiaca* 62 (=ACW 34 [1965] 144); for his connexion with Rufinus, cf. F. X. Murphy, *Rufinus of Aquileia, His Life and Works* (Washington, D.C. 1945) 83 ff.

[37] Cf. Augustine, *Ep.* 259.

[38] The subscription *Paullini epistula ad Macarium* is written in a second hand in the single manuscript in which it appears.

[39] Cf. in general E. Vacandard, *Saint Victrice, évêque de Rouen* (2nd ed. Paris 1903); A. Wilmart, RB 31 (1919) 333–47; E. de Moreau in *Revue belgique* (1926) 71 ff.; P. Grosjean in AB 63 (1945) 94 ff.

[40] Cf. Duchesne 2.44.

[41] Gregory of Tours, *Hist. franc.* 2.13, lists him as *episcopus Cadurcensis.*

[42] On this letter, cf. Fabre *Paulin* 181 ff.

[43] Cf. Letter 16.1. On Jovius, cf. the comments in Boissier, *op. cit.* 2.98 ff. For the view that Jovius was a Christian, cf. P. de Labriolle, *Latin Christianity* (London 1924) 329.

[44] On the controverted question of Crispinianus' rank and importance, cf. Fabre *Paulin* 203 n. 1.

[45] Cf. Letter 38.8.

[46] Cf. the texts cited in ML 61.895–6.

[47] As Letter 51 indicates. Honoratus became bishop of Arles in 426; cf. Duchesne 1.256. His monastery was on the island now known as Honorat.

[48] Cf. Duchesne 2.163.

[49] Cf. Cavallera 1.306.

[50] P. R. L. Brown, "Aspects of the Christianization of the Roman Aristocracy," JRS 51 (1961) 2.

[51] Cf. Jones 1.172: "The voluminous correspondence of Paulinus of Nola . . . contains less of interest to secular historians."

[52] The poems of Paulinus, however, contain references to such events; cf. e.g., *Carm.* 21.

[53] The whole tenour of Letter 1 illustrates this vividly.

[54] On Publicola, cf. Letter 45.3.

[55] Letter 28.5.

[56] Jerome, *Ep.* 58.8.

[57] Cf. Letter 49.

[58] Cf. Letter 31.3 ff.

[59] Cf. Letter 18.7.

[60] Cf. esp. Letter 48.

[61] We obtain general impressions not only of Delphinus and Amandus, but also, e.g., of church-building near Bordeaux (cf. Letter 20.3).

[62] On Siricius, cf. Letter 5 and n. 46 thereto; on Anastasius, cf. Letter 20.2.

[63] Cf. Letter 13.11 ff.

[64] Cf. Letters 31 and 32.

[65] The evidence for buildings is chiefly in Letter 32 and in *Carm.* 27 and 28 (though incidental information appears in Letter 29.13); all this is usefully assembled, translated, and annotated by R. C. Goldschmidt, *Paulinus' Churches at Nola* (Amsterdam 1940). The theory that Paulinus invented church-bells comes not from any evidence in his writings but from the use of the words *nola* and *campanile* for bells.

[66] On the singing during the day, cf. Letter 15.4; at night, Letter 29.13. For vigils introduced at Milan, cf. Augustine, *Conf.* 9.15.

[67] Cf. Letter 41.1.

[68] On clothing, cf. Letters 17.1 and 29.1; on hair, Letter 22.1 f.

[69] On the daily meal attended by the community, cf. Letters 15.4 and 23.8; for the vegetarian food, Letters 19.4 and 23.5 ff.; for the drink, Letter 15.4.

[70] On Paulinus' translating, cf. Letter 46.2; on the copying of texts, Letter 4.1.

[71] Cf. Letters 23.9 and 34.

[72] On the gifts of blessed bread, cf. below, n. 23 to Letter 3.

[73] Cf. Letter 29.5 ff.

[74] Cf. Letter 29.14. On Nicetas' revision of the *Te Deum*, cf. C. Mohrmann, *Études sur le latin des chrétiens* 1 (Rome 1961) 161 f.

[75] Cf. Letters 18.9, 32.6, etc.

[76] Cf. Letters 35.1 and 36.2.

[77] Cf. Letters 1.10 and 2.2.

[78] Cf. Letter 5.13.

[79] On this subject in general, see the useful collection of essays in *Paganism and Christianity in the Fourth Century*, ed. A. Momigliano (Oxford 1963).

[80] Letter 25.3.

[81] Letter 38.6.

[82] Letter 22.3.

[83] Letter 7.3.

[84] Cf. Letter 12.4.

[85] Cf. Letter 16.

[86] Cf. C. Mohrmann, *op. cit.* 1.369 and 2.247 ff.

[87] Cf. Quintilian, *Institutio oratoria* 10.2.1 ff.

[88] Cf. Letters 39, 19, 24.10 ff., 43.

[89] Cf. Letters 24.8 ff., 24.15, 32.22.

[90] Cf. G. Boissier, *op. cit.* 2.72.

[91] We find here the extraordinary conceit that hair betrays the man. "Hair was honoured under the Old Law, but now it is a burden" (Letter 23.23).

[92] Letter 23.14.

[93] For the significance of Hilary as a student of Origen, and for his allegorical interpretation of Scripture, cf. M. Simonetti, "Note sul *Commento a Matteo* di Ilario di Poiters," *Vetera christianorum* 1 (1964) 35 ff.

[94] Cf. Letters 5.2, 23.32, 13.4, 41.2, 23.16.

[95] Cf. Letter 13.8 f.

[96] Cf. P. Courcelle, *Les lettres grecques en occident de Macrobe à Cassiodore* (Paris 1943) 131 f.

[97] Cf. Ausonius, *Carm.* 5.8, 5.21, etc.

[98] Cf. Letters 16.4, 40.6.

[99] Paulinus calls the author St. Clement, but it is reasonable to infer from Rufinus' interests at this time that the document in question was the *Epistula ad Jacobum*, a letter wrongly attributed to Clement of Rome. Cf. F. X. Murphy, *op. cit.* 112 f.

[100] Letter 46.2.

[101] Cf. Letter 23.32–36.

[102] Compare Paulinus' Letter 24.7 with Ambrose's *De off. min.* 1.36.182 (ML 16.82); Paulinus' Letter 21.3 ff. with Ambrose's *De incarnatione* 3 (ML 16.857 ff.)

[103] Letter 44.1. On the other hand, the correspondence between Paulinus' Letter 30 and *Ep.* 186.40 in the Augustine collection is attributable to the fact that Augustine and Alypius wish Paulinus to recall his words written earlier to Severus, and so they quote them. The Paulinus letter was written in 401/2, the Augustine-Alypius letter, in 417; this is interesting evidence on the wide circulation of Paulinus' letters.

[104] For a longer analysis on this, cf. Fabre *Paulin* 53–135, to which this section of the Introduction is partly indebted.

[105] Cf. esp. Letter 21, where Paulinus speaks scathingly of sev-

eral heretical sects. On the more difficult problem of Paulinus' attitude to Priscillianism, cf. Fabre *Paulin* 108 ff.

[106] "Il a la foi, il connait le dogme, il en a médité les points essentiels; mais il n'éprouve pas le besoin, il ne voit pas l'utilité de l'approfondir" (Fabre *Paulin* 105).

[107] Cf., e.g., Letters 21.3 and 37.5 f.

[108] Cf., e.g., Letters 20.5, 23.43, 44.3.

[109] *Carm.* 19 is especially revealing in this connexion.

[110] Letter 18.3 is exceptional in this respect.

[111] Cf. Letters 9.4 and 23.29.

[112] Cf. Letters 12.5, 24.10, 30.2, 50.11, etc.

[113] Cf. Letters 18.6, 24.9, 34.5, 49.4, etc.

[114] Cf. Letter 38.7.

[115] Cf. Letters 11.2 f. and 12.10.

[116] Cf. Letter 40.2.

[117] Cf. esp. Letter 6.2; also Letters 2.3, 5.9, 18.1.

[118] Cf. Letters 13.3, 14.1, 15.1, 18.3.

[119] Cf. Letters 13.2 and 20.1.

[120] Eph. 4.3; 1 Cor. 12.26; etc.

[121] Cf. Letter 39.4.

[122] Cf. Letters 12.1, 32.21, 34. The scriptural reference here is 2 Cor. 8.14.

[123] Cf. Letter 39.4.

[124] Cf. Letter 13.20. The exposition is as old as Clement of Alexandria, *Quis dives salvetur?* (MG 9.609–32).

[125] Cf. Letter 40.11.

[126] *Carm.* 25.

[127] Cf. Letter 18.5.

[128] Letter 12.7.

[129] Cf. Letter 12.8.

[130] Cf. *Carm.* 16.234 ff., Letter 29.7, etc.

[131] Cf. Letter 25*.3.

[132] Cf., e.g., Letter 23.1.

[133] *Rom.* 13.10. Cf. Letters 11.14, 24.9, 34.8.

[134] Cf. R. C. Goldschmidt's remarks in his Foreword to *Paulinus' Churches at Nola* (Amsterdam 1940).

[135] C. de Santeul, *Les lettres de Paulin* (Paris 1703, published anonymously).

[136] Cf. above, nn. 29 and 65.

LETTER 1

[1] On the dating of this letter, in early 395 A.D., cf. Fabre *Chron.* 22. This letter was sent from Barcelona shortly after Paulinus' ordination at Christmas 394, and before he left for Nola, where he arrived late in the year 395. This dating rests chiefly on the series of *Natalicia* written annually in January by Paulinus to commemorate the death of St. Felix. The first of these was composed at Barcelona. Now the eighth in that series (*Carm.* 26) was written following the invasion of Alaric in 401 (cf. Jones 1.184; Démougeot, *De l'unité à la division de l'empire romaine* [Paris 1951] 267 ff.) and so was composed in 402; and the thirteenth in the series (*Carm.* 21) was written following the defeat of Radagaesus at Faesulae in 406 (cf. Jones 1.184), so its date is 407. Hence the first *Natalicium* was composed in January 395.

[2] This is Sulpicius Severus, long-time friend of Paulinus; cf. above, Intro. pp. 3 f.

[3] Ps. 118.103, with conflation also of Ps. 18.11.

[4] Prov. 15.30.

[5] Cf. Eph. 1.17 f.; Prov. 4.9.

[6] Some four years earlier Sulpicius Severus' wife had died, and he, after frequent visits to the monastery of Martin at Tours, had retired to a monastic life at Primuliacum (Prémillac in the Périgord). This was probably the home of his ancestors; cf. E. Mâle, *La fin du paganisme en Gaule* (Paris 1950) 61.

[7] Ps. 40.2.

[8] Cf. Matt. 25.37–40; Prov. 19.17.

[9] 2 Cor. 2.16.

[10] Cf. 1 Cor. 1.23.

[11] Cf. Matt. 16.17.

[12] 2 Cor. 2.16.

[13] Paulinus has in mind not only the taunts of non-Christians, but also the laments of such Christians as his own friend and former tutor Ausonius (cf., e.g., Ausonius, *Ep.* 18.27.).

[14] 1 Tim. 4.10.

[15] Matt. 18.6.

[16] Matt. 5.11.

[17] Ps. 81.5.

[18] Cf. Wisd. 5.6 and Mal. 4.2.

[19] Ps. 139.4.
[20] Ps. 5.10 f.
[21] Ps. 5.6.
[22] Ps. 17.26.
[23] 2 Tim. 2.19.
[24] Eccli. 28.28.
[25] Ps. 9.9.
[26] Ps. 7.16 f.
[27] 1 Tim. 6.11.
[28] Cf. Ps. 110.10; Prov. 1.7.
[29] 1 Cor. 1.27, 25.
[30] Cf. Matt. 10.33; Mark 8.38; Luke 9.26.
[31] Matt. 18.15.
[32] Cf. Matt. 13.24. The metaphor here is not so mixed as it may at first seem. The notion of creative fire animating plant growth derives from Stoicism. The fires within the barren crop symbolise the evil passions of worldly men.
[33] Matt. 18.17.
[34] Cf. Matt. 18.8, 5.29.
[35] Matt. 5.29 f.
[36] Matt. 10.24 f.
[37] John 15.20.
[38] John 15.19.
[39] Gal. 1.10.
[40] Matt. 25.44.
[41] Matt. 25.41. "Your father" is, of course, Paulinus' picturesque variation for "the devil."
[42] 2 Cor. 8.9.
[43] Tit. 1.16; 2 Tim. 3.5.
[44] Luke 16.8.
[45] Cf. Matt. 11.8.
[46] Ps. 72.5, describing the prosperity of sinners.
[47] Ps. 33.11.
[48] Cf. 2 Cor. 4.1 ff.
[49] Ps. 90.13.
[50] Matt. 13.32.
[51] Matt. 7.6; 2 Cor. 6.14.
[52] Eph. 6.14; 1 Thess. 5.8; Rom. 15.13.
[53] 1 Tim. 6.20; 2 Tim. 1.14, 2.22; 1 Tim. 4.8; 2 Tim. 4.5–8.
[54] 2 Tim. 4.3, 3.4.
[55] Cf. 1 Tim. 6.9.

[56] Ps. 113.4.

[57] Cf. 2 Tim. 2.23; 1 Tim. 4.7.

[58] Luke 14.30.

[59] Cf. Matt. 19.26.

[60] Gen. 12.1. Paulinus frequently urges Sulpicius Severus to leave Gaul and to make for Italy on a *peregrinatio pro Christo*, but without success.

[61] Cf. Prov. 18.19: "A brother that is helped by his brother is like a strong city."

[62] Paulinus had quitted Aquitania for Spain probably in the autumn of 389 (cf. *Carm.* 10.1 ff., which speaks of the passage of four winters, and which can be dated to 393; cf. Fabre *Chron.* 105). In 393 Therasia bore Paulinus a son, but the son died when eight days old and was buried at Complutum, the modern Alcala in New Castille (cf. *Carm.* 31.599 ff.). This sorrow may have provided the immediate impetus for Paulinus' espousal of monastic life and the sale of their property. A year later, in 394, Paulinus and Therasia proceeded to Barcelona (the most important city in Hispania Tarraconensis after the destruction of Tarraco by the Suebi and the Franks in the third century) to make their way to Nola.

[63] There is no need to regard *die domini* as meaning Sunday, an interpretation which led earlier scholars to date this ordination to Christmas 393. Christmas Day is the "day of the Lord" in a special sense.

[64] Such forcible ordination impelled by popular clamour has a number of parallels in the fourth century. Augustine was dragged before his bishop to be ordained (cf. Possidius, *Vita Aug.* 4). So, too, was strong pressure put on Jerome's friend Nepotian (cf. Jerome, *Ep.* 60.10). Similarly Ambrose and Martin were forced to accept office as bishops; cf. F. Homes Dudden, *The Life and Times of St. Ambrose* 1 (Oxford 1935) ch. 3.

[65] Translating *aedituus*, a word used often in the Vulgate for "temple warden." In Ezechiel 44.11 the *aeditui* are ranked with the *ianitores*. Paulinus protests that he wished to embark on his vocation at the humblest level.

[66] Paulinus had already decided to go to Nola.

[67] Ps. 18.8, 8.3.

[68] Therasia and himself.

[69] In 451 the Council of Chalcedon condemned this practice of nonspecific ordination (canon 6), and in his commentary on this

Zonaras states that it was the regular procedure to ordain a priest or deacon for a particular church. Cf. the texts in ML 61.835 f.

[70] Was Severus already ordained? Concelebration was a regular feature in the early church. Cf. L. Beauduin, "La concélébration," *Maison-Dieu* (1946) 7 ff.; J. A. Jungmann, *Missarum sollemnia* 1 (Paris 1954) 194, 244 ff.

[71] This town must have been in Narbonese Gaul for it to have been possible to journey from there across the Pyrenees in eight days. The distance from Narbonne to Barcelona as the crow flies is over 120 miles, which a Roman army would have considered a reasonable distance to cover in a week. Hence Ortel's reading *Elusa*, the city of the Elusates on the Adour west of Auch (cf. Duchesne 2.5), is misguided. There is an Elusone mentioned in the *Itinerarium Burdegalense* (ML 61.836) as lying between Toulouse and Narbonne, and it is reasonable to assume that this is the town indicated here.

LETTER 2

[1] Paulinus makes clear reference in this letter to his recent ordination, which suggests that this letter is roughly contemporaneous with Letter 1. Cf. Fabre *Chron.* 63; also n. 1 to Letter 1.

[2] On Amandus and Paulinus' correspondence with him, cf. above, Intro. p. 4.

[3] Prov. 25.25.

[4] Cf. Prov. 15.30; Ps. 106.9.

[5] Tit. 1.12.

[6] Ps. 67.7.

[7] Eph. 1.23.

[8] Cf. 2 Cor. 4.7.

[9] Gal. 1.15; Ps. 112.7 f.

[10] Cf. Isa. 61.10.

[11] Cant. 1.3.

[12] Ps. 132.2.

[13] Ps. 67.27.

[14] Ps. 21.7.

[15] Matt. 26.42; Mark 14.36; Luke 22.42.

[16] Matt. 20.28.

[17] Phil. 3.12.

[18] *Seniores* is here used by Paulinus in a double sense, both as

a literal translation of the Greek *presbyteroi,* "elders" or "priests," and in contrast to the *parvuli* and *lactantes* in the following clause. Compare Jer. 1.6.

[19] 2 Cor. 8.7.

[20] 1 Tim. 4.6.

[21] John 6.35; Rom. 1.17.

[22] 1 Tim. 2.5.

[23] Eph. 4.3.

[24] 1 Cor. 14.12.

[25] Cf. Eph. 2.19 f.

[26] Ps. 117.22; 1 Pet. 2.6; Matt. 21.42.

[27] 2 Tim. 4.8.

[28] This passage provides evidence that Amandus had instructed Paulinus for his baptism, which was administered by Delphinus, bishop of Bordeaux (cf. Letter 3.4). This must have taken place in or before 389, the year of Paulinus' departure for Spain.

LETTER 3

[1] This letter was written from Italy (see § 3 for Paulinus' visit to Rome) and doubtless from Nola. The time of composition is not certain, but the probable date is late 395; cf. the acute discussion in Fabre *Chron.* 14 ff. It would seem from § 1 that Paulinus had sent his courier Julianus to Africa with an earlier communication, and this probably is the second letter he sent to Alypius.

[2] On Alypius, bishop of Tagaste, and the correspondence between him and Paulinus, cf. above, Intro. p. 5.

[3] Eph. 1.4.

[4] Ps. 99.3.

[5] Joel 2.28.

[6] Ps. 45.5.

[7] Ps. 112.8.

[8] Cf. Ps. 145.8, 112.7.

[9] In Letter 4.2, addressed to Augustine, Paulinus describes these five books as "this Pentateuch" of Augustine "against the Manicheans." No such single work is known. Augustine mentions that the *De vera religione* was one of the books, and it therefore appears that this "Pentateuch" was a collection of Augustine's writings hostile to the Manicheans. A. Buse, *Paulin, Bischof von*

Nola 1 (Regensburg 1856) 272, suggests that the other works included were Augustine's two books *De Genesi contra Manichaeos*, the *De moribus ecclesiae catholicae*, and the *De moribus Manichaeorum*. All these were composed about 388–9. Augustine's three books *De libero arbitrio* (=ACW 22 [1955] 35–220), mentioned in Augustine's *Ep.* 31.7 as being sent to Paulinus, were dispatched by Augustine himself, and were therefore not in this consignment.

[10] The letter to Augustine is No. 4 in the present collection.

[11] Eusebius of Caesarea, author of the *Ecclesiastical History* and of the *Chronicle* here referred to, is here confused with Eusebius of Nicomedia, who was translated from that see to Constantinople in 339. On both men and their works, cf. Quasten *Patr.* 3.190–93, 309–45. The *Chronicle* was a summary of universal history with dates, especially valuable to scholars like Jerome because it attempted a correspondence between secular and sacred history.

[12] Jerome, *Ep.* 47.3, and Palladius, *Historia Lausiaca* 37.12 (=ACW 34 [1965] 108), both also mention this Domnio very favourably. Domnio is the addressee of Jerome's *Ep.* 50.

[13] St. Aurelius was bishop of Carthage for forty years until his death in about 430. Augustine (*Epp.* 22, 41, 60, 174) speaks of him with respect and affection. Cf. in general the article of A. Audollent in DHGE 5.726 ff.

[14] For other texts exemplifying the use of *corona* in the sense of episcopal rank, cf. ML 61.837.

[15] Virgil, *Aeneid* 8.114. Paulinus was steeped in classical poetry, as his verses show. Though he was to make a conscious effort to exclude the language of pagan culture from his writing (note his comments in Letter 7.3), there are in his letters over twenty quotations from Virgil alone. These are listed by Hartel in his Index in CSEL 30.377.

[16] 1 Pet. 2.9.

[17] Cf. above, n. 28 to Letter 2 and n. 64 to Letter 1.

[18] None of the correspondence between Ambrose and Paulinus has survived, and this passage is welcome testimony of the close relationship between the two men, suggesting that they had known each other prior to 389. In a celebrated letter (*Ep.* 58), Ambrose extols the conversion of Paulinus and the decision to sell his ancestral possessions. On the relations between Ambrose and Paulinus, cf. Lagrange 1.76 ff.

[19] Ps. 106.14.

[20] Prov. 18.19.
[21] Cf. Apoc. 1.13.
[22] Ps. 118.105.
[23] *In quo etiam trinitatis soliditas continetur.*—The custom of sending blessed bread as a mark of unity in faith was well established in the fourth century. It is discussed by Basil in his Rule (133). Augustine sent a loaf to Paulinus (cf. Augustine, *Ep.* 34), and Paulinus sent one to Severus (cf. Letter 5.21).

LETTER 4

[1] This letter was written at the same time as the preceding one to Alypius (cf. Letter 3.2), that is, probably in late 395. It is clear from § 1 of this letter that this is the first sent by Paulinus to Augustine.

[2] When Paulinus writes to old friends and acquaintances like Severus and Amandus, he is content to send the salutation in his own name. When he writes more formally to new acquaintances like Alypius and Augustine, he includes his wife in the expression of greeting.

[3] 2 Cor. 5.14.

[4] Paulinus implies that he will have copies made at Nola and sent to churches in Gaul and perhaps in Spain. We have no knowledge of how many servants or fellow monks had aided Therasia and Paulinus in their foundation of the monastic establishment at Nola.

[5] Cf. John 6.27.
[6] Cf. 2 Cor. 4.18.
[7] Cf. Matt. 5.13.
[8] Cf. Matt. 5.15.
[9] Cf. Apoc. 1.13 and 20.
[10] John 4.14.
[11] Cf. Ps. 35.9, 64.10.
[12] Virgil, *Aeneid* 7.338, referring to Allecto.
[13] Cf. Rom. 1.22.
[14] Ps. 6.8; Rom. 1.21; Ps. 120.1.
[15] Cf. Ps. 145.8.
[16] Phil. 3.12.
[17] Cf. Acts 4.22: "For the man was above forty years old. . . ." This is the main evidence for Paulinus' date of birth. If this letter

was in fact written in 395 and Paulinus had recently passed his fortieth birthday, his date of birth was 355. The additional evidence rests on the difficult question of his *depositio barbae* (*Carm.* 13.7 ff., written in 396, suggests that the ceremony took place in 381; but we cannot be certain of his age at the time). Cf. Fabre *Paulin* 14 ff., 18.

[18] The phraseology here suggests that of *Serm.* 374.3 among the *sermones dubii* of Augustine (ML 39.1667 f.); cf. also Augustine's *De libero arbitrio* 3.23.

[19] This passage (and the letter as a whole) shows that Augustine had not yet been made bishop, or at least that Paulinus had no knowledge of such a development.

[20] In fact Augustine was born in November 354, and so was almost exactly the same age as Paulinus. The phrase used here, *etsi forte sis aevo iunior*, suggests that Paulinus had no knowledge of Augustine's exact age.

[21] Cf. 2 Cor. 10.17; Rom. 7.18.

[22] Cf. Ps. 25.8, 83.11.

[23] Gal. 1.15.

[24] Ps. 112.8.

[25] Rom. 12.16.

[26] *Sacerdos*, a title which could designate either a priest or bishop. Paulinus here, as also in Letter 32.15, uses *sacerdos* for bishop; on this sense of the word, cf. H. Janssen, *Kultur und Sprache: Zur Geschichte der alten Kirche im Spiegel der Sprachentwicklung von Tertullian bis Cyprian* (Latinitas christianorum primaeva 8, Nijmegen 1938) 87 ff.

[27] Cf. above, n. 23 to Letter 3.

LETTER 5

[1] A probable date of composition is summer 396. Internal evidence suggests that this, the first letter sent to Severus from Nola, was dispatched when the cool reception accorded to Paulinus at Rome in 395 was still vivid in his mind (cf. §§ 13 f.). But he had been consoled by visits from Campanian bishops (including Memorius of Capua and Aemilius of Beneventum) and by fresh letters from African bishops sent "at the beginning of summer" (*prima aestate*). It is reasonable to conclude that this letter was sent later in 396. For a rebuttal of the argument in

Reinelt 10 in favour of 397, cf. Fabre *Chron.* 19 ff. His main reason for delaying a whole year in writing to his dearest friend is given in § 11; he had received a letter, but illness postponed the reply.

[2] 2 Tim. 4.8.

[3] Cf. 1 John 4.20.

[4] John 13.1, 10.15.

[5] This is the queen of Saba whose visit to Solomon is mentioned in 3 Kings 10. The phrase *regina Austri* echoes Christ's words at Matt. 12.42: *The queen of the south shall rise in judgment with this generation, and shall condemn it; because she came from the ends of the earth to hear the wisdom of Solomon.* Josephus, *Jewish Antiquities* 8.6.1, calls her Nicaulis, queen of Egypt and Ethiopia, but she is now generally considered to have come from northern Arabia.

[6] 2 Cor. 3.3.

[7] Ps. 44.10.

[8] This emphasis on the typological significance of the queen of Saba is found already in Hilary's *Comment. in Matt.* 12.20: *sed et Austri regina nunc in exemplum Ecclesiae praesumpta, sapientiam admirata Salomonis, ex ultimis terrae partibus venit audire quam erat admirata sapientiam.* Paulinus may have read Hilary, or the similar interpretation in Ambrose, *Expos. in Luc.* 7.96. Just as the queen of Saba showed reverent love for Solomon by her gifts, so the Church with similar wisdom (or does *ecclesia providens* convey the notion of provision of gifts?) reveres and loves Christ.

[9] Rom. 13.10.

[10] Luke 14.14; cf. Matt. 25.40.

[11] Matt. 10.41.

[12] Cf. Rom. 2.13.

[13] We have little information of Paulinus' secular career before 379, the year in which Ausonius was consul. Membership of the senatorial order was hereditary, so Paulinus was a senator by right. Moreover, Paulinus held curule office before Ausonius, and so held it in or before 378. This need not have been the consulship, as has often been supposed. More probably, the curule office designated in the Fasti would have been the governorship of Campania (so Reinelt 60 ff.). Paulinus then would have been *consularis sexfascalis Campaniae* (for Campania as a proconsulate by the decree of Gratian, cf. Jones 1.161 and the references there).

The tenure of the governorship of Campania would normally
have been preceded by a less exacting administrative office, so
that Paulinus' official career could have begun several years before
378.

¹⁴ The calumny referred to here arose out of the violent death
of Paulinus' brother in Aquitania (cf. Paulinus, *Carm.* 21.416 ff.),
an event which had important repercussions, inducing Paulinus
finally to be baptised and to leave Aquitania (cf. *Carm.* 21.421 ff.).
The precise circumstances of the murder of his brother are unknown. E. Babut, RHLR (1910) 98 ff., believed that Paulinus
and his brother were charged with Priscillianism; against this, cf.
H. Delehaye, AB 38 (1920) 107. Others believe that a political
accusation against his brother also implicated Paulinus; cf.
U. Moricca, *Didaskaleion* (1926) 85 ff. The only certainty in this
is that after the murder of Gratian in 383, that emperor's protégés
were exposed to attack from Maximus, who was prone to accept
capital charges in order to confiscate the property of the accused
(cf. Sulpicius Severus, *Dial.* 3.11). It is possible, therefore, that an
attempt was made to pin his brother's murder on Paulinus in
order to seize his property.

¹⁵ Ps. 1.1.

¹⁶ Cf. Rom. 2.13.

¹⁷ Cf. Gal. 2.19.

¹⁸ In Letter 31.1 Paulinus emphasises the close relationship between Severus and his mother-in-law Bassula. She seems to have
played the same role in the foundation of the monastery at
Primuliacum as Therasia played at Nola.

¹⁹ Cf. Matt. 4.22, etc.

²⁰ Cf. John 1.47.

²¹ Various patristic authorities propound the meaning of Israel
as "seeing God"; cf. the texts in ML 61.838.

²² Cf. Gen. 22.24.

²³ Eph. 6.12.

²⁴ Cf. Gal. 1.10.

²⁵ Cf. 1 Cor. 1.19–23.

²⁶ 1 Cor. 1.18.

²⁷ Matt. 16.17.

²⁸ 1 Cor. 1.27.

²⁹ Cf. Matt. 5.15, etc.

³⁰ Cf. Apoc. 1.12.

³¹ Lam. 28.3.

[32] Ps. 53.7, 42.14.
[33] Cf. Rom. 8.34.
[34] Deut. 13.3.
[35] Cf. Matt. 26.41.
[36] Matt. 5.25; Ps. 37.4, 83.3, 15.9.
[37] Apoc. 3.11.
[38] Rom. 8.28.
[39] Cf. 1 Cor. 12.26.
[40] Ps. 117.18.
[41] Cf. Matt. 10.29.
[42] On Vigilantius, cf. the article by G. Bardy in DTC 15.2992; also W. Schmidt, *Vigilantius: Seine Verhältnis zum heiligen Hieronymus* (Münster 1860); A. Réville, *Vigilance de Calagurris* (Paris 1902). A native of Aquitania, Vigilantius attained notoriety a decade after this letter when, after attacking Jerome for being an Origenist, he was labelled "Dormitianus" and roundly abused in Jerome's *Contra Vigilantium* and in the same scholar's *Epp.* 61 and 109. (We cannot be absolutely certain that this is the same Vigilantius, but there is no inconsistency involved in making the assumption; cf. Fabre *Chron.* 22, n. 1.)
[43] The notion of the mystical unity of Christians extending even to sympathetic illness is one repeatedly alluded to by Paulinus. Cf. Fabre *Paulin* 288.
[44] Cf. 2 Cor. 12.10; Gal. 5.17.
[45] Ps. 106.42.
[46] When Paulinus reached Rome on his way from Spain in the summer of 395, he was coldly ignored by Pope Siricius and his entourage of clerics. The reason for this has been the subject of much speculation. Did Siricius look coldly on Paulinus' irregular ordination? This is the view in Lagrange 1.198. Did he suspect Paulinus of Priscillianism? Cf. above, n. 14. This is a highly dubious thesis, however, especially as Siricius was deeply disturbed about the execution of Priscillian; cf. F. Homes Dudden, *op. cit.* 233. Was Siricius jealous of the popular stir aroused by the arrival of this celebrated convert to monasticism? This was suggested by Baronius, quoted in ML 61.838 f. Siricius was also hostile to Jerome, and the most likely explanation is that Siricius had some distrust of the rapidly developing cult of monasticism in the West, especially as this movement had repercussions in the internal rivalries and factions within the Church.
[47] Phil. 4.7.

[48] Ps. 34.19.

[49] Ps. 119.7; 1 Cor. 11.16.

[50] Cf. Eccli. 28.28.

[51] This was Romanianus, who came with a letter from Augustine (*Ep.* 27) sent before his consecration as bishop, and also with replies from Aurelius and Alypius to Paulinus' letters, as we may assume. Cf. Fabre *Chron.* 19.

[52] 2 Cor. 5.6.

[53] Luke 4.24.

[54] The anxiety of Paulinus for Severus' coming is partly motivated by a desire to increase his small community; note the later delight at the prospect of Severus' bringing other monks with him.

[55] A reminiscence of Cicero, *Pro Milone* 69, a passage concerned with friendship and loyalty.

[56] Devotion to St. Felix had led Paulinus to establish his community at Nola. A native of that town but the son of a Syrian, Felix had distributed most of his possessions to the poor before being ordained. He was imprisoned during the persecution of Decius in 250. After Decius' death, he refused a pressing invitation to become bishop of Nola. His sale of property and renunciation of the world first directed Paulinus' thoughts to the monastic life when he was governor of Campania; it had been a predecessor in that office who had persecuted Felix. The details of his patron's life are recorded by Paulinus in his *Carm.* 15, 16, 18, 21, 23, 24, 26, 27, 28, and 29. For a good account of Felix based on these poems, cf. Lagrange 1.204 ff.

[57] Ps. 117.24, 132.1.

[58] Cf. Matt. 20.9.

[59] Cf. Luke 10.35.

[60] Cf. Matt. 20.4.

[61] 1 Cor. 5.8; Eph. 5.19; Col. 3.16 f; Ps.. 67.7.

[62] Eph. 2.14; John 12.32.

[63] Cf. Col. 1.20.

[64] Ps. 125.3, 117.26.

[65] Cf. Ps. 115.13; Luke 14.15.

[66] Ps. 22.4.

[67] Isa. 35.3; Ps. 17.33, 18.6.

[68] Cf. Sallust, *Catiline* 1. Paulinus quotes from Sallust, acknowledging his source, in his *Carm.* 3.2.

[69] 2 Cor. 12.9.

[70] Ps. 44.5, 88.15.

[71] Ps. 40.31.

[72] Ps. 40.31.

[73] Cf. Mark 6.8; Luke 9.3; Matt. 10.10.

[74] Cf. Exod. 12.11. Severus' journey is compared with that of the Israelites out of Egypt.

[75] Ps. 67.20; Isa. 40.4; Ps. 90.11 f.

[76] Ps. 120.5.

[77] Ps. 88.16, 90.4, 16.8, 120.6.

[78] Cf. Ps. 120.8; Luke 10.6.

[79] Ps. 125.6 f.

[80] 2 Cor. 13.13.

[81] Cf. 2 Cor. 5.1 and 6.16; Eph. 2.20.

[82] I.e., Bassula. Cf. above, n. 18.

[83] This is Therasia. Throughout this section Paulinus consciously imitates the characteristic conclusions of St. Paul's Epistles.

[84] The reading of the MSS here, *salutant vos omnes qui in domino nobiscum sunt, ut ex Hebraeis Proforus et Restitutus, amans dominum et te in Christo compertum diligens* . . . , is accepted without question by Hartel. Yet it is suspect. The participles suggest that only one person is mentioned. I propose: . . . *ut ex Hebraeis Proforus restitutus.* . . , and I have translated accordingly. Lagrange (1.218, n. 2) proposes: . . . *ex Hebraeis Proforus: Restitutus amans dominum.* . . . Paulinus does not mention this Jewish convert again, but in Letter 29.13 he gives the Hebraic etymology of Cedar, "ut comperi." Was Proforus perhaps his authority?

[85] 1 Tim. 1.5; Matt. 5.37.

[86] Eph. 1.17.

[87] 1 Cor. 13.7.

[88] Cf. above, n. 23 to Letter 3.

[89] The meaning of Paulinus' word here, *nigellatum*, is uncertain, but the context indicates that oil or wine is meant. *Nigellatum* may well be the Latin equivalent of the Greek *melanthelaion*, the oil of the *nigella sativa*, which Paulinus may have required for medicinal purposes. Cf. the learned note of Rosweyde in ML 61.841.

[90] Cf. 2 Cor. 4.7.

[91] Ps. 13.3, 52.4; Matt. 10.36. Narbo (Narbonne) was the most convenient Mediterranean port for the shipment of Aquitanian wine, and though Valentinian had forbidden wine-exports, it

seems certain that these restrictions were not observed. It seems probable that the wine had been sent to Narbo for shipment before Paulinus sold his estates. The sell-out displeased his family and dependents, who were accordingly slow to carry out his wishes.

LETTER 6

[1] This letter was composed a few months before the preceding one, for Paulinus has not at this time received his first letter from Augustine (see § 1). Since the courier from Augustine arrived at the beginning of the summer (cf. n. 1 to Letter 5), this letter presumably was written in the spring of 396.

[2] 1 Cor. 2.15.

[3] 1 Cor. 12.6.

[4] Cf. above, n. 9 to Letter 3.

[5] On Alypius, cf. above, Intro. p. 5; on Aurelius, cf. n. 13 to Letter 3.

[6] Cf. 1 Cor. 12.12, 10.17; 2 Cor. 5.1.

[7] Reading *omne quod sumus* instead of the *in omne quod sumus* in the MSS and editions.

[8] These couriers brought Augustine's reply to Paulinus; cf. Augustine, *Ep.* 31.2 f.

[9] I punctuate: *Romanus et Agilis, quos ut nos alios commendamus in nomine domini, revertentur.* . . . On the word order, compare Ps. 117.26, etc.

[10] Cf. Prov. 18.19.

[11] For Paulinus' gift of bread, cf. Letter 4.5.

[12] Acts 4.32.

LETTER 7

[1] The date of this letter cannot be before late 396, and this has an important bearing on the date of Augustine's consecration as bishop, usually assigned to 395 after Prosper of Aquitaine (cf., e.g., G. Morin, "Date de l'ordination épiscopale de s. Augustin," RB [1928] 367), but which in view of the evidence of Paulinus more probably was in 396. We have seen that the sequence of Paulinus' correspondence with African ecclesiastics was as fol-

lows. After his arrival at Nola in 395 (cf. n. 1 to Letter 1), Paulinus received a letter from Alypius, and sent him a book from Rome (cf. Letter 3.3). At the same time he wrote to Augustine. After the lapse of a winter (cf. Letter 6.1) he had still not received a reply, so he wrote a second letter to Augustine; the time probably was early 396. Later Romanianus brought Augustine's first letter (*Ep.* 27), and later still Paulinus' own couriers brought Augustine's second letter (*Ep.* 31), which had the news of Augustine's elevation to bishop. Paulinus immediately wrote this present letter to inform Romanianus. The time is late 396, or possibly early 397.

² This is the Romanianus who was friend and patron of Augustine. Cf. above, Intro. p. 5 f. Romanianus was probably at Rome at this time, since Paulinus' letter to Romanianus' son Licentius, which was sent at the same time, speaks of the seductions of the capital (cf. Letter 8.3).

³ For Romanus and Agilis, cf. Letter 6.3.

⁴ On Aurelius, cf. above, n. 13 to Letter 3. On Alypius, cf. Intro. p. 5. Profuturus was a member of Augustine's monastic community at Hippo before he was consecrated bishop of Cirta (Constantine); cf. Augustine, *Ep.* 38. Severus, too, had been a member of that monastery before being appointed bishop of Milevis (Mila, west of Constantine); cf. Augustine, *Ep.* 110.

⁵ Ps. 67.36.

⁶ Valerius, bishop of Hippo, was a Greek who had authorised Augustine whilst still a priest to assist him with preaching (cf. Augustine, *Ep.* 21; Possidius, *Vita Aug.* 5). Megalius, bishop of Calama and primate of Numidia, consecrated Augustine bishop (cf. Augustine, *Serm.* 355.2). The consecration was irregular because according to the Council of Nicaea (canon 8) two bishops were forbidden to administer the same see; but, as Augustine later wrote (*Ep.* 213.4), neither he nor Valerius knew of the prohibition at that time. Perhaps Augustine, as a result of this, was influential at the Council of Carthage in drafting canon 3, which stipulated that new bishops should be reminded of the decrees of past councils. By then, however, Valerius had retired.

⁷ Matt. 19.26.

⁸ Ps. 71.18, 67.7.

⁹ Cf. Deut. 26.7; Ps. 30.8; Luke 7.16.

¹⁰ Luke 1.69.

[11] Ps. 74.11.

[12] Augustine had begun his attacks on the Donatist schism with the *Psalmus contra partem Donati*, an alphabetic composition written in 393. This was followed in the next year by his *Contra epistolam Donati haeretici*. The evidence of Paulinus' earlier letters suggests that he had no firsthand acquaintance with these, since the anti-Manichean works were the first writings of Augustine which he had read (cf. Letter 6.2; also n. 9 to Letter 3).

[13] On Licentius, cf. above, Intro. pp. 5 f.

[14] Cf. Matt. 13.3 ff.

[15] Cf. Terence, *Adelphi* 96 ff. Aeschinus in this play is the adopted son of Micio.

[16] This is an example of that antagonism to the distractions of classical literature which was frequently expressed in the writings of the fourth-century Christian humanists, e.g., Jerome, Augustine, Ambrose. For further evidence of Paulinus' attitude, cf. in this volume Letter 22.3.

LETTER 8

[1] This letter was sent as an enclosure with Letter 7 to Romanianus; cf. n. 1 to Letter 7.

[2] Licentius was Romanianus' son. Cf. above, Intro. pp. 5 f.

[3] Cf. Prov. 1.8: *My son, hear the instruction of thy father, and forsake not the law of thy mother.*

[4] Prov. 1.9.

[5] Cf. 4 Kings 2.2 ff.; 2 Tim. 1.3 ff.; Acts 16.1 ff.

[6] Of this letter nothing is known. It may have been inspired by Paulinus' correspondence with Augustine. Hearing that this well-known public figure and poet was now in Nola, Licentius, who fancied himself a litterateur, may well have introduced himself by letter.

[7] The language here recalls Ciceronian translations of Platonist ideas in the *Timaeus* and the *De natura deorum*.

[8] Phil. 2.9.

[9] The rest of this letter, 108 lines in the Latin, is in elegiacs. The reason for this is given in the preceding paragraph. Paulinus wishes to interest and win over Licentius through his poetic interests, and to demonstrate that Christian themes are at home in classical metres.

[10] Paulinus, in his retirement from the active life of state service, exemplifies the sharp dichotomy in the minds of his Christian contemporaries between service in the military and civil administration and the monastic vocation. The results of this abandonment of the secular world are well studied in A. Momigliano's essay, "Christianity and the Decline of the Roman Empire," in *Paganism and Christianity in the Fourth Century* (Oxford 1963) 1–16. See Paulinus' critical comments about the military dress which symbolises such service in Letters 17.1 and 22.1. There is further criticism of military life in Letter 25.3 ff.

[11] Matt. 11.30.
[12] A reminiscence of Virgil, *Georgics* 3.188.
[13] For the sentiment, cf. Juvenal, *Sat.* 10.8 ff.
[14] Cf. Luke 16.13.
[15] Cf. Eph. 4.5 f.
[16] An echo of Virgil, *Aeneid* 4.336.
[17] Cf. Rom. 8.1 ff.

LETTER 9

[1] As is noted in Fabre *Chron.* 62 ff., it is impossible to specify precisely the date of this letter and of Letter 10 to Delphinus, both of which were composed at the same time (cf. § 2 of this letter and § 3 of Letter 10). But the general tone of the two letters, especially at Letter 10.2, suggests that they were written shortly after Paulinus' decision to retire into monastic life. The introductory comment in this letter shows that Paulinus had not hitherto written regularly to Delphinus. The inference is that these letters were sent before Paulinus' arrival at Nola; note that there is no Italian detail in them. Accordingly I assume, with Fabre, that they were written from Spain. Letter 2 to Amandus was sent in early 395 from Spain; Letters 9 and 10 may have been written a year or two earlier, that is, in 393 or 394.

[2] Cf. Matt. 10.27.
[3] Cf. Wisd. 10.21.
[4] Cf. Col. 4.6.
[5] The baptismal imagery recalls Paulinus' baptism by Delphinus in or before 389; cf. above, n. 28 to Letter 2.
[6] Matt. 5.13.
[7] Luke 14.24. Cf. Ps. 33.9; 1 Pet. 2.3.

[8] Prov. 22.13. The Vulgate reads: "The slothful man saith: There is a lion without; I shall be slain in the midst of the streets."

[9] In this passage on the "mystical" bee and the ant, Paulinus probably has in mind the passage of Ambrose in his *Hexaemeron* 5.67 ff. (ML 14.248): *apes, quae solae in omni genere animantium communem omnibus subolem habent, unam omnes incolunt mansionem, unius patriae clauduntur limine . . . communis omnibus generatio, integritas quoque corporis virginalis. . . .* Ambrose next quotes Prov. 6.8 in the version of the Septuagint, and comments: *propheta mittit utique te ut apiculae illius sequaris exemplum, imiteris operationem.* So the bees in this sense symbolise the working of the Mystical Body. In Letter 23.16, in discussing the passage at Judges 14.8–14 (where Samson finds a honeycomb in the lion's carcass and poses the riddle: "Out of the eater came forth meat and out of the strong came forth sweetness"), Paulinus presents an allegorical interpretation. The lion is Christ, and in His body, which is the Church, the apostles like bees stored the honey of wisdom. For the symbolic meaning of the bee in the Old Testament, cf. the article by Vigouroux in DB 1, s.v. "abeille."

[10] Cf. Prov. 6.6.

[11] Prov. 24.33 f.

[12] 2 Cor. 8.9.

[13] Ps. 29.10.

[14] Ps. 76.11.

[15] Tit. 1.12; Ps. 118.25; Eph. 5.14.

[16] Cf. Matt. 8.24.

[17] Cf. Ps. 106.30.

[18] Cf. Ps. 38.8, 54.9.

[19] Matt. 24.20.

[20] The phrase *opus servile*, "servile work," derives from the Vulgate translation of Lev. 23.21 and 35 f., Num. 28.18, etc. The interesting symbolic interpretation put upon it here can be paralleled in Augustine's *Tract. in Joann.* 3.19 (ML 35.1404), which, however, was not preached until A.D. 413 (so H. Pope, *Saint Augustine of Hippo* [London 1937 (repr. Westminster, Md. 1949)] 378).

[21] John 8.35.

[22] Rom. 12.11 f.

[23] Cf. Luke 21.34; 2 Cor. 5.3.

[24] Ps. 147.17.

[25] Cf. Wisd. 1.15.

[26] Cf. Phil. 3.12 f.

[27] The symbolism of the cross as plough, bringing fresh life to the earth, was already a commonplace in fourth-century times. The Latin fathers took it over from such Greeks as Justin (cf. his *Apologia* 1.55). For a collection of such passages from Minucius Felix, Tertullian, and others, cf. H. Rahner, *Greek Myths and Christian Mystery* (London 1962) 56. But the use of the symbol here in exegesis of Phil. 3.12 may be novel.

[28] Ps. 120.1, 67.36.

[29] John 14.6; Ps. 17.34.

[30] Ps. 103.18.

[31] The scriptural reference here is Gen. 10.9, which, however, reads in the Vulgate *robustus venator coram Domino*, "stout hunter before the Lord." In this letter, as also in Letter 38.9, Paulinus uses Nemrod as a symbol of Satan, and calls him *contra dominum venator*. Clearly the pre-Vulgate version used by Paulinus had the alternative translation of the Greek *enantion*, which could be translated either "before" or "against."

[32] Cf. Ps. 67.16 f.

[33] Ps. 29.2, 17.49, 53.9.

[34] Cf. Ps. 103.18.

[35] Eccli. 28.28.

[36] Cf. Ps. 16.5.

[37] Phil. 4.1. Note the characteristically ingenious way with which Paulinus passes from the imagery of hart and hedgehog, which is admirably sustained, to that of laurel and crown.

[38] Cf. Isa. 61.3; Matt. 15.13.

[39] Ps. 76.11, 72.26.

[40] Cf. 1 Cor. 15.46.

[41] Ps. 141.6.

[42] Eph. 4.23.

[43] Ps. 72.26.

LETTER 10

[1] On the dating of this letter, cf. above, n. 1 to Letter 9.

[2] On Delphinus and Paulinus' correspondence with him, cf. above, Intro. p. 4.

[3] 2 Cor. 12.14.

[4] Cf. Matt. 25.18; Luke 19.12–23.

[5] Cf. Matt. 25.9.

[6] Matt. 12.34.

[7] Cf. Matt. 7.16.

[8] Jer. 2.21.

[9] Cf. Isa. 5.4.

[10] Cf. Eccli. 28.28.

[11] Compare Hilary's *Comm. in Ps.* 57.10 (ML 9.371): *Rhamnus sentium genus est, quod plures ex se condensasque spinas modo rubi effert: florescit autem cum ceteris vere confotum.*

[12] Cf. Matt. 13.7.

[13] Ps. 91.14.

[14] Cf. Ps. 79.14.

[15] Cf. Matt. 21.33.

[16] Cf. Luke 13.8.

[17] Cf. Matt. 3.10.

[18] Cf. Luke 13.8.

[19] Cf. Matt. 13.30; Isa. 18.5.

LETTER 11

[1] As Reinelt (15) has demonstrated, this letter follows in order after Letter 5 in the group of letters to Severus, because the topic of Paulinus' modest garden (cf. Letter 5.16) has been taken up jokingly by Severus, who is answered here in § 14. At this time Paulinus was writing yearly to Severus (cf. Fabre *Chron.* 23). So this letter was written in 397, while Paulinus still had hopes of Severus' coming to Nola.—It will be noted that Severus has sent his life of St. Martin to Paulinus, who acknowledges it in § 11 of this letter. If the date of Martin's death was November 397, as the sources suggest, the *Vita* was composed in the saint's lifetime (so Duchesne, *Histoire ancienne de l'église* 3 [Paris 1910] 164). The comments of Paulinus lend support to this view.

[2] Eccli. 6.15; Prov. 16.23.

[3] Eccli. 6.16; Prov. 16.24.

[4] Prov. 25.25.

[5] Prov. 16.30.

[6] Ps. 115.12.

[7] Severus was, like Paulinus, a native of Aquitania. We do not

know if they were intimates during their early years, but Paulinus' letters provide abundant evidence for the period between Paulinus' return from Campania and his departure to Spain. Cf., e.g., § 5 below.

[8] Matt. 12.48.

[9] John 1.13.

[10] Cf. Col. 1.16 f.; John 1.12.

[11] Phil. 3.21.

[12] Cf. Gen. 12.1 ff.

[13] 1 Cor. 13.8.

[14] Cf. 1 Cor. 13.4 ff.

[15] Matt. 11.29.

[16] Ps. 68.9.

[17] Ps. 37.12. Such passages as this and the end of Letter 5 show that Paulinus' decision to retire to monastic life caused a rift not only with his worldly friends like Ausonius but also with his family.

[18] Cf. Ps. 37.12; Eph. 2.13.

[19] Ps. 44.17.

[20] Ps. 52.7.

[21] Cf. Matt. 19.29.

[22] Paulinus thinks primarily of the messages that he has received from Africa (cf. Letters 3 and 6). He was also in communication with Jerusalem (cf. P. Courcelle, "Paulin de Nole et saint Jérôme," REL 25 [1947] 250 ff.).–By "our own region," *orbis*, Paulinus may mean either Aquitania or the Romanised West.

[23] Ps. 48.8.

[24] Matt. 10.36.

[25] Cf. Acts 4.32.

[26] The concept of Christian friendship as transcending the most noble human friendship (as described, e.g., in Cicero's *Laelius*) has a key position in Paulinus' thought. It is well treated in Fabre *Paulin* ch. 3, "La théorie de l'amitié."

[27] Cf. Luke 1.48.

[28] Matt. 24.40.

[29] Cf. Rom. 7.23.

[30] Eph. 2.14.

[31] Cf. Rom. 13.10.

[32] Matt. 24.40.

[33] Cf. Matt. 24.41; Luke 17.35.

[34] This allegorical interpretation may have been derived from Ambrose, *Expos. in Luc.* 8.48: *in hoc ergo postremo vel synagoga . . . at vero sancta ecclesia*, etc.

[35] Cf. Origen, *In Matt. comm. ser.* 57 (MG 13.1691): *Duo in agro, sensus hominis boni et sensus hominis mali. Sensus bonus assumitur, sensus malus relinquitur.*

[36] Rom. 11.29.

[37] *Adsumpti autem non nostro merito sed gratia dei, cuius dona et vocationes sine paenitentia sunt, neque ex operum praerogativa sed ex fide bonae voluntatis. . . .*

[38] Though Paulinus reached his decision first, Severus followed shortly afterwards, probably on the death of his wife, while Paulinus was in Spain; cf. Fabre *Paulin* 278.

[39] Ps. 135.25.

[40] John 6.33.

[41] Cf. Eccli. 24.29.

[42] 1 Tim. 1.5.

[43] 1 Cor. 5.8.

[44] Reading here *voluntatum eius effectu*, where Hartel reads *effectus*. (Cf. Letter 4.4: *vide quando adsequatur effectum dei voluntatum. . . .*)

[45] 1 Cor. 6.17.

[46] 1 Cor. 15.49.

[47] 2 Cor. 2.15; Rom. 12.1.

[48] Cf. Lev. 5.6 ff.

[49] This eloquent expression of the Christian transformation of the idea of sacrifice, implicit in Rom. 12.1 (cf. Ps. 39.7 f.), by which the individual consciously makes sacrifice by obedience to the divine will, has many parallels elsewhere (e.g., Jerome, *In Gal.* 4.8; Augustine, *De civ. Dei* 10.6; etc.). Cf. also the article of A. Gaudel in DTC 14.662 ff.

[50] On the symbolism of the fleece, cf. the note at ML 61.844.

[51] Rom. 14.13.

[52] Cf. Judges 6.37 f.

[53] Cf. Eccli. 24.41.

[54] Ps. 71.6.

[55] Cf. John 4.6.

[56] Cf. Ps. 90.6, 16.8.

[57] Isa. 53.7.

[58] Cf. John 10.17 f.

[59] Cf. Hebr. 10.10 f.

[60] Cf. Luke 15.5.—On the Good Shepherd motif on chalices, cf. Tertullian, *De pudicitia* 7 (=ACW 28 [1959] 68); also the remarks of W. P. Le Saint in ACW 28.217, n. 174.

[61] Ps. 15.2.

[62] Cf. 1 Cor. 4.7.

[63] Cf. Matt. 19.29.

[64] Cf. 1 Tim. 6.7.

[65] Cf. 1 Cor. 7.31.

[66] Cf. Gal. 6.8.

[67] Cf. 2 Thess. 3.10.

[68] Cf. John 6.27.

[69] Cf. Ps. 127.2.

[70] Cf. 1 Cor. 5.7.

[71] Cf. Exod. 12.11.

[72] 1 Cor. 7.29, 32, 26.

[73] Cf. Luke 12.36.

[74] Cf. Ps. 31.6.

[75] Cf. Matt. 13.38.

[76] Matt. 24.40.

[77] Cf. Gal. 5.17.

[78] Cf. Rom. 7.23.

[79] Cf. 1 Cor. 5.7.

[80] Paulinus here acknowledges receipt of Severus' biography of Martin written in verse. This work may be found in CSEL 1 (ed. Halm, Vienna 1864). Martin, born the son of a pagan (the date cannot be established), obtained his discharge from the Roman army to enter monastic life near Milan. In about 360 he went to Poitiers where he founded the first Gallic monastery at Locociagum. In 372 he became bishop of Tours, and a few years later built a monastery there at Marmoutier. About eighty monks followed the regimen of prayer and spiritual life, and many bishops originated from this monastery. The fundamental article on St. Martin is that of H. Delehaye, "Saint Martin et Sulpice Sévère," AB 38 (1920) 5–136. The biography by P. Monceaux (Paris 1926) includes a translation of the *Vita* by Severus. For a briefer portrait, cf. G. Boissier, *La fin du paganisme* 2 (Paris 1891) 66 ff. For the meeting of Paulinus and Martin, cf. Letter 18.9.

[81] Inserting, with Sacchini, *membra* into the text.

[82] Cf. 1 Cor. 15.54.

[83] Cf. Luke 9.62.

[84] Phil. 3.14.
[85] Cf. Matt. 13.25.
[86] 1 Tim. 6.8; Matt. 6.34.
[87] Luke 9.23.
[88] Cf. Matt. 8.20.
[89] There is a similar reference to Paul in § 7 above.
[90] Cf. Gal. 6.14.
[91] Deut. 8.3; Matt. 4.4.
[92] Cf. Gal. 3.11.
[93] 1 Cor. 6.13.
[94] Cf. Matt. 7.26.
[95] Matt. 6.34, 33; Luke 12.31.
[96] Cf. Rom. 2.29.
[97] This passage may mark the beginning of the estrangement between the two friends, the immediate cause of which was the bantering tone used by Severus about the jejune hospitality at Nola and the tiny garden (cf. § 14 below) to which he had been invited. Paulinus was hurt because Severus did not manifest the same *desiderium* as he himself had shown; and undoubtedly the mention of visits to Martin's monastery at Marmoutier led him to suspect that Severus had found a closer comrade in the spiritual life.
[98] Rom. 13.10.
[99] This is Paulinus' native estate. Its location has not been established with certainty. Perhaps it is Embrau on the Garonne (so Fabre *Paulin* 295, n. 2).
[100] 2 Cor. 6.10.

LETTER 12

[1] The dating of this letter, in 397 or 398, can be speculatively established by analysing the order of the surviving correspondence with Amandus and Delphinus. Letters 19, 20, and 21 seem certainly to have been sent in 401, or possibly late in the year 400. In Letter 19.1 Paulinus complains of a lack of news from Bordeaux of almost two years, and expresses delight at the return of the courier Cardamas. Now Letters 14 and 15 portray Cardamas at an earlier stage of his reformed life (cf. Letter 15.4), and it is reasonable to assume that he carried these letters to Aquitania in 399. The present letter was written earlier than Nos. 14 and

15, because the final sentence requests aid for a priest, and Letter 14.3 acknowledges that aid. So this letter was written in 398 (so Reinelt) or earlier. Now the courier who journeyed to Aquitania with letters in 398 was Amachius, subdeacon of Delphinus (cf. Letter 17.3), whereas the present letter was carried by Sanemarius (cf. § 12), so that a date of 397 is more probable (so Fabre *Chron.* 61).

2 1 Tim. 1.5; 1 Cor. 5.8.

3 Ps. 15.2.

4 2 Cor. 8.14.

5 Ps. 38.2; cf. Prov. 10.19.

6 Cf. Eph. 6.19; Ps. 118.105, 138.12.

7 Cf. Num. 22.28; Ps. 44.2.

8 Cf. Luke 19.40.

9 Ps. 99.3.

10 Cf. Gen. 4.25.

11 Cf. Gen. 7.1 ff.

12 Cf. Rom. 5.12 ff.

13 I.e., Abraham. Cf. Rom. 4.12 f.; Gal. 3.7.

14 Cf. Hebr. 1.1; Matt. 5.17.

15 Cf. Wisd. 16.12.

16 Cf. Phil. 3.21.

17 Cf. Eccli. 33.13 ff.; Jer. 18.6; Rom. 9.21.

18 Cf. Phil. 2.7.

19 Ps. 87.5.

20 Ps. 87.6.

21 Isa. 53.12.

22 John 1.29; Isa. 53.7.

23 Ps. 75.5.

24 The concept of the cross as the second tree, and Mary as the second Eve, had already been formulated by Justin, Irenaeus, Tertullian, and Ambrose. For the cross as the tree of life, cf. H. Rahner, *Greek Myths and Christian Mystery* (London 1962) 59 ff.

25 Phil. 2.7.

26 Deut. 2.27; Num. 21.22.

27 Cf. 1 Tim. 2.5.

28 The doctrine of humility and magnanimity developed here and again in §§ 7 and 8 has interesting correspondences with Chrysostom's injunction "to be great in good deeds and humble oneself in thought" (*Hom. de incomprehensibili* 5.6 [MG

48.745]). On the topic in general, cf. R. A. Gauthier, *Magnanimité* (Paris 1951) 436 f.

[29] Cf. Ps. 16.11, 31.9; Eccli. 2.22, 26.

[30] Rom. 12.16; 2 Cor. 10.13.

[31] Cf. 1 Cor. 1.19.

[32] Ps. 63.6.

[33] Letter 16 to Jovius is devoted largely to this topic.

[34] Isa. 60.1; Ps. 111.4, 72.9.

[35] *Scrutantur caeli plagas*, an echo of Ennius, *Tragedies* fr. 244 Vahlen³.

[36] Cf. Letter 16.2 and nn. 7–9 thereto.

[37] Ps. 63.7 f. There is here a play on the words *plagae*, "wounds," in the Psalm, and *plagas*, "quarters," used immediately above (cf. n. 35).

[38] 1 Cor. 3.19; Ps. 8.3; 1 Cor. 4.20.

[39] Cf. Matt. 11.25.

[40] Eph. 2.14; 1 Cor. 1.27; 2 Cor. 8.14.

[41] Cf. 1 Cor. 1.31.

[42] Cf. Ps. 2.11; Matt. 11.29; Phil. 2.5.

[43] Cf. Rom. 6.4.

[44] Cf. Eph. 2.14, 4.8.

[45] Rom. 8.3.

[46] John 1.14.

[47] Gal. 3.13.

[48] Cf. Rom. 8.3 f.

[49] Cf. Eph. 2.14.

[50] Cf. Rom. 7.21 f.

[51] Col. 3.5.

[52] 1 Cor. 9.27; Phil. 3.13.

[53] Matt. 4.7. Cf. Luke 4.8; Deut. 6.13, 10.20.

[54] For such condemnation of false humility, compare Origen, *Contra Celsum* 3.62; Basil, *In ps.* 33.12 (MG 29.380 f.).

[55] Cf. Isa. 1.22.

[56] Cf. Isa. 5.20, 23.

[57] Cf. Eccli. 19.23.

[58] Ps. 130.1 f.

[59] Ps. 50.19.

[60] Ps. 72.28.

[61] Phil. 2.5 ff.

[62] Col. 3.1.

[63] Cf. Matt. 11.30.

[64] Ps. 37.5.

[65] Rom. 7.24; Ps. 50.3.

[66] Ps. 16.7.

[67] Ps. 39.13.

[68] Cf. Isa. 6.5 ff.

[69] Exod. 32.31 f.

[70] 1 John 4.4.

[71] Mentioned only here, but obviously a former slave of Paulinus.

[72] The letter sent to Delphinus at this time has not survived.

[73] *In Galliis*, i.e., not in Aquitania, but in Gallia Lugdunensis or Belgica.

[74] On the left bank of the Garonne, not far from Bordeaux. Delphinus was at this time engaged in building a church there; cf. Letter 20.3.

[75] The priest in question is Basilius of Capua, to whom Paulinus refers in greater detail in Letters 14.3 f. and 15.2. Cf. also n. 13 to Letter 14.

LETTER 13

[1] This inspiring meditation on the Christian attitude towards death was written by Paulinus to console Pammachius (on whom, cf. above, Intro. p. 6.) on the death of his wife Paulina (cf. n. 12 below). We know that the death of Paulina occurred two years before Jerome sent his condolences to the bereaved husband (cf. Jerome's *Ep.* 66.1: *per biennium tacui*). Since that letter of Jerome has been firmly dated to spring 398 (so Cavallera 1.229), Paulina must have died early in 396, or possibly late in 395. The winter, then, to which Paulinus refers in § 2 of this letter, is that of 395–6, and this letter can be dated securely in early 396.

[2] Eccle. 3.7.

[3] Not otherwise known.

[4] For Paul as *vas electionis*, cf. Acts 9.15.

[5] Rom. 12.15.

[6] Gal. 6.2.

[7] Prov. 18.19.

[8] Cf. Matt. 26.41.

[9] This is a favourite theme in Paulinus' development of the notion of Christian friendship. Cf. esp. his *Carm.* 11.49 ff.

[10] Ps. 61.5.

[11] Matt. 12.34; cf. Luke 6.45.

[12] Paulina was the second daughter of the celebrated St. Paula of Rome. Paula had been widowed in her early twenties, and shortly afterwards gave up patrician luxury to convert her Roman house into a kind of monastery. There Paulina, with her sisters Blesilla and Eustochium, shared in the life of prayer, scriptural study, and charitable works, until she married Pammachius, the leading Christian senator of the day.

[13] Cf. Tob. 12.9: "For alms delivereth from death. . . ."

[14] Eccli. 38.16.

[15] Cf. Gen. 23.2.

[16] Cf. Gen. 23.16–19.

[17] Cf. Gen. 12.1.

[18] Rachel died in childbirth in Bethlehem; cf. Gen. 35.19.

[19] Rom. 10.4.

[20] Cf. Tob. 2.3 ff.

[21] Cf. Gen. 50.1.

[22] Cf. Ps. 6.7.

[23] Cf. John 11.35.

[24] Eccli. 26.16.

[25] Prov. 31.18.

[26] Prov. 31.19, 26.

[27] Wisd. 4.1.

[28] Wisd. 4.7.

[29] Wisd. 4.8 f.

[30] Wisd. 4.14, 11.

[31] 1 John 5.19; 1 Cor. 15.33; Eccli. 13.1.

[32] Ps. 119.5.

[33] Ps. 119.5.

[34] The same comment is made by Paulinus in Letter 29.13.

[35] Cf. 2 Kings 12.22 f.

[36] Cf. 2 Kings 18.33.

[37] Cf. 2 Kings 13.29.

[38] 2 Kings 12.23.

[39] Ps. 41.6, 40.9.

[40] Matt. 22.32; cf. 1 Cor. 15.18.

[41] Eccle. 3.1.

[42] Eccli. 38.17.

[43] Eccli. 38.17, 19.

[44] 2 Cor. 7.10.

[45] 1 Cor. 1.24.

[46] 2 Cor. 2.7.

[47] The church here described as the scene of the feast was the basilica built by Constantine on the site of St. Peter's crucifixion. F. Homes Dudden, *The Life and Times of St. Ambrose* 1 (Oxford 1935) 51, gives a lively description of the scene on occasions such as this, when the basilica was used to give food to the needy of Rome.

[48] Cf. Matt. 14.19; John 6.11.

[49] This rather bizarre reconstruction of the miracle of the loaves and fishes has no parallel, so far as I know, in earlier commentaries.

[50] Cf. Matt. 14.19; Mark 6.39; Luke 9.14 f.; John 6.10.

[51] Cf. Mark 8.19 f.

[52] Cf. Matt. 8.11, 22.12.

[53] Matt. 8.20.

[54] For a description of Constantine's basilica, cf. F. X. Kraus, *Geschichte der christlichen Kunst* 1 (Freiburg 1896) 683.

[55] For *solium* in the sense of tomb, see Rosweyde's note in ML 61.848.

[56] On the *cantharus*, which provided water for washing for those entering the church, cf. R. C. Goldschmidt, *Paulinus' Churches at Nola* (Amsterdam 1940) 114; also Rosweyde's note in ML 61.850.

[57] As Paulinus later explains, the *mystica species* of the four columns symbolises the four evangelists.

[58] John 4.14.

[59] Luke 24.32.

[60] Cf. Lev. 6.14; Par. 1, 29.21; etc.

[61] Ps. 26.6, 49.14.

[62] Worthy of note here is the literary manner in which Paulinus adds to the first three corporal works of mercy an allusion to visiting the imprisoned.

[63] Cf. Matt. 13.8.

[64] Eccli. 35.21.

[65] Cf. Apoc. 3.3.

[66] Ps. 1.1.

[67] Ps. 90.13.

[68] Luke 16.9.

[69] Luke 16.25. The parable of the rich man and Lazarus is one to which Paulinus returns again and again (cf. Letters 25*.2, 32.21, etc.). This and the passage of Corinthians quoted at the end of § 19 had an important influence in his conversion and in his writings.

[70] Cf. Luke 10.32 f.

[71] Cf. Luke 16.21.

[72] Ps. 140.3; Prov. 18.21; Matt. 12.37.

[73] Cf. Matt. 5.3.

[74] Prov. 18.11.

[75] Ps. 15.4.

[76] Cant. 1.1.

[77] Luke 12.20.

[78] Matt. 19.22.

[79] Cf. Matt. 19.23: "Amen, I say to you that a rich man shall hardly enter into the kingdom of heaven."

[80] Matt. 6.19.

[81] 1 Cor. 1.7.

[82] Hilary, *Comm. in Matt.* 19 (ML 9.1020) states that the young man in Matt. 9.16–22 symbolises the Jews.

[83] Cf. Gen. 18.1 ff.; Job 1.3 ff.

[84] Cf. Matt. 27.57.

[85] Ps. 40.2.

[86] Acts 2.44.

[87] An echo of the proverbial phrase in Terence, *Heautontimoroumenos* 77.

[88] Acts 4.32.

[89] Cf. Gen. 18.3, 19.2 f.; Job 42.10.

[90] Cf. John 8.56. The normal patristic exegesis of this theophany suggests that the three men represent the Trinity.

[91] Cf. Gen. 19.8.

[92] Matt. 19.29.

[93] Cf. Wisd. 10.6.

[94] Segor, which was, however, a "little" city; cf. Gen. 19.20.

[95] Cf. Ps. 65.10.

[96] Job 29.15.

[97] Job 1.21; 1 Tim. 6.7.

[98] Ps. 127.2.

[99] Cf. Job 42.12.

[100] Cf. Luke 16.9. Later, in Letter 32.21, Paulinus develops this

idea, that we must utilise worldly riches to win such friends as will ensure by their prayers that we attain heaven.

[101] Ps. 67.19.

[102] Cf. Matt. 16.17.

[103] Cf. 1 Cor. 1.24.

[104] Cf. Matt. 25.40.

[105] Ps. 40.2.

[106] Ps. 40.3 f.

[107] Ps. 29.12.

[108] Ps. 50.14, 17.35.

[109] Ps. 17.34.

[110] Eccli. 5.12.

[111] Ps. 114.8 f.

[112] Ps.144.13, 19.4.

[113] Cf. Exod. 29.41, etc.

[114] John 4.35.

[115] I propose, and translate here, *satio* for the *ratio* of the MSS.

[116] Paulinus here passes in brief review the more popular of the contemporary pagan notions of life after death. Transmigration of souls is a Pythagorean doctrine; the notion of disembodied souls is Platonist; and the doctrine of the soul dying with the body is Epicurean. The other major school, Stoicism, had by this time moved from its earlier rigorous view (that at death the soul of the individual merges with the world-soul) towards a more Platonist stand; the development can be observed in the second book of Cicero's *De natura deorum*. In Letter 16 Paulinus makes a more extended criticism of the doctrines of these schools; cf. that letter and the notes thereto.

[117] Wisd. 2.5.

[118] Ps. 26.13.

[119] John 11.25 f.

[120] John 20.27; Luke 24.39.

[121] Cf. 1 John 1.1.

[122] Cf. 2 Cor. 1.22.

[123] Cf. 1 Tim. 2.5.

[124] Cf. 1 Cor. 15.54.

[125] Cf. John 14.6.

[126] Cf. Matt. 11.12.

[127] Phil. 3.12.

[128] Cf. Matt. 7.14.

[129] Ps. 44.10.

[130] Cf. Luke 16.24.
[131] Cf. n. 12 above.

LETTER 14

[1] On the dating of this letter, cf. above, n. 1 to Letter 12.

[2] In various letters Paulinus provides sundry details of Cardamas, who was his favourite courier. He had been an actor or mime (cf. Letter 19.4) and a drunkard (cf. Letter 15.4), who reformed and eventually took orders. Letter 15 to Amandus gives a vivid and humorous picture of his early struggles with the rigour of the monastic routine; and later letters (esp. Letter 21.5 f.) extol his virtues as courier.

[3] Eccli. 26.16.

[4] Ps. 125.3, 40.4, 114.8.

[5] Cant. 1.3.

[6] John 11.4.

[7] Cf., e.g., Gen. 27.1 and 48.10.

[8] Cf. Job 1.14 ff., 2.10, 13.

[9] Ps. 36.7.

[10] Eccli. 5.4.

[11] 1 Pet. 4.18.

[12] Ps. 65.12. Is there here something of that humorous quotation of Scripture observable in Letter 15.4?

[13] Basilius, described in Letter 12.12 as *sanctissimus presbyter . . . et vita et aetate venerabilis,* appears to have been dispossessed of his house in Capua by the Daducius mentioned in Letter 12.12. Through Delphinus and Amandus (cf. Letter 15.2), who interceded with Daducius, his property was restored to him.

[14] Ps. 106.7.

[15] Cf. Luke 16.9.

LETTER 15

[1] This letter was sent at the same time as Letter 14, as the common topics of the recovery of Delphinus (§ 1), Basilius (§ 2), and Cardamas (§ 4) indicate. On the dating, cf. above, n. 1 to Letter 12.

[2] Ps. 20.4.

[3] Cf. above, n. 2 to Letter 14.

[4] Ps. 18.9 and 11.

[5] Ps. 50.10, 47.10, 71.12, 34.10.

[6] Cf. above, n. 43 to Letter 5.

[7] Cf. above, n. 13 to Letter 14.

[8] Ps. 29.12, 91.11.

[9] Ps. 117.15.

[10] Luke 1.48; Ps. 146.3, 34.26, 29.12.

[11] I propose, and translate here, *quos a te rogari poposceramus*, though all the MSS and editions have *ante* instead of *a te*.

[12] On obedience as preferable to sacrifice, cf., e.g., 1 Kings 15.22.

[13] It would appear that Basilius owned a house in the Capua area abutting on land owned by the Daducii.

[14] Eccli. 31.10.

[15] The passage suggests that the Daducii had land interests in Campania, and that their employees made frequent visits there. The Daducius mentioned in Letter 12.12 is yet another correspondent of Paulinus the letters to whom have not survived.

[16] Even outside Lent only one meal was taken daily at Nola, and that in the evening. Such was the regular practice in early Italian monasticism; cf. Augustine, *De mor. eccl.* 1.70 (ML 32.1340). In this respect at Nola the Rule of Basil was closely followed. On the general subject of early monastic life in Italy, cf. Speizenhofer's *Die Entwicklung des alten Mönchtums in Italien* (Vienna 1894); C. Butler, *The Lausiac History of Palladius* 1 (Cambridge 1898) 248 ff., sets it in the context of Egyptian, Greek, and Gallic monasticism.

[17] In the Rule of Basil the drink at the evening meal was water. This passage suggests that at Nola a modest draught of wine was permitted.

[18] Cf. 1 Tim. 5.23.

[19] Cf. Eccli. 31.32 ff.; also Ambrose, *De fide* 1, of which there is perhaps a reminiscence here.

[20] A reminiscence of Ps. 118.171: *eructabunt labia mea hymnum. . . .*

[21] Ps. 71.18, 113.8.

[22] Paulinus jokingly represents himself as a doubting Thomas (cf. John 20.24–29) who could not believe the facts of the matter on hearsay.

[23] Not in the monastery, but in the Christian community at large.

²⁴ Cf. Ps. 21.16.

²⁵ Ps. 118.81, 101.6.

²⁶ Eccli. 2.4, 23.6; Deut. 8.3.

²⁷ Ps. 37.14, 57.5.

²⁸ Cf. Luke 15.16.

²⁹ Paulinus tells us more about the assembly for the singing of hymns in Letter 29.13, though in that later passage the communal service is during the night hours.

LETTER 16

¹ There is nothing in this letter to permit an exact dating of it. One pointer, however, is the fact that Posthumianus and Theridius were the couriers. In Letter 27 we read that Posthumianus and Theridius had then just returned from Aquitania; Letter 27 was written in or after 400, perhaps in 401 or 402, and we may assume that this present letter to Jovius was sent before Letter 27. Paulinus' *Carm.* 23, the seventh in the series of *Natalicia* and composed for January 401, indicates that Theridius had been recently at Nola, where he sustained an eye injury. Hence Posthumianus and Theridius may have taken this letter to Jovius in 399, returning later that year or in 400. But on the other hand, they may have set out after the healing of Theridius' eye in 401. Cf. Fabre *Chron.* 47.

² On Jovius, cf. above, Intro. p. 8.

³ Posthumianus and Theridius were Gauls, and perhaps Aquitanians, as this passage and Letter 27.2 suggest. Is the Posthumianus here the character in the *Dialogues* of Sulpicius Severus, who describes the wonders of eremitic life in Egypt? The identification is by no means certain. Reinelt 26, n. 2, and Fabre *Chron.* 45, n. 5, both raise the powerful objection that the Posthumianus of the *Dialogues* was an intimate friend of Severus, whilst the Posthumianus in Paulinus had barely made Severus' acquaintance (cf. Letter 27.2).

⁴ I agree with Lagrange (2.71) that "the silver of that holy commerce" probably means that the silver was being transported to Nola for church building and furnishing.

⁵ The concepts of *fortuna* and *fatum* ("fortuna omnipotens et ineluctabile fatum" [Virgil, *Aeneid* 8.334]) held an obsessive place

in Hellenistic literature and philosophy, and consequently in Roman thought as well. A famous passage from Pliny (*N.H.* 2.22) describes how everywhere and constantly Fortune was invoked by all lips, and the philosophers were much concerned with the question. Paulinus was familiar with such discussions as that in Cicero's *De natura deorum* 2.81 ff., where the Stoic spokesman discusses his school's notion of providential government, and the Epicurean idea of the fortuitous collision and sundering of atoms. The topic was early taken up by Christians, e.g., Tertullian in his now-lost *De fato*, and Clement of Alexandria, who defends the Christian concept of Providence in his *Strom.* 1.16.

⁶ Rom. 1.21.

⁷ The description of Epicurean theology is reminiscent of Cicero, *De natura deorum* 1.53 (*in omnium vacatione munerum*).

⁸ Here Paulinus continues his attack on the Epicureans, who posited innumerable atoms moving in the infinite void. In the Epicurean view, these atoms cannot be created or destroyed, but they combine, initially by chance, to form countless worlds; the gods neither create nor supervise, but live a life of quietism in the *intermundia*.

⁹ Here the assault switches to Stoicism. Following Heraclitus, the Stoics believed that the universe originated from the *pneuma*, the fiery breath in the aether which they deified.

¹⁰ The order of this polemic (Epicureans, Stoics, astrology) follows that of Tacitus, *Annals* 6.22. Some Stoics believed in the influence of the stars, but Paulinus is thinking more generally of the astrological superstition condemned by Christian bishops and emperors.

¹¹ I translate here *careat* (thus Sacchini), finding it much preferable to *pareat*, which is retained by Hartel.

¹² The Roman *fatum*, besides translating the Greek *heimarmene*, or "destiny," also carries the traditional Roman sense of divine utterance through dreams, oracles, and the like.

¹³ For Occasio as goddess, cf. e.g., Ausonius, *Ep.* 19.12.3.

¹⁴ Fortuna (Tyche) is commonly represented in literature and art with a wheel or ball to symbolise her variability.

¹⁵ Cf. his *Republic* 617b.

¹⁶ This literal interpretation of the myth of Ur and Paulinus'

utter misunderstanding of Plato's use of myth are especially surprising in a writer who is himself so preoccupied with the symbolism of the writings he quotes. In this lack of philosophical sophistication Paulinus can be strikingly contrasted with Augustine. We can conclude that Paulinus had read Plato, but more as a literary exercise than a philosophical study.

[17] Cf. Sallust, *Catiline* 1.

[18] Cf. Ps. 110.10; Eccli. 1.16.

[19] Cf. Rom. 5.3 f.

[20] By the pun on "Peripatetic" Paulinus means that Jovius should stop being a mere Aristotelian, but should travel to preach the truth of Christ. He would become a "Pythagorean" towards the world by espousing monastic life.

[21] Cf. Homer, *Odyssey* 9.84 ff., 12.39 ff.

[22] For Odysseus at the mast in early Christian literature, as symbolising the Christian on life's voyage, cf. H. Rahner, *Greek Myths and Christian Mystery* (London 1962) ch. 7. Of particular interest for its possible influence on Paulinus is Ambrose's use of the image of the Sirens in a letter to Gratian (*De fide ad Gratianum* 3.1.4), in which he calls the temptations surrounding the young a *dulcem sed mortiferam cantilenam*, the very noun that Paulinus has used to describe the song of Necessity in the Platonic passage.

[23] Here Paulinus achieves a happy synthesis of Pauline teaching (cf. 1 Tim 6.7) and the Epicurean doctrine of necessary desires (cf. Cicero, *De finibus* 1.45).

[24] Such contempt for riches was especially characteristic of Cynics such as Antisthenes and Diogenes. It is interesting to note here that Jerome, in his *Ep.* 58.2 to Paulinus, speaks of Crates of Thebes, who *magnum auri pondus abiecit*, and in exemplifying pagan philosophers who despised riches Jerome on two occasions (*Epp.* 66.8 and 71.3) mentioned Antisthenes and Crates of Thebes. Socrates was also commonly depicted in this light under Cynic influence; cf., e.g., A.-H. Chroust, *Socrates, Man and Myth* (London 1957) ch. 5.

[25] Cf. 1 Cor. 4.7; Job 1.21.

[26] Ps. 49.14.

[27] Ps. 110.10; Eccli. 1.16.

[28] Virgil, *Aeneid* 4.188.

[29] Cf. 2 Tim. 3.7.

[30] Compare Augustine's similar image in his *De doctrina christiana* 2.40.

[31] What is notable in this survey of Christian and pagan notions of God and Providence is the conscious attempt made by Paulinus to avoid mere citation of scriptural authority, and his appeal to Jovius by argumentation familiar to Jovius from classical philosophy, especially that of Aristotle and Cicero, adorned by reminiscences from Homer and Virgil.

LETTER 17

[1] This letter marks a crisis in the friendship of Paulinus and Severus. Paulinus has at last realised that there is little prospect of Severus' coming to Nola, and his friend has not bothered to write for "nearly two years" (§ 1). This rift was clearly foreshadowed in Letter 11.12 ff. (cf. n. 97 to that letter), and it is reasonable to assume that the present epistle is next in sequence in the correspondence with Severus. Since Letter 11 was written in 397, this letter was composed either in 399 (so Lebrun in ML 61.748), or more probably in late 398 (cf. Fabre *Chron.* 25), for Paulinus writes late in the year after returning from Rome and after a lengthy bout of sickness.

[2] Each year from his arrival at Nola till about 406, Paulinus visited Rome for the feast of Saints Peter and Paul on June 29. Later he changed the time of his annual visit to the period immediately following Easter (cf. Letter 45.1: *iuxta sollemnem meum morem post Pascha Domini . . .*).

[3] The courier was wearing military dress, which those in monastic life frowned upon (cf. Fabre *Paulin* 206 f.; also above, n. 10 to Letter 8). The courier here is the Marracinus whom Paulinus pillories in Letter 22, where again the boots, crimson cloak, and ruddy cheeks are scathingly mentioned.

[4] Cf. John 11.25; Ps. 117.18.

[5] Ps. 31. 10.

[6] Ps. 146.3.

[7] Doubtless, as Fabre *Paulin* 296 suggests, these phrases are a sarcastic echo of Severus' excuse for not writing earlier; cf. § 1 of this letter.

[8] Isa. 58.9 (LXX).

[9] Mark 9.22.

LETTER 18

[1] Of the two extant letters to Victricius, bishop of Rouen, the other, Letter 37, can be securely dated to 403/4, and it is obvious that the present letter is earlier, since Paulinus introduces himself to Victricius in § 1. Now in §§ 1–2 Paulinus talks of having been in Rome for June 29, and of his illness later at Nola. These are precisely the circumstances under which Letter 17 was written, and this letter can be confidently ascribed to the same period, i.e., in 397 or 398. Cf. Fabre *Chron.* 68.

[2] On whom, cf. above, Intro. p. 7. Paulinus' sources for the unique evidence in this letter on Victricius' early life presumably were the deacon Paschasius (§§ 1–3) and Tychicus (§ 4).

[3] Not mentioned elsewhere.

[4] 1 Tim. 1.5.

[5] 2 Cor. 7.6; Ps. 146.3.

[6] Cf. Eccli. 6.16.

[7] Cf. Matt. 18.20.

[8] Cf. Luke 1.48.

[9] Cf. Rom. 6.18.

[10] Ps. 134.7.

[11] Isa. 9.1.

[12] The Morini dwelt in the Ostend-Calais region. Virgil's phrase, *extremique hominum Morini (Aeneid* 8.727), was doubtless in Paulinus' mind here.

[13] Ps. 64.13.

[14] For a brief account, cf. E. Mâle, *La fin du paganisme en Gaule* (Paris 1950) chs. 1–2.

[15] Wisd. 6.17, 7.27.

[16] A slightly loose phrase, for the Nervii, another Belgian tribe, lived further to the southeast.

[17] Ps. 18.5.

[18] For the importance of this evidence in the assessment of missionary work amongst the barbarians of Belgica Secunda, cf. E. A. Thompson, "Christianity and the Northern Barbarians" in *Paganism and Christianity in the Fourth Century* (ed. A. Momigliano, Oxford 1963) 64. This missionary activity received a stimulus in 382 with the edict of Gratian, which deprived pagan religions of many of their privileges. Martin's example of destroy-

ing pagan temples and replacing them with Christian churches was sedulously followed. On the remains of pagan temples discovered beneath Christian churches, cf. E. Mâle, *La fin du paganisme en Gaule* (Paris 1950) 39.

[19] On the early history of Rouen, cf. R. Hertal, *Histoire de Rouen* 1 (Rouen 1947).

[20] Ps. 148.14.

[21] Ps. 46.8.

[22] As Paulinus and Therasia were themselves living.

[23] Cf. Luke 1.78.

[24] 1 Tim. 2.4.

[25] Isa. 52.7.

[26] Ps. 18.6.

[27] Eph. 6.15; Ps. 90.13.

[28] Cf. Matt. 5.15.

[29] *Comiti.* Constantine had created the title *comes* as official recognition of the status of those invited to accompany an emperor on his journeys. Subsequently a *comes* was frequently appointed to take charge of a diocese. But there were also military *comites* who commanded detachments of the field army in the provinces, and Paulinus here obviously is referring to a military *comes*. Cf. Jones 1.105 and n. 61 there.

[30] Ps. 23.8.

[31] Cf. Luke 23.34.

[32] Cf. Luke 22.51.

[33] Cf. 1 Kings 19.23.

[34] This would have been in the early years of Julian's hegemony as Caesar in Gaul (he became Caesar in November 355), or perhaps in the years immediately preceding, when Constantius II was in effective control.

[35] Ps. 54.7.

[36] Cf. Luke 7.38.

[37] Prov. 27.6.

[38] Isa. 6.5.

[39] The precise date of this meeting has not been determined. There is general agreement that it must have occurred after Paulinus' return from Italy to Gaul, and before his final departure to Spain (i.e., between 384 and 389). Martin does not seem to have met his fellow bishops after 386 (cf. Fabre *Paulin* 30, n. 2, and the references there) and Paulinus was preoccupied with his

marriage in the period after his return from Italy. The most likely date is therefore 386. Cf. further Lagrange 1.74.

⁴⁰ Martin had become bishop of Tours in 372. This letter proves that Victricius was bishop of Rouen by 386, and suggests that Victricius was much older than Martin had been when he became bishop.

⁴¹ Ps. 11.7; Wisd. 3.6.

⁴² Cf. Matt. 13.8.

⁴³ One of Victricius' sermons, *De laude sanctorum*, has survived; cf. ML 20.443–58.

LETTER 19

¹ It is clear from Letter 20.1, also addressed to Delphinus, that Paulinus sent two letters at the same time to the bishop of Bordeaux. Letter 20 can be dated without hesitation to between late 400 and June 401 (cf. below, n. 1 to Letter 20), and it can reasonably be assumed that Letter 19 accompanied it. Note that the final section of this present letter includes a quotation from Proverbs enjoining us to avoid loquacious utterance, and that Letter 20 begins with a repetition of the same theme, most likely a deliberate reminiscence. Moreover, the description of Cardamas' spiritual progress shows that the sequence of letters to Bordeaux during this period is 12, 14/15, 19. Cf. above, n. 1 to Letter 12.

² Cf. Joel 1.20; Ps. 142.6.

³ Paulinus appends in § 2 some bitter comment on the delinquency of Uranius. There would be a certain irony if this were the same Uranius who attended Paulinus so faithfully on his deathbed, and who wrote of his *felicem ad superos transitum* (cf. ML 61.152, 53.859).

⁴ Ps. 110.4, 145.7; 2 Cor. 7.6.

⁵ Luke 1.44; Ps. 34.10, 8.5.

⁶ Ps. 84.2, 35.9.

⁷ Ps. 118.171, 54.18, 12.6.

⁸ Prov. 25.25.

⁹ Ps. 89.15.

¹⁰ Ps. 106.8, 49.14, 106.9.

¹¹ Ps. 26.12.

¹² Ps. 102.10, 13, 11.

[13] Ps. 142.2.

[14] Cf. Luke 17.10.

[15] Cf. Rom. 11.17. As in Letter 10, also addressed to Delphinus, Paulinus develops this image from arboriculture, comparing his former life to that of a wild vine, before Delphinus planted him in the Lord's vineyard.

[16] Cf. Matt. 3.7.

[17] Cf. Heb. 6.8.

[18] Cf. Deut. 32.32 f.

[19] Luke 1.49; Ps. 56.4.

[20] Ps. 103.30.

[21] Ps. 79.15 f.

[22] John 14.6, 15.1.

[23] Ps. 103.13.

[24] Ps. 67.10.

[25] On this exegesis of Ps. 71.6 ("He shall come down like rain upon the fleece"), compare the following from the *Brev. in psalmos*, attributed to Jerome: *sicut enim in vellus Gedeonis pluvia descendens, cum terra arida defecit, ita et hic illapsus est in uterum virginalem per infusionem Spiritus Sancti* (ML 26.1090).

[26] Ps. 102.3, 35.20, 106.20.

[27] Ps. 67.10.

[28] Phil. 2.8.

[29] Ps. 53.8.

[30] Ps. 67.10; cf. Ps. 106.35.

[31] 2 Cor. 13.4.

[32] At baptism, those to be baptised were clothed in a white robe, now represented in the Roman rite by a white stole.

[33] Cf. Ps. 125.6.

[34] Isa. 8.18.

[35] Prov. 10.19.

[36] I propose for the text here: *ut in eo ante ridicula mimici nominis levitatem, nunc adsumpta de exorcistae nomine gravitas reverentiam dederit.* The change from *ridicula* (nominative) to *ridiculam* is easily explained. There is a touch of desperation about Hartel's *in eo ante <dante>*.

[37] Cardamas had been admitted to the second of the Minor Orders, on which cf. J. Forget in DTC 5.1762 ff.

[38] As in Basil's Rule, the single meal at Nola was vegetarian.

LETTER 20

¹ In this letter we have precise evidence for dating. In § 2 Paulinus mentions the kindness he is receiving from Anastasius, who invited him to the anniversary celebration of his election as pope. That celebration was in November 400, because the election was in November 399. Paulinus says in this letter that he did not accept the invitation, but will try to see Anastasius on his yearly visit to Rome the following June. Hence this letter was written between November 400 and June 401.

² Cf. Eccli. 28.28; Prov. 10.19.

³ Ps. 119.5.

⁴ Rom. 8.35.

⁵ Cf. Rom. 8.38 f.

⁶ Rom. 2.28.

⁷ 2 Cor. 7.3.

⁸ Anastasius, elected as successor to Siricius in late 399, died in November 401. He was a Roman, highly regarded for his frugal and abstemious life. This made him especially sympathetic in the eyes of Paulinus, to whom he showed particular affection because he knew how Paulinus had been snubbed by Siricius (cf. above, Letter 5.13 f.). Cf. in general the article of H. Hemmer in DTC 1.1162 f.

⁹ I.e., on June 29, 400.

¹⁰ Venerius had succeeded Simplicianus, who died in June 400.

¹¹ Cf. Luke 7.5. This passage suggests that Paulinus had some years earlier lent financial help to this project of church-building in the Bordeaux area.

¹² Cf. above, n. 74 to Letter 12.

¹³ Ps. 80.2 f., 95.8.

¹⁴ Ps. 131.8, 117.27.

¹⁵ Wisd. 2.24; Ps. 111.10. These opponents of the building of churches, if the parallel of Jerusalem and the Assyrians has any point, would have been representative of the final pagan resistance to Christianity in Gaul.

¹⁶ Cf. 1 Esd. 4.4.

¹⁷ 1 John 4.4; Ps. 111.10.

¹⁸ Ps. 146.11.

¹⁹ Ps. 126.1.

[20] Cf. 1 Cor. 10.4.
[21] Cf. Matt. 21.12.
[22] Cf. John 2.14 f.
[23] Prov. 14.4.
[24] Cf. Gen. 3.6; Rom. 7.14.
[25] Cf. 1 Cor. 6.20.
[26] Cf. 1 Pet. 2.9.
[27] Cf. Rom. 8.17.
[28] Ps. 9.10, 17.28.
[29] Cf. 1 Cor. 5.8.
[30] Ps. 8.9.
[31] Cf. Matt. 17.26.
[32] Cf. Matt. 22.20, etc.
[33] Ps. 11.7.
[34] Cf. Lev. 10.1 f. There is a notable correspondence here with Origen, *In Levit. hom.* 9 (MG 12.509).
[35] Luke 12.49.
[36] Lev. 10.1.
[37] Heb. 12.29; Ps. 26.1.
[38] Ps. 22.4.
[39] Ps. 41.2.
[40] Ps. 35.10.

LETTER 21

[1] Though we cannot be certain, it is highly probable that this letter to Amandus was sent to Bordeaux together with Letters 19 and 20 to Delphinus. Cardamas is the courier, and Paulinus emphasises that he has now been admitted to the order of exorcist (§ 6), a point also made in Letter 19.4. Moreover, Cardamas' progress in fasting is described in similar terms in Letter 19.4 ("he consistently dined at our poor board") and in Letter 21.6 ("there was scarcely a day on which he shrank from dining with us"). On the dating, therefore, cf. above, n. 1 to Letter 19 and n. 1 to Letter 20.
[2] Cf. 2 Kings 2.18.
[3] Cf. 2 Kings 21.20.
[4] Cf. John 20.4.
[5] Cf. John 13.23, 21.20.

[6] Cf. Gal. 2.9.

[7] John 1.1.

[8] Cf. Gen. 1.1 ff.

[9] Cf. Matt. 1.1; Luke 1.5; Mark 1.2.

[10] Cf. Eph. 1.21.

[11] It is worth noting that Paulinus is ambiguous on the *Filioque* issue in his exposition of the Trinity here; but elsewhere, in *Carm.* 27.93 (*spiritum ab unigena sanctum <et> patre procedentem*), he specifically states that the Spirit proceeds from both Father and Son. For a general discussion of the question, cf. J. N. D. Kelly, *Early Christian Creeds* (London 1950) 358–67.

[12] 1 Cor. 2.10.

[13] On Arius, who argued that God is eternal and unknowable, and that the Son could not be God in the same sense, cf. J. H. Crehan's magisterial article in CDT 1.134–42; also Quasten *Patr.* 3.7–13.

[14] Sabellius was a third-century "modalist" Monarchian who believed that the Persons of God were not distinct, but reflected only a succession of modes or actions. Thus he held, with Praxeas, that the Father was crucified on Calvary. Cf. G. Bardy in DTC 10.2194 ff., and esp. 2204 ff., s.v. "Monarchianisme."

[15] It is worth noting that Ambrose, *De Incarnatione* 3 (ML 16.857 ff.), likewise calls John *piscator noster* in a similar discussion on the opening words of the Johannine Gospel. This passage of Ambrose may well have inspired Paulinus' wording here.

[16] On Photinus, the fourth-century bishop of Sirmium who denied the preexistence of Christ, see G. Bardy in DTC 12.1532–6.

[17] Marcion, a second-century heretic from Sinope, rejected the God of the Old Testament and the Creator of the material world as having nothing in common with the God of the Gospels. The Marcionite heresy survived vigorously into the fifth century. On Marcion and his doctrine, cf. Quasten *Patr.* 1.268–72.

[18] On the Manichees, cf. the discussion of J. J. O'Meara, *The Young Augustine* (London 1954) 61–79. The Manichees attacked the God of the Old Testament as immoral, and also ridiculed the New Testament claims that God was born of a woman and died on the cross. For them, God did not become truly man but assumed human shape. For a full discussion, cf. H. Ch. Puech, *Le manichéisme, son fondateur, sa doctrine* (Paris 1949).

[19] John 1.3.

[20] It was characteristic of Gnosticism to identify evil with the world of matter. As spirits, human beings must, according to the Gnostics, seek to escape to the illumination of celestial revelation. On pre-Christian and early Christian Gnosticism, cf. Quasten *Patr.* 1.254–77.

[21] John 1.14.

[22] Paulinus has already castigated Arius and Photinus for claiming that Christ was merely human; here he is attacking the rather different notion that God renounced His divine nature when He took on human form. This is an idea more characteristic of the Antiochenes, finally quashed at the Council of Ephesus in 431. The words used by Paulinus here suggest that he had recently been informed of such heretical views.

[23] 2 Cor. 11.19; 1 Cor. 13.7 f.

[24] Ps. 38.1 f.

[25] Cf. 2 Kings 2.18; Ps. 17.34.

[26] Cf. Ps. 102.5.

[27] Ps. 16.4.

[28] Cf. Ps. 54.7.

[29] Prov. 15.19.

[30] Cf. Ps. 18.6; Prov. 6.11.

[31] Prov. 15.30; Ps. 117.15, 113.12.

[32] Ps. 117.24, 20.3 f.

[33] Matt. 12.34.

[34] Cf. Ps. 91.11.

[35] On Cardamas as a reformed alcoholic, cf. Letter 15.4; also n. 2 to Letter 14.

LETTER 22

[1] The dating of this letter is somewhat speculative. The courier Marracinus mentioned on this occasion as having avoided coming to Nola is obviously the same person as that mentioned in Letter 17; compare the descriptions in § 1 of this letter and in Letter 17.1. It is clear that this letter, which describes Marracinus' conduct on that earlier occasion, was written later than Letter 17. This reinforces the argument that the chronology of the letters to Severus can be traced by the development of the quarrel between

the two friends. The seeds of the quarrel were already sown at the time of Letter 11. Further development of the quarrel is evident in Letter 17. The present epistle, a relatively brief, frigid, and censorious letter, comes next when the estrangement is at its height. And this is followed by a letter of reconciliation, Letter 23, which begins with protestations of boundless affection and which is the longest surviving letter. Letter 11 was written in 397 (cf. n. 1 to Letter 11), and Letter 23 can be assigned to the year 400. It is therefore reasonable to assume that Letter 17 belongs to the year 398 (or possibly 399; cf. n. 1 to Letter 17) and that Letter 22 was composed in 399. For a more complex analysis, cf. Fabre *Chron.* 27 ff.

² Sorianus is mentioned again as a courier in Letter 27.

³ Cf. n. 1 above.

⁴ Such garments of goat or camel's hair, worn in imitation of John the Baptist (cf. Paulinus' Letter 49.12), were the regular clothing of fourth-century monks in both the Eastern and Western worlds. St. Martin likewise recommended such a garb; cf. Severus, *Vita s. Martini* 7: *plerique camelorum saetis vestiebantur, mollior ibi habitus pro crimine erat.* In Letter 29.1 Paulinus acknowledges a gift from Severus of garments of camel's hair. Letter 29 probably was written in the year following this, and it is natural to assume that these comments of Paulinus gave Severus the idea of sending the present.

⁵ It is difficult to imagine what contrast is being made between the *chlamys* and the *sagulum* here. Perhaps the *sagulum* is used of the military cloak worn by private soldiers, and the contrast would then be between an effeminate and a rough garment.

⁶ Since the contrast is between the monk's shorn locks and the long hair of men like Marracinus, I take "shameless (*improba*) brow" to refer to the artificial curls much affected in imperial times, as the statuary and the literature of the period both attest. For a lively description of such male hair styles, cf. J. Carcopino, *Daily Life in Ancient Rome* (London 1941) 158 ff.

⁷ Unkempt hair is another monastic requirement put forward by Basil, *Ep.* 2.

⁸ Cf. 2 Cor. 2.16; Isa. 5.20.

⁹ Cf. 2 Cor. 2.15.

¹⁰ The swaggering soldier in Terence's *Eunuch.*

¹¹ Cf. Virgil, *Aeneid* 7.323 ff., where Juno summons the Fury

Allecto, "to whom grim wars are dear"; her shapes are many, her appearance fierce, her hair composed of snakes.

[12] Cf. above, n. 16 to Letter 7.

[13] Virgil, *Aeneid* 3.493.

[14] Cf. Plautus, *Aulularia* 2.

INDEXES

1. OLD AND NEW TESTAMENT

2. AUTHORS

Ambrose, St., 3, 5, 14, 20, 46, 206, 216, 226, 235
  De fide 1: 243; 3.14: 246; *De incarn.*, 21; 3: 209, 254; *De off. min.*, 21; 1.36.182: 209; *Ep.* 58: 216; *Expos. in Luc.*, 21; 7.96: 219; 8.48: 232; *Hexaemeron* 5.67 ff.: 228
Antisthenes, 246
Aristotle, 247
Audollent, A., 216
Augustine, St., 5, 6, 13, 14, 16, 21, 44, 48, 70, 73 ff., 76 ff., 217 f., 225 f., 246
  Conf. 9.15: 208; *C. ep. Donati haer.*, 226; *De civ. Dei* 10.6: 232; *De doct. christ.* 2.40: 247; *De Gen. c. Manich.*, 216; *De lib. arb.*, 216; 3.23: 218; *De mor. eccl.*, 216; 1.70: 243; *De mor. Manich.*, 216; *De vera relig.*, 215; *Epp.* 21: 225; 27: 222, 225; 31: 206, 225; 31.7: 216; 45: 206; 110: 225; 186: 206; 186.40: 209; 213.4: 225; 259: 207; *Ps. c. part. Donati*, 226; *Serm.* 355.2: 225; *Serm. dub.* 374.3: 218; *Tract. in Joann.* 3.19: 228
Ausonius, 2, 20, 209, 211, 245

Babut, E. Ch., 206, 220

Bardy, G., 206, 221, 254
Baronius, C., 221
Basil, St., 217, 251
  Ep. 2: 256; *In ps.* 33.12: 236
Beauduin, L., 214
Boissier, G., 205 f., 209, 233
Brown, P. R. L., 206, 207
Buse, A., 215 f.
Butler, C., 243

Carcopino, J., 256
Cato the Elder, 158
Cavallera, F., 203, 207, 237
Chroust, A.-H., 246
Cicero, 57, 158, 247
  De finibus 1.45: 246; *De nat. deorum*, 226, 241; 2.81 ff.: 245; *Laelius*, 231; *Pro Milone* 69: 64, 222
Clement of Alexandria, St., 210, 245
Clement of Rome, St., 209
Courcelle, P., 205, 209, 231
Crates, 246
Crehan, J. H., 254

Delehaye, H., 206, 220, 233
Demosthenes, 158
Dill, S., 205
Diogenes, 246
Duchesne, L., 203, 207, 230
Dudden, F. Homes, 221, 239

267

3. GENERAL INDEX

Aaron, 40, 189

Abel, 106

Abraham, 129, 131; attitude towards death, 19, 120 f.; exemplar of pilgrim, 37; on use of riches, 132, 136; entertains strangers, 137

Absalom, 124

abstractions, Roman deification of, 16, 155

Adam, 69

aedituus, meaning of, 213

Aemilius, bishop of Beneventum, 218

Aeschinus, character of Terence, 74, 226

Agilis, courier, 71, 223

agriculture, imagery drawn from, 17, 32, 41 f., 88 f., 101, 140, 180

Alaric, 211

Alethius, bishop of Cahors, 7

Allecto, 217, 257

alms-feast, 11, 130 ff.

Alypius, bishop of Tagaste, letter to, 5, 43, 215; letters from, 5, 73, 222; sends Paulinus works of Augustine, 48, 70; kinsman of Licentius, 80 f.

Amachius, subdeacon of Delphinus, 164, 235

Amanda, wife of Aper, 9, 21

Amandus, confessor of Paulinus, letters to, 4, 39, 82, 105, 147, 191; revitalises Christianity at Bordeaux, 2

Amandus, comrade of Sanctus, 9

Ambrose, St., connexions of, with Paulinus, 46, 206, 216; with Alypius, 46; forced to become bishop, 213; source for Paulinus, 228, 232, 243, 246, 254; intermediary of Greek thought, 20

Anastasius, Pope, 3, 4, 11, 186, 208, 252

Antiochene heresy, 255

Aper, letters to, 9, 21; his career, 9

Apocalypse, threats in, 131

Apollinarianism, 7

Aquileia, 6

Aquitania, native country of Paulinus, 1; spiritual awakening in, 8 f.; Paulinus' education in, 20

Arcadius, emperor, 206

Arian persecution, 13

Arius, 193, 254, 255

Arles, 9

Asael, 191, 194

asceticism, 24

Assyrians, 187

astrology, 154, 245

athlete, image of, 17

Greek, Paulinus' knowledge of, 12 f., 20 f.

habits, monastic, see clothing
hair, 21, 29; monastic cut, 12, 197, 208, 256
heaven, nature of, 5
Hebromagus, 104, 234
Helena, St., 11
Heraclitus, 245
Hippo (Bône), 5, 45, 47, 74
Holy Cross, finding of, 11
Holy Spirit, 141, 153, 168
Honorat (Lérins), 207
Honoratus, bishop of Arles, 9, 207
Honorius, emperor, 15
humanism, Christian and pagan, 14
humility, in Paulinus, 25 f., 108, 111 f., 235 ff.; misguided, 112
hymns at Nola, 12, 244; Gallic hymnary, 12

imagery in Paulinus, 17
Innocent I, Pope, 7
Isaac, 129, 131
Israel, meaning of, 220
Itinerarium Burdegalense, 214

Jacob, 19, 58, 129, 131; buries Rachel, 121; well of, 97
Jerome, St., Paulinus' letters to, lost, 3, 205; attacks Vigilantius, 9, 221
Jerusalem, 13, 132, 171, 187
Jews, 95, 111, 185; symbolised, 240
Joab, 191

Job, tested, 145; patient, 138; his right use of riches, 136 ff.
John, St., apostle, 191 f.; Gospel of, 192
John the Baptist, 192, 256
Joseph, 19, 121
Joseph of Arimathea, 136
Jovius, letter to, 8, 15 f., 25, 151 ff., 207, 244
Julian, emperor, 249
Julianus, courier, 43, 215
justice in sharing wealth, 24 f.

Lampius, bishop of Barcelona, 46
Lazarus, 26, 133 f., 240
Lent at Nola, 149 f.
letters, importance of Paulinus', 10 ff.
Licentius, 74, 226; Paulinus' letter to, 76, 225; kinsman of Alypius, 80
liturgy in fourth century, 11, 12, 208, 244
Locociagum (Ligugé), 233
Lot, 136, 137
Lotus-eaters, image of, 158

Macarius, Paulinus' letter to, 6 f., 207
Mammon, 15
Manicheans, 193, 254; attacked by Augustine, 49, 70, 74
Marcion, 193, 254
Marmoutier, 233 f.
Marracinus, courier, 164, 196 f., 199, 247, 255
marriage, 25
Martin, St., founder of Gallic monasticism, 3, 13, 206; career of, 233; forced to be-

come bishop, 213, 250; destroys pagan temples, 248 f.; visited by Severus, 103, 165; by Paulinus, 176, 209; recommends habit of camel's hair, 256; life of, by Severus, 100 f.
Mary Magdalen, type of Church, 19, 21
Maximus, emperor, 220
meals, monastic, 12, 149 f., 198 f., 208, 243, 251
Megalius, bishop of Calama, 225
Melania the Elder, portrait of, 13; humility of, 25
Memorius, bishop of Capua, 218
Micio, character of Terence, 74, 226
Milan, 45, 186
Milevis (Mila), 73, 225
Monarchianism, 254
monastic school at Primuliacum, 3
Morini, 170, 248
Moses, 192
Mystical Body, Paulinus' notion of, 24, 71

Naples, 1
Narbo (Narbonne), 69, 214, 223 f.
Natalicia, 23, 211, 244
Necessity, 155
neighbour, defined, 133
Nemrod, 85, 229
Nephthali, 170
Nepotian, friend of Jerome, 213
Nervii, 170, 248
Nicaea, council of, 225
Nicaulis, 219

Nicetas of Dacia, 13
nigellatum, meaning of, 223
night-raven, image of, 18
Nola, site of Paulinus' monastery, 1; provenance of letters, 2; in barbarian invasions, 10; monastic life at, 11 f.; visited by Melania, 13; by Nicetas, 13

Occasio, deified, 245
Odysseus, see Ulysses
Olympius, friend of Pammachius, 117
ordination of Paulinus, 14, 37, 39, 46; date of, 213
ordination, forcible, 213
orthodoxy of Paulinus, 22, 209 f.
Ostia, 6

Pammachius, Paulinus' letter to, 6, 10, 19, 117 ff., 237
Pasch, 99
Paschasius, deacon of Victricius, 167 f., 177, 248
Paul, St., mentor of Paulinus, 22, 87, 113; of Timothy, 77
Paula, mother of Paulina, 143, 238
Paulina, wife of Pammachius, 6, 120, 142; dies young, 123; date of death, 237
Pauline epistles as basis of Paulinus' thought, 24, 26
Paulinus, St., birth and provenance of, 1 f.; secular career of, 1, 56, 219; lateness of his vocation, 114; leaves Gaul for Spain, 1, 213, 220; marries Therasia, 1; death of his son,